# Tibet as I Knew It

**Studies in Modern Tibetan Culture**
Series Editor: Gray Tuttle, Columbia University

*The Nine-Eyed Agate: Poems and Stories*
Translated by Heather Stoddard; by Jangbu

*Labrang Monastery: A Tibetan Buddhist Community on the Inner Asian Borderlands, 1709–1958*
By Paul Kocot Nietupski

*The Hidden Life of the Sixth Dalai Lama*
By Simon Wickham-Smith

*The Disempowered Development of Tibet in China: A Study in the Economics of Marginalization*
By Andrew Martin Fischer

*The Social Life of Tibetan Biography: Textuality, Community, and Authority in the Lineage of Tokden Shakya Shri*
By Amy Holmes-Tagchungdarpa

*The Rise of Gönpo Namgyel in Kham: The Blind Warrior of Nyarong*
By Yudru Tsomu

*Oral and Literary Continuities in Modern Tibetan Literature: The Inescapable Nation*
By Lama Jabb

*Tibetan Environmentalists in China: The King of Dzi*
By Liu Jianqiang. Translated by Ian Rowen, Cyrus K. Hui, and Emily T. Yeh

*Muslims in Amdo Tibetan Society: Multidisciplinary Approaches*
Edited by Marie-Paule Hille, Bianca Horlemann, and Paul K. Nietupski

*Tibet as I Knew It: The Memoir of Dr. Tsewang Yishey Pemba*
By Tsewang Yishey Pemba

# Tibet as I Knew It

## The Memoir of Dr. Tsewang Yishey Pemba

Tsewang Yishey Pemba

Foreword by the Dalai Lama

LEXINGTON BOOKS

*Lanham • Boulder • New York • London*

Published by Lexington Books
An imprint of The Rowman & Littlefield Publishing Group, Inc.
4501 Forbes Boulevard, Suite 200, Lanham, Maryland 20706
www.rowman.com

86-90 Paul Street, London EC2A 4NE

British Library Cataloguing in Publication Information Available

**Library of Congress Cataloging-in-Publication Data**
Names: Pemba, Tsewang Y., author. | Bstan-'dzin-rgya-mtsho, Dalai Lama XIV, 1935– writer of foreword.
Title: Tibet as I knew it : the memoir of Dr. Tsewang Yishey Pemba / Tsewang Yishey Pemba.
Other titles: Memoir of Dr. Tsewang Yishey Pemba
Description: Lanham : Lexington Books, 2023. | Series: Studies in modern Tibetan culture | Includes bibliographical references and index.
Identifiers: LCCN 2022042890 (print) | LCCN 2022042891 (ebook) | ISBN 9781666908565 (cloth) | ISBN 9781666908589 (paper) | ISBN 9781666908572 (epub)
Subjects: LCSH: Pemba, Tsewang Y. | Tibet Autonomous Region (China)—Biography. | Physicians—China—Tibet Autonomous Region—Biography. | Authors, Tibetan—Biography. | Tibet Autonomous Region (China)—Social life and customs—20th century. | Tibet Autonomous Region (China)—Description and travel.
Classification: LCC DS786.3 .P463 2023  (print) | LCC DS786.3 (ebook) | DDC 951/.505092 [B]—dc23/eng/20220907
LC record available at https://lccn.loc.gov/2022042890
LC ebook record available at https://lccn.loc.gov/2022042891

# Contents

*Contents*

# FOREWORD

Doctor Tsewang Y. Pemba's life story is that of a man who had made the most of the opportunities offered to him, dedicating himself to the well-being of others. As a young medical officer in Darjeeling, Doctor Pemba volunteered to provide much needed treatment to Tibetan refugees.

I am delighted that the remarkable story of Dr. T.Y. Pemba's life is being published. It sheds highly informative light on modern Tibetan history as experienced by one of the early Tibetans to become a doctor of western medicine. I hope that readers will find it interesting and draw inspiration in his autobiography.

15 October 2021

# 1

~

# Historical Background

Before I begin the narrative of the Tibet that I knew, the country in which I was born and grew up, I think it will be interesting for the reader to know something of the relevant geographical, historical, and political background to my account.

Tibet is the highest country in the world, with most of its towns lying at altitudes over 10,000 feet (3,050 meters). It has been colorfully called "the Roof of the World." Gyantse in Central Tibet, where I was born, is 13,100 feet (3,965 meters); Yatung, where I spent many years of my early boyhood, is nearly 10,000 feet (3,050 meters); and Lhasa, the capital, where I lived for over three years, lies at an altitude of 12,000 feet (3,660 meters).

The country of Tibet lies north of India, with China to its east and Mongolia to its northeast, and its latitude is approximately that which passes through Louisiana in the United States of America. The size of the country of the Cholka-Sum (Three Provinces) of U-Tsang, Kham, and Amdo is roughly 2.5 million square kilometers, and, historically, the population consisted of 6 million. It includes the present-day Chinese administrative areas of the so-called Tibet Autonomous Region (TAR), Qinghai Province, two Tibetan Autonomous Prefectures and one Tibetan Autonomous County in Sichuan Province, one Tibetan Autonomous Prefecture and one Tibetan Autonomous County in Gansu Province, and one Tibetan Autonomous Prefecture in Yunan Province. Tibet Autonomous Region (TAR), made up of U-Tsang and a small part of Kham, has an area of 1.2 million square kilometers and a population of over a million. Hence the bulk of Tibet, in both area and population, lies outside of TAR, of which Lhasa is the capital.

Because of its altitude, the climate is cold, but I think any impression that the country is an Arctic wasteland is wrong. I remember that in Lhasa and Yatung, one could go out and play even in the middle of winter. I was in Milwaukee and Green Bay in the United States in the winter of 1989, and I found these places colder than Lhasa or Yatung.

Tibetans believe that, as a race, they have descended from a monkey who was an emanation of *Chenresig* (*Avolokiteshvara* in Sanskrit), the Bodhisattva of Compassion, the patron deity of Tibet, of whom the Dalai Lama is believed to be an incarnation. The divine monkey took the demoness as a spouse and beget the Tibetan race. Gradually, with disuse, the tails of descendants fell off and they became less hirsute. Originally, they inhabited the Tsethang area close to Lhasa. Thus, our Tibetan belief seems to have anticipated both Charles Darwin and Jean-Baptiste Lamarck, and perhaps Alfred Russell Wallace was not the only contender to Darwin's theory. This legend of the origin of the Tibetan race was firmly believed in by most Tibetans when I was in Tibet, and from an early age my grandmother told me this intriguing story many times.

The exact political status of Tibet, whether it is part of China or not (which is nowadays such an inflammable subject, much debated and argued), is open to discussion. The Tibetans dress, eat, and behave differently from the Chinese. They have their own language, traditions, customs, and religion. There is very little about them that can be called Chinese. Throughout history they have retained their cultural, religious, and racial identity, but their political status appears to me one of the strangest in Central Asia. From Nepal and India, they obtained their religion, Tibet's most precious possession, but India played very little part in the politics of Tibet until the latter half of the nineteenth century. The countries that made decisive impacts on its history were Mongolia and China.

At one time Tibet had been a great military power in central Asia, and in 763 (dates in CE), during the fabulous Tang Dynasty, they had even captured the Chinese capital of Chang'an (modern Xi'an). But then we read of a lama from the Sakya school of Tibetan Buddhism visiting the court of Kublai Khan, the first Mongol emperor of China, in 1270, perhaps even converting him to Tibetan Buddhism, and the khan rewarding the priest with the sovereignty of Tibet. It says very little for the political power or status of Tibet that a Mongol emperor could dispense a whole country as a gift, and it says very little for the pontiffs of religion that a Sakya lama should readily accept such a gift. Another priest, Sonam Gyatso, who converted the Mongols to Tibetan Buddhism, was given the title *Tale* (meaning "Ocean" in Mongolian) in 1578 by Altan Khan, a Mongol chief. *Tale* has now become "Dalai" to the rest of the world, but Tibetans still pronounce the title as *Tale*. It was thus Mongolia that gave the spiritual and temporal ruler of Tibet his title. In 1642, Gushri Khan, another Mongol chief, granted the Dalai Lama complete spiritual and temporal power over the whole of Tibet, which is another example of Mongol dominance.

Until the coming of the Chinese Communists into Tibet and the building of modern roads, Tibet was very far from China, remote and inaccessible, making it difficult for China to wield power and direction over an inhospitable, infertile, unrewarding country. It took twenty-one days on horseback and two months if one carried a load from Markham in eastern Tibet, where my grandmother was born, to travel to Lhasa. The Chinese frontier is still a considerable distance away from Markham. China's control over Tibet right into the middle of the twentieth century was therefore loose, uncertain, and flimsy.

I do not wish to burden my readers too much with statistics, dates, and the minutiae of Tibetan history and politics, as this book is not meant to be an encyclopedia or catalog of such details. For those readers interested in such matters concerning Tibet, there is no dearth of books providing ample and rewarding reading to any such assiduous scholar. However, as I am writing this book to give an intimate glimpse into the Tibet that I knew, some historical and political background is essential for the enjoyment and understanding of the narrative. I must now enter a stage of Tibetan history directly connected to my own account and which also shaped the destiny of my family and myself.

In the nineteenth century, Tibet lay there brooding over the Himalayas, a remote, inaccessible country, unknown, untraced, and unexplored, following its own secret life, guarded against all intrusion, with no desire whatsoever to have any relations with any neighboring countries. Whatever had happened in the past centuries, Tibet in the nineteenth century pursued a policy of distance and isolation, an indrawn recluse among the nations of the world. The power of Mongolia was no more; Genghis and Kublai Khan were long dead, and in 1368 the Mongol Yuan dynasty had been replaced by the Ming, and in 1644 the Ming were supplanted by the Ching or Manchu dynasty, which still held sway two centuries later. Tibet lay under the shadow of Manchu China, but Manchu China herself was struggling to maintain some semblance of power and independence against the relentless intrusions of European imperialism, such as the British, Dutch, German, French, and Portuguese, boasting modern arms, mighty in sea power, and fed by the inexhaustible wealth engendered by the Industrial Revolution. China could do very little to control and steer Tibet when she herself, ragged and tattered from their wolfish attacks, was at the mercy of the European imperialists.

In 1858, China suffered the humiliation of being forced to make treaties with Great Britain, France, Russia, and the United States of America, granting special privileges and extraterritorial rights to each of these nations. In 1860, the British and France occupied Peking. In 1895, China was defeated by the Japanese. Such a chain of national calamities, abjection, and humiliation helped to keep the Middle Kingdom away from Tibet, and this situation was totally in Tibet's interests, for Tibet desired nothing but isolation and withdrawal from contact with other nations. A theocratic country obsessed with religion, it felt certain that imperialist countries had sinister designs on it, and Christian nations would destroy and disintegrate its treasured possession, the Tibetan religion. It was comforting to Tibet that China was reeling from European imperialist blows, but the chief danger lay to the south. British India was a vast, utterly powerful nation, and between this imperialist power and Tibet lay the small countries of Nepal, Bhutan, and Sikkim. Nepal was friendly with the British and even as far back as the Indian Mutiny of 1857 had supplied Gurkha soldiers for their armies. Bhutan was mountainous, inaccessible, and peopled by a tough vigorous race. It was only through little Sikkim that the British might enter Tibet.

Sikkim, with an area of nearly 3,000 square miles (7,770 square kilometers), is wedged between Nepal and Bhutan. At one time, it had been almost a province of Tibet. Its rulers and aristocracy were of Tibetan blood. Sir Joseph Dalton Hooker—a doctor, botanist, and director of Kew Gardens—had been in Sikkim in the late 1800s and made some interesting collections. Sikkim is even mentioned in Darwin's *On the Origin of Species*.[1] Mrs. Margaret Williamson, the wife of a former British political officer of Sikkim, says the state had four thousand species of flowering plants, including 450 varieties of orchids and 40 rhododendrons.[2] The vegetation varied from subtropical to alpine. There were seven hundred bird and six hundred butterfly species. Dr. R. R. Marett, rector of Exeter College, Oxford, in a foreword to Walter Evans-Wentz's book *Tibetan Yoga and Secret Doctrine*, has referred to "that carefully protected dependency of the British Empire, Sikkim."[3]

In 1860, the British annexed Sikkim and, in a war with the Bhutanese in 1865, did the same with portions of Bhutanese territory, including Kalimpong, which is close to the southern border of Tibet. The British were getting uncomfortably close to Tibet. In vital government affairs, the Delphic oracle of Tibet—the Nechung Chökyong—was consulted. I shall in a later chapter say something about the monastery of Nechung close to Lhasa and its oracle, for I spent a few days there in 1940 and met the incumbent soothsayer of that time. The oracle commanded the Tibetans to attack in Sikkim and regain what was legitimate Tibetan territory, and the Tibetans, obeying with a blind faith, did so around 1887. The British would have none of it, accusing accused the Tibetans of encroaching eighteen miles into British-Sikkimese territory and demanding an immediate withdrawal. When the Tibetans failed to comply, General Graham attacked them in 1888 and drove them right across the border and, by capturing the Chumbi valley, advanced about fifteen miles into Tibet. This was the first encounter between the Tibetan troops armed with swords, slings, and muzzle-loaders and modern British troops. In spite of the inspired assurances of the Nechung oracle, Tibet suffered an ignominious defeat. General Graham, having driven the Tibetans out of Sikkim, however, withdrew from the Chumbi valley. We are told that he was ordered to evacuate Tibetan territory "in order to avoid Chinese susceptibilities," but this explanation is hardly plausible, for the British had no such compunction when they occupied Peking in 1860![4]

However, the British did not want a repetition of such incidents. Since the Tibetans were reluctant to negotiate, and since China was considered Britain's suzerain and could be bullied into anything (had not the British taken Peking in 1860), a convention was signed between Great Britain and China that related to Tibet and Sikkim. This was done in Calcutta in 1890 and had the two following specific clauses:

Article 1. The boundary of Sikkim and Tibet shall be the crest of the mountain range separating the waters flowing into Sikkim Teesta. . . .

Article 2. It is admitted that the British government, whose protectorate over the Sikkim State is hereby recognised, has direct and exclusive control over the internal administration and foreign relations of that State, and except through and with the permission of the British Government, neither the Ruler of the State nor any of its officers shall have official relations of any kind, formal or informal, with any other country.[5]

Having manipulated the wedge in skillfully, the British, in a chess-like move, now brought in the question of trade with Tibet. *Trade* has always been a keyword in the diplomatic maneuvers of imperialist powers. We were taught in school that "trade follows the flag." I think putting it the other way around would be more appropriate. Nobody must be reluctant or averse to trade even if it meant forcing that trade down somebody's throat. Like a tiff between husband and wife, it takes two to trade, but imperialism disagrees. Thus was added the Regulation of 1893 regarding Trade, Communications and Pasturage to be appended to the Sikkim-Tibet convention of 1890:

Article 1. Trade-mart shall be established at Yatung, on the Tibetan side of the frontier, and shall be open to all the British subjects for purposes of trade from the first day of May 1894. The Government of India shall be free to send officers to reside at Yatung to watch the conditions of British trade at that mart.

Article 2. British subjects trading at Yatung shall be at liberty to travel freely to and fro between the frontier and Yatung, to reside at Yatung, and to rent houses and godowns for their own accommodation and the storage of their goods.[6]

The agreement was signed at Darjeeling in the Himalayas close to the Tibetan border, a town famous for its tea throughout the world, and where I was destined to spend many decades of my life.

But the Tibetans now began to get up to their usual tricks. They wanted to be recluses, not traders. They were more interested in religion and the preservation of their own way of life than in rendering to the British Caesar what was Caesar's. They were more xenophobic than any Han Chinese of the Middle Kingdom. *Chö Nangpa*, meaning "Inner Religion" (Tibetan Buddhism), must not be contaminated—not at all—by adherents of *Chö Chipa*, meaning "Outer Religion" (every other religion except Tibetan Buddhism). They made it clear that they did not recognize the 1890 convention, nor the regulations of 1893, as they had not been consulted or been a signatory. They did not recognize the Sikkim-Tibet boundary and began dismantling boundary markings. What Sir Charles Bell, a British political officer in Tibet and a great friend and advisor of the thirteenth Dalai Lama, says is perhaps more pertinent: "But the Tibetan government desired at all costs to keep us at arm's length, for they feared and distrusted us. To them we were a pushful people, forcing ourselves in where we were not wanted, and harboring ulterior designs on their country and their religion."[7]

Around that time, the formidable, redoubtable, celestial *Pukkah* Sahib George Nathaniel Curzon (a very superior person), or Lord Curzon, as he was known, was viceroy of India, a position that in those days of the British Raj was next to the divine. He is reported as saying when he saw a bunch of British Tommies taking a bath somewhere in a military station in India, "Dear me! I have no conception that the lower class had such white skins!"[8] Curzon stood no nonsense from the recalcitrant Tibetans. He sent off a letter in 1900 to the thirteenth Dalai Lama, the predecessor of the present. The Dalai Lama was hesitant and noncommittal, saying that he could not do anything for fear of Chinese objections. Another letter followed in 1901, but the letter was not even opened.

In dispatching these letters, Curzon was merely playing the "Great Game," a name coined by Rudyard Kipling for the clash of Britain and Russian imperialist ambitions in Central Asia, and Tibet was a vital pawn in the "game."[9] Tsarist Russia (or *Urusu*, as Russia is called by the Tibetans) possessed a subtle attraction for the Tibetans during the first decade of the twentieth century. This was before the guns of the "Great October Revolution," an event now being hastily relegated to the limbo of

forgotten things. Tibetans realized they could obtain isolation and reclusive seclusion only if they had a strong card to play against the persistent
demands of British imperialism. Already Great Britain had made several
forays into Tibet, and now there was this "trade mart" in Yatung, well
within the precincts of *Chö nangba* (Tibetan territory).

There was no alternative but to seek Tsarist Russia as a patron, doing
what Tibetans had always done throughout its history, seeking patrons
and benefactors to outwit and outplay rival religious and secular fac-
tions. The Dalai Lama had a tutor who was from a Buddhist community
in Siberian Russia. He was a *Tsannyid Khenpo*—that is, a learned profes-
sor of Tibetan metaphysics, very high in Tibetan Buddhist hierarchy. He
was sent to Russia to woo the tsar and make the correct overtures, and
he appears to have been successful. The tsar smiled benevolently, and
Curzon was alarmed. To have Tsarist Russia at the very doors of Imperial
India, the crown jewel of the British Empire, was unthinkable.

Curzon took preemptive action. The velvet glove of diplomacy and the
guise of "trade" had not worked, and now the only alternative was to
resort to gun-boat diplomacy. The military action known as the "Younghusband Expedition" was launched in 1904 under the leadership of Francis (later Sir Francis) Younghusband, who was destined to mature into
an explorer and mystic. And it is here that history and my own life meet,
for I would get to know extremely well, when I was a student in Britain,
Lieutenant-Colonel F. M. Bailey, CIE, a young lieutenant in the 32nd Sikh
Pioneers and who later became an explorer, ornithologist, spy (in the
"Great Game"), and botanist, and who fought in most of the battles of the
expedition. I stayed many times at his homes in Stiffkey and Cromer. It
was a privilege for me to discuss the Younghusband Expedition with him,
and I felt that I was in the presence of living history.

On the Tibetan side too, I knew many men and women who remembered the *Shing-Druk lo kyi ma*, the war of the Wood Dragon year (1904).
The British army fought battles at altitude where no such battles had been
fought in their annals. The Tibetans for the second time clashed against
a modern well-trained army that had Lee-Enfield rifles and Howitzers,
against which their swords, slings, muzzle-loaders, and raw untrained,
undisciplined courage were no match. The British advanced easily from
the Chumbi valley to Gyantse (the town where I was born) and then to
Lhasa. The "Forbidden City" of Lhasa, they claimed, had been breached,
and a book was written about the *Unveiling of Lhasa*.

Just before Younghusband entered Lhasa, the thirteenth Dalai Lama
was only twenty-eight years old and, in the midst of a three years, three
months, three days meditation was advised to flee; he left for Urga in
Mongolia, 1,500 miles (2,400 kilometers) away. The British concluded a
convention with the Tibetans, signed by Ganden Tri Rinpoche on behalf

of the Dalai Lama during his absence, on September 7, 1904, the twenty-seventh day of the seventh month of the Tibetan Wood Dragon year. Some parts of this convention are worth quoting:

> Whereas doubts and difficulties have arisen as to the meaning and validity of the Anglo-Chinese Convention of 1890, and the Trade Regulations of 1893, and as to the liabilities of the Tibetan Government under these agreements; and whereas recent occurrences have tended towards a disturbance of the relations of friendship and good understanding which have existed between the British Government and the Government of Tibet; and whereas it is desirable to restore peace and amicable relations, and to resolve and determine the doubts and difficulties as aforesaid; the said Governments have resolved to conclude a Convention with these objects, and the following articles have been agreed upon by Colonel F. E. Younghusband, CIE, in virtue of full powers vested in him by His Britannic Majesty's Government and on behalf of that said Government, and Lo-sang Gyal-tsen, the Ga-den Ti-Rimpoche, and the representatives of the Council, of the three monasteries Se-ra, Dre-pung, and Ga-den, and of the ecclesiastical and lay officials of the National Assembly of the Government of Tibet.

I. The Government of Tibet engages to respect the Anglo-Chinese Convention of 1890 and to recognise the frontier between Sikkim and Tibet, as defined in Article 1 of the said Convention and to erect boundary pillars accordingly.

II. The Tibetan Government undertakes to open forthwith trade marts to which all British and Tibetan subjects shall have free right of access at Gyantse and Gartok, as well as at Yatung. . . .

V. The Tibetan Government undertakes to keep the roads to Gyantse and Gartok from the frontier clear of all obstruction and in state of repair suited to the needs of the trade. . . .

VI. As an indemnity to the British Government for the expense incurred in the dispatch of armed troops to Lhasa, to exact reparation for breaches of treaty obligations, and for the insults offered to and attacks upon the British Commissioner and his following and escort, the Tibetan Government engages to pay a sum of pounds five hundred thousand. . . .

VII. As security for the payment of the above-mentioned indemnity and for the fulfilment of the provisions relative to trade marts . . . the British Government shall continue to occupy the Chumbi Valley until the indemnity has been paid and until the trade marts have been effectively opened for three years. . . .

IX. The Government of Tibet engages that, without the previous consent of the British Government—
   a. no portion of Tibetan territory shall be ceded, sold, leased, mortgaged or otherwise given for occupation, to any Foreign Power;
   b. no such Power shall be permitted shall be permitted to intervene in Tibetan affairs;

    c. no representative or Agents of any Foreign Power shall be admitted
       to Tibet;
    d. no concessions for railways, roads, telegraphs, mining or other
       rights, shall be granted to any Foreign Power, or to the subject of
       any Foreign Power. In the event of consent to such concessions
       being granted, similar or equivalent concessions shall be granted to
       the British Government;
    e. no Tibetan revenues, neither in kind or in cash, shall be pledged
       or assigned to any Foreign Power, or to the subject of any Foreign
       Power.[10]

The above document is extremely interesting for me, both from a historical-political point of view and from a personal one. It was the first document of such a nature signed directly between the British and the Tibetans without the intermediary of the Chinese. Curzon must have realized that the direct dealings with the Tibetans were necessary, as China's hold over Tibet was nebulous. The preamble speaks of the "doubts and difficulties" and "the liabilities of the Tibetan Government under these agreements," but the plain fact was that Tibetans wanted to have no dealings with the British, and they ignored any agreements made over their heads with the Chinese.[11] "Disturbances of the relations of friendship and good understanding which have existed between the British Government and the Government of Tibet"—these touching expressions make one smile in disbelief, for such relations were nonexistent.[12] Tibetans were the most xenophobic of peoples at that time, and the last thing they wanted was "relations of friendship and good understanding" with *Chö chiba* ("the outsiders"), least of all the imperialistic, colonizing Christian British.[13] The thirteenth Dalai Lama's overtures to the Russian tsar were merely gestures of desperation.

    It was strange treaty in many ways. There were no protracted negotiations. The British dictated their terms in great detail, dotting all their "i"s and crossing all their "t"s, and the Tibetans accepted everything. I think the Tibetans were most anxious to get the *Enjis* (British) to depart from Lhasa as quickly as they came and lead their own isolated lives. They were willing to sign any terms as long as they were left alone. In this sense, the Tibetans proved to be right, for the British left Lhasa almost immediately after signing the treaty. There were no atrocities, no mass executions or reprisals, and very little looting. Tibetan prisoners of war were treated kindly; their wounds were tended, and when they were released, they were given cigarettes and small sums of money. It was as if the British began to suffer from qualms of conscience at attacking a defenseless country that desired nothing but to be left alone.

    The treaty was also quite unique for the British in that the chief signatory on the other side of the table was a priest of the highest rank and learning. I wonder what went through the Ganden Tri Rimpoche's mind as he signed the document. He was the abbot of the monastery of Ganden, close to Lhasa, and was nominated to this position on account of his learning, integrity, disciplined behavior, and spotless monastic career. It was one of the few positions in Tibet to which anybody in the land, be he beggar or serf, could aspire through sheer learning and merit. In fact, Tibetans have a saying: "For any mother's son who has tenacity and determination, the Seal of the Throne of Ganden is within his grasp." The signing took place in the Potala, the vast administrative edifice that rears above Lhasa (and also the winter palace of the Dalai Lama). It must have been a strange confrontation between Colonel Younghusband and the Ganden Tri Rimpoche: the *Pukkah* Sahib, soldier, explorer, adventurer with his feet planted solidly on imperialist foundations and duties of bearing "the white man's burden,"[14] serving God, King, Country, and the Empire, and facing his adversary, an austere ascetic Tibetan monk, pursuing the path to spiritual salvation and versed in the doctrine of emptiness and believing that the taking of any form of life to be a sin.

The treaty must also have been one of the few in the world requiring the signatures of the heads of monasteries. One does not usually associate monasteries with such mundane matters, but Tibet was a completely theocratic country dominated by monks, and these three monasteries were the largest in the world and had immense influence on Tibetan political affairs—shades of Archbishop Thomas Becket and Tudor England.

We also notice once more that "trade" was being forced down the throats of obstinate Tibetans, and political agencies were shrouded under the camouflage and euphemism of "trade marts." Having spent many years at such British "trade marts," I know how much "trade" was carried out. One also finds the poor Tibetans having to pay an indemnity of £500,000. This is not a princely sum by present-day standards (American heavy-weight boxing champions earn many times that sum in a knock-out bout lasting less than three minutes), but it was a vast sum for an impoverished country to pay in 1904.

The British had forced "trade" down the Tibetans' unwilling throats, had invaded their country, and had killed their slings and muzzle-loader carrying men with howitzers and Lee-Enfield rifles, and now they had to pay this indemnity "for expenses incurred in the dispatch of armed troops to Lhasa, to exact reparation for breaches of treaty obligations, and for the insults offered to and attacks upon the British commissioner and his following and escort."[15] Tibetans, too, one must remember, "fought for the ashes of their fathers and the temples of their gods."[16]

On November 11, 1904, Lord Curzon was "pleased to direct as an act of grace that the sum of money which the Tibetan Government have bound themselves under the terms of Article VI of the said Convention to pay to His Majesty's Government as an indemnity . . . be reduced . . . and to declare that the British occupation of the Chumbi valley shall cease after the due payment of three annual installments . . . provided, however, that the trade marts . . . shall have been affectively opened for three years . . . and that, in the meantime, the Tibetans shall have faithfully complied with the terms of the said Convention in all other respects."[17] Eventually, as a matter of fact, the indemnities were paid by the Chinese government in 1907, and presumably the subdued Tibetans "faithfully complied with the terms of the said Convention in all respects" because the British withdrew from the Chumbi valley (redolent with idyllic memories for me) on February 9, 1908.[18] I think this is the only instance when Great Britain occupied Tibetan territory for any length of time.

The Younghusband Treaty had been signed without consulting China, and presumably to make sure that the Chinese also came into the picture, a convention was signed between Great Britain and China in Peking on April 27, 1906, which in my opinion effectively demolished any Tibetan ambitions for international recognition of nationhood, independence, and the abolition of those terms of "suzerainty" and "autonomy" that are obnoxious to Tibetan national sentiment.[19] It destroyed any hopes of what the Tibetans call *rangzen* (independence) and usually qualified by the emphatic adjective *tsangma* (pure). It is worth quoting in some detail because of its obliteration of Tibetan aspirations for independence and on account of its charmingly ostentatious baroque style, which sugarcoated much of brutal cloak-and-dagger diplomacy affecting the lives and happiness of millions in the days of imperialism and colonialism.

Whereas His Majesty the King of Great Britain and Ireland and of the British Dominions beyond the seas, Emperor of India, and His Majesty the Emperor of China are sincerely desirous to maintain and perpetuate the relations of friendship and good understanding which now exist between their respective Empires;

And whereas the refusal of Tibet to recognise the validity of or to carry into full effect the provisions of the Anglo-Chinese Convention of March 17th, 1890, and Regulations of December 5th, 1893, placed the British Government under the necessity of taking steps to secure their rights and interests under the said Convention and Regulations;

And whereas as Convention . . . was signed at Lhasa on September 7th, 1904, on behalf of Great Britain and Tibet. . . .

His Britannic Majesty and His Majesty the Emperor of China have resolved to conclude a Convention on this subject and have for this purpose named Plenipotentiaries, that is to say:—

His Majesty The King of Great Britain and Ireland:

Sir Earnest Mason Satow, Knight Grand Cross of the Most Distinguished Order of St. Michael and St. George, His said Majesty's Envoy Extraordinary and Minister Plenipotentiary to His Majesty the Emperor of China;
and His Majesty The Emperor of China.

His Excellency Tong Shoa-yi, His said Majesty's High Commissioner Plenipotentiary and a Vice-President of the Board of Foreign Affairs,

who having communicated to each other their respective full powers and finding them to be in good and due form have agreed upon and concluded the following Convention in ix articles:—

Article I. The Convention concluded on September 7th, 1904 . . . is hereby confirmed . . . both of the High Contracting Parties engage to take at all times such steps as may be necessary to secure the due fulfilment. . . .

Article II. The Government of Great Britain engages not to annex Tibetan territory or to interfere in the administration of Tibet. The Government of China also undertakes not to permit any other foreign state to interfere with the territory or internal administration of Tibet.

Article III. The concessions which are mentioned in Article 9 (d) of the Convention concluded on September 7th, 1904, by Great Britain and Tibet are denied to any state or to the subject of any other state other than China, but it has been arranged with China that at the trade marts specified . . . Great Britain shall be entitled to lay down telegraph lines connecting to India.

Article IV. The provisions of the Anglo-Chinese Convention of 1890 and Regulations of 1893 shall . . . remain in full force.[20]

The convention was signed in Peking on April 27, 1906, which was the fourth day of the fourth month of the thirty-second year of the reign of Kuang-hsu. The inscrutable Chinese must have smiled and nodded their approval. Tibet was firmly in their pocket, and that, too, with the connivance and the blessings of the British imperialists.

A final convention drove the last nails into the coffin of Tibetan independence. This was between Great Britain and Russia, signed at St. Petersburg on August 18, 1907. It said:

The Governments of Great Britain and Russia recognising the suzerain rights of China in Thibet, and considering the fact that Great Britain, by reason of her geographical position, has a special interest in the maintenance of the status quo in the external relations of Thibet, have made the following arrangement.

Article I. . . . respect the territorial integrity of Thibet and to abstain from all interference in the internal administration.

Article II. . . . Great Britain and Russia engage not to enter into negotiations with Thibet except throughout the intermediary of the Chinese Government. . . .

Article IV. . . . engage neither to seek nor to obtain whatever for themselves or their subjects any Concessions for railways, roads, telegraphs, and mines or other rights in Thibet.[21]

The "Great Game" between Britain and Tsarist Russia regarding Tibet, or "Thibet" (as spelled in the convention), thus ended with China taking the spoils.

In December 1909, the thirteenth Dalai Lama, who had fled from the British in 1904, after an exile in Mongolia and China, returned to Lhasa. During his exile in China, he met in 1908 William Rockhill, the United States of America's minister to China, and this was historic in being the first meeting between an American official and a Dalai Lama.

The Dalai Lama was barely two months in Lhasa when a Chinese army approached the city as if to put into reality all the rights China had obtained from the treaties and conventions. The Dalai Lama had to flee once more, but this time he sought refuge in British India. It was an irony of history that his former enemy should now become his only hope. While escaping, the Dalai Lama, from the monastery of Samding located on the shores of Yardrok lake, sent an urgent message to Basil Gould (later Sir Basil), who was then the British trade agent at Gyantse. Gould met the Dalai Lama at Phari and accompanied him to Yatung, where David Macdonald, with Scots and Tibetan blood in him, was the British trade agent.[22] The supreme pontiff of Tibet took shelter at the British Residency in Yatung, insisting on sharing Macdonald's bedroom, as he could feel secure only in the presence of a British official.

David Macdonald retired to Kalimpong, where I used to meet him often in the Himalayan Hotel, which was run by his daughters. He was a benign old gentleman who spoke perfect Tibetan, always talked to me in Tibetan instead of English, and played cards every evening with his family. I little realized that he had once given asylum to the thirteenth Dalai Lama, who is considered by some to have been Tibet's greatest Dalai Lama: Ngawang Lobsang Thubten Gyatso.

The Dalai Lama crossed into India over the 14,300-foot Jelep La pass, arriving at Gnatong just over the Indian side of the border close to Kalimpong. This was the very area that had been in dispute and precipitated the first clash of arms between Tibetans and the British in 1888 and started the train of events that led to the Younghusband Expedition. The Gnatong outpost—bleak, remote, and inhospitable—was manned by two ex-sergeants of the British army, Luff and Humphries. The Tibetans in the Dalai Lama's entourage, exhausted after an arduous journey, covering the 270 miles from Lhasa to Gnatong in nine days (which normally would have taken twice that time), rushed in great excitement toward the two ex-sergeants, seeking asylum for their god-king, insisting, as at Yatung, that His Holiness should sleep in their bedroom. They were terribly agitated, gesturing wildly and everybody speaking out at once. Above the bedlam, one of the sergeants, phlegmatic and displaying admirable British sangfroid, shouted the question that has now become a minor classic: "Which of you blighters is the Dally Lama?"

The Dalai Lama spent two years in Darjeeling at a site now occupied by the Tibetan Refugee Self-help Centre and hospital. At one time in the 1970s, I used to see Tibetan refugee patients at the hospital. In 1911, Sun Yat-sen's revolution broke out in China, and the Manchu emperor was deposed. In Tibet, fighting broke out between the isolated Chinese garrisons and Tibetan monks and laymen. Many of the Chinese units, deprived of their salaries because of the civil war in China, openly mutinied. The Dalai Lama left Kalimpong in June 1912 and made a triumphant return to Lhasa, traveling leisurely on the same route down which he had made such a wearisome and hazardous escape two years previously.

There followed a period from 1912 until 1950 when Tibet was de facto independent. After the return of the Dalai Lama, China tried to assert her rights of suzerainty over Tibet, and there were spells of fighting on the eastern borders where the Tibetans held the Chinese at bay, Tibetans boasting that one Tibetan armed with a modern rifle could take on a dozen Chinese. To end the sporadic fighting on the Sino-Tibetan border, the Simla Conference of 1913–1914 was convened at the instigation of the British. It was held at the British summer hill station of Simla (now Shimla), and the British, Chinese, and Tibetans met as equal conferees. It was inconclusive, as the agreement was only initialed and not formally signed by the Chinese, and then the First World War intervened, and the Sino-Tibetan dispute was shelved. What resulted from this conference and provided a modus vivendi between the Tibetans and Chinese were as follows:

1. Tibet was divided, and the British claim that this was at their suggestion, into "Outer" and "Inner," with reference to China: Lhasa, Gyantse (my birthplace), Yatung, and Markham (my grandmother's birthplace) falling into the former category.
2. Chinese suzerainty over the whole of Tibet was recognized, but she was to refrain from converting Tibet into a Chinese province.
3. Great Britain was not to annex any part of Tibet, but she could retain all the trade marts, appoint officials in these areas, and maintain an escort of troops at all these marts.
4. The autonomy of "Outer Tibet" was recognized, with China agreeing not to send any troops, settlers, or officials into this region.
5. The British trade agent at Gyantse was authorized to visit Lhasa to settle matters that could not be settled in Gyantse.[23]

Such was the Simla Conference, which my grand-uncle Tashi Tsering attended as a minor clerk to Sir Charles Bell, the British advisor on Tibetan affairs for Sir Henry McMahon, secretary in the Indian Foreign Department, who was the British plenipotentiary at the conference and for whom the famous McMahon Line is named, in delineating the Indo-Tibetan boundary that even to this day (1992) is a matter of ferocious dispute between the Chinese Communist government and India and led to the Sino-Indian war of 1962. Only an uneasy lull prevails, with alert, tense armies armed to the teeth facing each other across the controversial hotly disputed McMahon Line. The Berlin Wall may be obliterated, but the McMahon Line persists, a legacy of the Simla Conference. The political status of Tibet became a conundrum, well expressed by Mrs. Margaret Williamson: "H. M. Government . . . recognised the de facto autonomy of Tibet within the theoretical suzerainty of China."[24]

During the 1914–1918 Great War, the Dalai Lama offered one thousand Tibetan soldiers to fight for the British and ordered prayers to be said throughout the land, invoking a swift and total victory for the armies of Great Britain, his former enemy.

*Left to right: Late Prime Minister Jigme Dorji of Bhutan; his wife Ashi Tess la; Kumar Palden Namgyal of Sikkim; King Jigme/Ugen Wangchuk of Bhutan; Political Officer Sir Basil Gould; Princess Kula of Sikkim; Dr. Henricks of Sikkim; and author's father, Rai Sahib Pemba Tsering (Deothang, Bhutan 1943). Photo by author's father, Rai Sahib Pemba Tsering*

Around 1919–1920, China sent delegates to Lhasa to try and bring Tibet closer to the Han Motherland and to put an end to the fighting that had persisted in eastern Tibet, where Tibetan troops (many of them armed with imported British rifles) were gaining the upper hand, to the great humiliation of the Han Motherland. The delegates met the Dalai Lama several times, but he maintained a noncommittal statesmanlike attitude and declined to join the Chinese republic. Tibetans were now leaning more toward British India, and a close friendship that began with his exile in Darjeeling during 1910–1912 developed between the Dalai Lama and the political officer, Sir Charles Bell, although the British appear to be rather guarded and coy in their relations with the Himalayan neighbor with whom India, their crown jewel, shared the longest boundary. Sir Charles Bell appears to have been a charming, courteous, cultured gentleman in the true British sense, the "Waterloo was won on the playing fields of Eton"[25] type, who had very great sympathies for Tibet and always "played cricket" in his political dealings with her. I remember an old Tibetan man in Darjeeling who worked as a bearer (servant) for Sir Charles, and he spoke of him as a deity: "A *Pukkah* Sahib in every sense of the word," he told me.

Sir Charles Bell wrote many books on Tibet that have now become classics. He visited Lhasa in 1920 and renewed his cordial relations with the Dalai Lama, but the British did very little to modernize Tibet or to support her claims to independence. All they could do was display sympathy; sell a limited quantity of arms to her (knowing that they would be used against the Chinese in eastern Tibet); establish an English school in Gyantse in 1923 for children of the nobility, with Frank Ludlow, an Englishman, as headmaster (the school was closed because of Tibetan priestly opposition in 1926); foster amicable relations with Tibetans; and allow British thoughts and ways to permeate into Tibet through their trade agencies, example being better than precept. Such British hesitancy and caution must have disillusioned the Dalai Lama, and his eyes had no choice but to turn toward China, careful not to please or rebuff the Han Republic, though his heart lay with the British.

His Holiness the Thirteenth Dalai Lama, born in 1876, was getting old by Tibetan standards. In 1931, he made it known that he was giving up all secular affairs and devoting himself entirely to religion. The Nechung oracle prophesied that His Holiness would soon pass into the Fields of Bliss—that is, die. All Tibet fell into gloom; prayers were recited everywhere; rites and rituals performed for his continued existence in order to guide the affairs of Tibet, but to no avail, for on December 17, 1933, the Great Thirteenth passed away at the age of fifty-seven.

In 1934, the Chinese Republic dispatched a "condolence mission" led by General Huang Mu-sung, ostensibly to pay respects to the Tibetan government on the passing away of the Dalai Lama. Some of the officials stayed on permanently to continue to "pay their condolences." But here I am coming close to my own personal narrative, and I think it is good place to end this chapter.

## NOTES

1. Charles Darwin, *The Origin of Species* (New York: P. F. Collier & Son Company, 1909), 417.

2. Margaret D. Williamson and John Snelling, *Memoirs of a Political Officer's Wife in Tibet, Sikkim and Bhutan* (London: Wisdom, 1987), 12.

3. W. Y. Evans-Wentz, ed., *Tibetan Yoga and Secret Doctrine*, 2nd ed. (New York: Oxford University Press, 1958), xxiv.

4. Charles Bell, *Tibet Past and Present* (New Delhi: Motilal Banarsidass, 1992), 60.

5. Francis Edward Younghusband, *India and Tibet: A History of the Relations which Have Subsisted Between the Two Countries from the Time of Warren Hastings to 1910; with a Particular Account of the Mission to Lhasa of 1904* (London: John Murray, 1910), 439.

6. Ibid., 440.

7. Bell, *Tibet*, 61–62.

8. Harold Nicolson, *Curzon: The Last Phase 1919–1925* (London: Constable & Co., 1934), notes 1, 47–48.

9. Rudyard Kipling, *Kim* (New York: Doubleday, Page & Company, 1901), 279.

10. C. U. Aitchison, comp., *A Collection of Treaties, Engagements and Sanads. Relating to India and Neighbouring Countries*, Vol. II (Calcutta: Superintendent Government Printing, 1909), 344–346.

11. Ibid., 344.

12. Ibid.

13. Ibid.

14. Rudyard Kipling, *Stories and Poems from Rudyard Kipling* (New York: Grosset & Dunlap, 1909), 359.

15. Aitchison, *Collection of Treaties*, 344–346.

16. Thomas Babington Macaulay, *Lays of Ancient Rome* (London: Longman, Brown, Green, and Longmans, 1847), 56.

17. Aitchison, *Collection of Treaties*, 348.

18. Ibid.

19. Aitchison, *Collection of Treaties*, 342.

20. Ibid., 348–350.

21. Bell, *Tibet*, 290.

22. Basil John Gould, *The Jewel in the Lotus: Recollections of an Indian Political* (United Kingdom: Chatto & Windus, 1957), 23.

23. Bell, *Tibet Past and Present*, 154–155.

24. Williamson and Snelling, *Memoirs of a Political Officer's Wife*, 209.
25. George Orwell, *The Lion and the Unicorn* (London: Penguin Books, 1982), 55.

# 2

~

# Family Background

Tashi Tsering, my granduncle, used to tell me vaguely that my ancestors from my father's side came from Gartok in the Kham region of eastern Tibet. He related that there had been three brothers who were wild and iconoclastic, of dubious character, possibly even bandits or robbers; one of them, known as Gartok Tsering (presumably the more notorious), fathered the children from whom we are descended. Sometime in the eighteenth century, Gartok Tsering and his brothers fled Kham and migrated southward as far as they could. Reasons for migration? Possibly pillage, high-handed robbery, murder, manslaughter, inciting rebellion, refusal to pay taxes—I am not certain! However, they migrated very far and must have had cogent reasons for doing so, because they settled in Kyirong, in Tibetan territory but close to the Nepal border. By present-day standards, this is almost like migrating to the moon because, until the Chinese built motorable roads in Tibet in the 1950s, it took almost two to three months on horseback from Kham to Kyirong. A safe distance, certainly, even for murder! But perhaps my ancestors were wily and cunning and calculating to boot, because just in case officialdom and the long arm of the law should catch up with them (and Tibetan methods of punishment were barbarous in the extreme), they encamped within sprinting distance of the Nepalese border and thence sanctuary and asylum. I think that is possibly why they chose Kyirong.

I have never been to Kyirong, but from all accounts regarding the place, I don't think my ancestors could have chosen a better place than Kyirong. Heinrich Harrer of *Seven Years in Tibet* fame, who knew my father well and whom I met for the first time in the Himalayan Hotel

(David Macdonald's hotel, which my readers have come across in the last chapter) in Kalimpong in 1990, has this to say about Kyirong, where he spent some time during his escape from India to Tibet:

> The name Kyirong means "the village of happiness" and it really deserves the appellation. I shall never cease thinking of this place with yearning, and if I can choose where to pass the evening of my life, it will be Kyirong. There I would build myself a house of red cedar-wood and have one of the rushing mountain streams running through my garden, in which every kind of fruit would grow, for though the altitude is over 9000 feet Kyirong lies on the twenty-eighth parallel. When we arrived in January the temperature was just below freezing; it seldom falls below –10 degrees centigrade. The seasons correspond to those in the Alps, but the vegetation is sub-tropical. One can go skiing the whole year around, and in the summer there is a row of 20,000 footers to climb.[1]

Despite Heinrich Harrer's rapturous description, my ancestors left the village of happiness. Why? Perhaps their nightmares of the law catching up with them really came true! There are no Canadian Mounties in Tibet, but it could be that things got a bit too hot for them. Or perhaps I am being unfair; their nomadic spirit might have stirred, and they could have got tired of their Shangri-La, for the chief defect of all Shangri-Las and utopias is their intrinsic boredom. My ancestors traveled farther into Nepal, and then we find their children settled in present-day Pashupati in Nepal, close to the Indian town of Darjeeling.

The next link in the story is a wild rider. (Tibetans who have settled in Sikkim and Darjeeling areas are called Bhutia, by the way.) This gentleman had a long pigtail, and he often rode from Pashupati to Ghoom-Jorebungalow, a small town close to Darjeeling. At one time, Ghoom, nearly 8,000 feet (2440 meters), boasted the highest railway station in Asia. Alas, I am told that this pigtailed gentleman, a Tibetan John Peel, one night while returning to Pashupati from Ghoom-Jorebungalow saw a ghost on the roadside, causing his horse to bolt; he was thrown and suffered such serious injuries that he died within a few hours. He had four sons, the oldest marrying Rhida Lhamo, the sister of Tashi Tsering and niece of Tashi Wangdi, about whom I shall write soon. I was told that Rhida Lhamo's family also came from Kyirong, and possibly this was a kind of marriage within the same clan. One of his other sons, Dawa Lama, became a Gurkha officer in the 2nd Battalion of the 10th Gurkha Rifles— "Shekend Ten," as we knew it in Tibet (all aspiring southern Tibetans wanting to join the Gurkhas seemed to go into the "Shekend Ten"). He saw action in the Third Afghan War of 1919.

I am not sure what my great-grand-uncle Tashi Wangdi was under the British Raj, but he must have been directly responsible for getting my grand-uncle Tashi Tsering to join the British Trade Agencies in Tibet, and later Tashi Tsering was the man who forced my father to do the same. During his exile in India in 1910–1912, the thirteenth Dalai Lama traveled to Calcutta to meet Lord Minto, the viceroy of India, on March 14, 1910, at Hastings House. Perhaps a photograph was taken on that very day, because the only photograph I have seen of Tashi Wangdi is in a group at Hastings House. In it the Dalai Lama, surrounded by officials, is seated in the front; behind him stands Sir Charles Bell, and close to Sir Charles Bell is Tashi Wangdi: short, unsmiling, firm mouthed, rather shrewd look-ing, in official Tibetan clothes, hatted, silk jacketed, with a long pendant turquoise earring hanging from his left earlobe. I may sound a bit child-ish when I say this, and it may indicate disrespect for an ancestor, but he looked very much like the film actor Herbert Lom (Napoleon and other cameo roles).

Some years ago, while rummaging through some old boxes in my house in Gangtok, the capital of Sikkim, I came across the British Raj "Service Book" belonging to my grand-uncle Tashi Tsering, nephew of Tashi Wangdi. It was very interesting, and I shall give some extracts from this book:

Race: Tibetan          Residence: Jorebungalow, Darjeeling District.
Birth: 1886            Exact height: 5 feet 4 inches
Attesting officer—Lieutenant F.M. Bailey, Assistant Political Officer, Chumbi.
     Appointed Trade Registration Clerk at Chema, Chumbi Valley on 27 December 1906 at a salary of Rupees 100/-per month. [equivalent in 1992 to 3.5 US dollars or £2 sterling per month]

"This officer has served under me for three years. He is capable man and understands his work."
     Signed: David Macdonald, British Trade Agent, Yatung, Tibet, on 9 Janu-ary 1913.

"Babu Tashi Tsering worked with me on the Tibet Conference in Simla and Delhi from September 1913 to July 1914. He worked hard, intelligently in all respects rendered me thoroughly capable assistance."
     Signed: C.A. Bell, Political Officer on-Special Duty, Tibet, 14 December 1921.

"I agree with the remarks made by Sir Charles Bell. Since his return from Lhasa, he discharged his duties with conspicuous ability and to my entire satisfaction. He is fitted for a higher post of trust and responsibility."
     Signed: David Macdonald, British Trade Agent, Yatung Tibet, 13 October 1924.

"I have found Babu Tashi Tsering an exceptionally able clerk. He is tactful, full of common sense and thoroughly reliable and sound."
    Signed: F. Williamson, British Trade Agency, Yatung, Tibet, 2 September 1925.

"During the six months he has worked under me in Gangtok, I have found no reason to alter the high opinion I had already formed of him."
    Signed: F. Williamson, British Trade Agent, Yatung, Tibet, 9 December 1926.[2]

Then, after all the above superlatives, and with his career taking a meteoric rise and Tashi Tsering not yet forty-three years old, something happened, and the rocket plummeted ignominiously to earth. I am even not sure of what happened, but I think it had something to do with an affair with the wife of a senior Tibetan officer working in a British Trade Agency. The subject was seldom discussed in our family except for some comments from my father about *ashang* (maternal uncle) Tashi Tsering wasting all his talents because of bad behavior: "He was an exceptionally gifted man and could easily have become a Political Officer in Tibet [the highest post in the British Trade Agencies]. But he threw it all away—a sheer waste."

On January 4, 1929, Tashi Tsering's appointment was terminated by Lieutenant-Colonel J. Weir, British political officer in Sikkim. There is a terse note from Weir that reads, "An invalid pension not exceeding Rupees 59 and 4 annas [about 2 US dollars or £1 sterling in 1992] per mensem is reported to be admissible with effect from the 5 January 1929."[3] Since Tashi Tsering was in perfect health at that time, I think "invalid pension" was a euphemistic camouflage to smooth over a painful scandal. Then, in a fitting finale to the whole episode, on April Fool's Day of 1930, in a memorandum from Weir, his account was finally closed; his "Service Book" was dispatched to him, and he was told to acknowledge its receipt. Knowing Tashi Tsering well, he most likely disdained to acknowledge and tossed his "Service Book" into the nearest wastepaper basket. Fortunately for posterity, it must have been retrieved and locked away in an old trunk.

My father, Pemba Tsering, was born in Jorebungalow on June 1, 1905, in the same year as Jean-Paul Sartre and a year after the Younghusband Expedition. This was also the year in which Albert Einstein, working as an unknown official in a Swiss patent office in Zurich, had submitted a paper on the Special Theory of Relativity. Pemba Tsering's father died soon after his birth and his mother when he was about eight years old. Rendered an orphan, he came under the guardianship of Tashi Tsering, his maternal uncle. My father used to say that his parents had been very rich, but Tashi Tsering squandered away all the family wealth. Throughout his life, he

*Sitting on floor (left to right): Norzin (author's sister) and author; standing: author's father and Mingmar (maternal cousin); seated: author's mother (Yatung, Tibet, 1935). Courtesy of the author*

had an intense dislike for his *ashang*. My father was educated at the Darjeeling High School, and as soon as he had obtained his matriculation, Tashi Tsering forced him to join the British Trade Agency in Yatung in 1924. My father, all his life, regretted that he had not been to a university. In those days it was extremely rare for young Tibetans of Darjeeling to possess college degrees. My father used to say that he could easily have gotten one. This was a recurring topic in our family, my father never ceasing to envy anybody with a degree after his name.

I have an old notebook of my father, dated 1924, and in it he made some brief autobiographical entries. There are also some English maxims in it written in his neat handwriting: "Adversity flatters no man. Adversity makes a man wise, not rich. Anger may glance into the breast of a wise man but rests only unto the bosom of fools."[4] There is also a recipe on frying fish to "a golden colour." Something awry must have happened to my genes, or else the hand of the Eternal Saki must have shaken, because I can barely make a cup of tea! Here are some excerpts from the notebook that are of interest:

> Born 1 June 1905. Admission to the Scandinavian Alliance Mission, Middle English School, Ghoom, on 19 July 1911. Finished the course in this school on 19 December 1918, after appearing in the District Higher English Scholarship Examination. Admission to the Government High School, Darjeeling, on 1 March 1919 and finished my course on 6 March 1923. Worked as a third master in the above-mentioned school from 1 October 1923 to 30 November 1924. Then from 1 December 1924 until 6 April 1926 as Second Clerk in the British Trade Agency, Yatung, Tibet. From 7 April 1926 to 6 August 1926, I was deputed to Tehri-Garhwal as temporary Tibetan clerk of the Tehri-Garwal Boundary Commission. From 28 August 1926 till 17 September 1926, I went to hand over the Kharita of the Viceroy of India to His Highness the Maharaja of Bhutan. Went with Mr. Hopkinson, Indian Civil Service tour to Gyantse in March 1927 for the first time. Wife delivered a still-born child in August. I was transferred to Gyantse as Tibetan youth under training in November 1927. On Wednesday 14 August 1929, 10th day of the seventh month of the Earth-Snake year son Lhawang Phuntso was born, who died on 22 October 1930. On 5 June 1931, third son, Tsewang Yishey was born. I was promoted to Head Clerk, Yatung, where I arrived on 3 August 1931. I have been very lucky in getting it. On 12 November 1932 I went to Gangtok to see Uncle Tashi Tsering.[5]

When I was a medical student in London in 1951, I received a letter from my father. The envelope was interesting, for there was a King George VI six annas Indian stamp on it. India became independent in 1947, but British-Indian stamps were still being used in Tibet. The letter had been dispatched from Lhasa on February 4, 1951, but was postmarked Gyantse, Tibet, February 10, 1951. The Chinese Communists had occupied Tibet for nearly a year then. My father wrote, "I am glad that you met Col. Bailey. He was the officer who appointed me in this department in December 1924. Please convey my respects to him when you see him next."[6]

Mr. Hopkinson was the British political officer in Tibet and Sikkim who took over from Sir Basil Gould. I met him once in London, and we spent a pleasant afternoon at Kew Gardens. He was a kind of a soft-spoken, subdued man.

My maternal grandmother, born in 1868, came from Markham in the Kham region of eastern Tibet. She had come to Yatung as a young woman from Lhasa, and when my father and my mother met each other, she was living in Pipithang, a few miles south of Yatung. In those days, it took nearly two months to travel from Markham to Lhasa and another sixteen days from Lhasa to Yatung. She had certainly come a long way from home, and I never found out why she had left home and come so far. I was told that my father first met my mother at the house of the Governor Meru Gyalpo at Pipithang, the representative of the Tibetan government in the Chumbi Valley. Meru Gyalpo was harsh, authoritative, and an arrogant autocrat. I have seen a photograph of him with some British officers taken in his house in 1931. He is balding, heavy lidded, silk gowned, and proud. There are glasses, decanters, and what looks suspiciously like a bottle of Scotch whiskey arrayed on his table. His wife is ostentatiously bejeweled, wearing two *gaus* (a square box-like ornament worn as a necklace) when it was customary to wear only one, like a British duchess wearing two tiaras!

The bottle of Scotch reminds me of an amusing story told to me by Lieutenant-Colonel F. M. Bailey. I cannot vouch that the Tibetan official involved in the story was Meru Gyalpo, but it could very well have been him. Colonel Bailey recounted how Tibetans always admired the medals (called *takma* in Tibetan) worn by British officers on their chests. A certain official in Pipithang wanted the colonel to present him with a medal. Bailey protested, saying that the medals weren't given around like biscuits. People had to earn them, and for some medals, like the Victoria Cross, one even gave up one's life. The Tibetan official would listen to none of this and insisted that he be presented with a large medal; not only that, but it also had to bear an appropriate inscription similar to "For Valour" on a Victoria Cross. Seeing that there was danger of Anglo-Tibetan good relations being jeopardized, the colonel had no option but to reluctantly agree. The next time he visited Calcutta, he had a suitably impressed medal made and, on his return to Tibet, presented it to the Tibetan official in a formal solemn ceremony. The official was delighted and would wear the medal over his gorgeous silken clothes every time the British passed through Yatung, and he made sure that the medal was inspected and admired. The British officers, on doing so, could hardly restrain their laughter. Now the Tibetan was a notorious drunkard, and Scotch whiskey was his favorite. British officials made it a point to present him with some bottles whenever the occasion demanded it. The inscription at the back of the medal read *Nunc est bibendum!* (Now is the time to drink!)

## NOTES

1. Heinrich Harrer, *Seven Years in Tibet*, trans. Richard Graves (London: Rupert Hart-Davis, 1953), 56.
2. British Service Book. Personal access.
3. Pemba Tsering, personal conversation with the author, n.d.
4. Pemba Tsering's Notebook, 1924.
5. Ibid.
6. Pemba Tsering, letter to the author, February 10, 1951.

# 3

~

# Early Glimmerings in Gyantse and Yatung

History with its flickering lamp stumbles along the trail of the past, trying to reconstruct its scene, to revive its echoes, and kindle with pale gleams the passion of former days.

—Winston Churchill[1]

My narrative begins in 1931. What was Tibet back then? The thirteenth Dalai Lama, the predecessor of the present spiritual leader, was the absolute autocratic ruler of the land of "Outer Tibet" in both the spiritual and the secular fields. However, he had just then expressed a wish to give up his secular powers and devote himself entirely to the spiritual side. He was fifty-five years old. The oracles of Nechung prophesied that His Holiness would die soon—that is, pass into the Fields of Bliss. Despite being beseeched by his devotees to continue to rule Tibet, and despite prayers and rituals conducted in every monastery and household, he died on December 17, 1933.

He left behind a land strange in many ways and anachronistic certainly for the twentieth century. Tibet was, to quote a cliché, "a land where time stood still." There were in "Outer Tibet" no motor roads, railways, or aerodromes; there was no electricity, plumbing, or sanitation, no hospital except the small ones at Yatung, Gyantse, and Lhasa run by the British Trade Agencies, and no modern schools. I saw electric lines and piped water for the first time in my life when I came to Gangtok, Sikkim, in 1941. It was then also that I saw a motorcar for the first time. Telegraph lines had been laid by the British up to Gyantse after the Younghusband Expedition, and by 1924 they had been extended to Lhasa by the Tibetans.

There was no radio in any part of the country until 1934, when the Chinese under General Huang Mu-sung (the "condolence mission" to pay respects on the death of the thirteenth Dalai Lama) brought in their sets. There was a postal system of mail runners and horse couriers from Lhasa to Gyantse run by the Tibetan government and from Gyantse to Sikkim and Kalimpong under the British.

There were half a million monks and nuns in a country with a population perhaps of four million, and almost half the entire revenue of Tibet went toward maintaining the clergy, with Lhasa alone boasting the three largest monasteries in the world: Drepung (7,700 monks), Sera (5,500 monks), and Ganden (3,300 monks)—and these were only official figures, which were usually exceeded in practice.

In "Outer Tibet," there were no Chinese soldiers or officials anywhere except a representative in Lhasa with a small escort. Tibet was as independent as any country in the world, for China was involved in her own problems with the rising tide of Communism under Mao Tse-Tung and would soon be engulfed by the Sino-Japanese War, which began in 1937. The British were in favor, and the British Trade Agencies in Yatung and Gyantse flourished, permeating their surroundings with Anglo-Indian thoughts, culture, customs, habits, and philosophies, and there was a permanent mission in Lhasa. The British had obtained all they wished to get from their conventions and treaties commencing from 1890, the Younghusband Expedition of 1904, and the Simla Conference of 1913–1914. By now, the British had cordial relations with "Outer Tibet," a benign backward buffer nation that shielded the crown jewel of India from Soviet Russia and Republican China along a vast 2,000 miles of shared frontier. It still took nearly two months on horseback from my grandmother's birthplace of Markham in eastern Tibet to Lhasa, and from Lhasa to the frontiers of India it was another three weeks. It was in the interests of the British to keep Tibet backward and medieval, and for time to stand still there, and, in the words of Sir Charles Bell, to form a "powerful buttress for India against those who sought to attack her with rifles or revolutionary propaganda."[2]

Years earlier, Adolf Hitler had emerging from obscurity to become a fanatic national savior, and Einstein's theory of relativity had been confirmed by Sir Arthur Eddington's expedition to photograph an eclipse of the sun. The 1930s were the decade of the twentieth century when the greatest war mankind has ever known would begin, and within a few years the atom would be split and the atomic age ushered in. But Tibet lived in another age. Before the Younghusband Expedition of 1904, no white man had entered Lhasa during the previous fifty years. Sir Charles Bell in 1920, while spending a year in Lhasa (and my grand-uncle Tashi Tsering was also there working under him), wrote, "I was destined to stay

*Standing: unknown; seated (left to right): author's mother (with author on lap) and grandmother; sitting in front: Mingmar (maternal cousin) and Tibetan apso Sinto (?) (Yatung, Tibet, 1932). Courtesy of the author*

longer than any other white man has stayed for a hundred and seventy-five years."[3] Mrs. Weir, the wife of Lieutenant-Colonel J. Weir, British political officer for Tibet and Sikkim (the man who sacked Tashi Tsering in 1929), became the first British woman to come to Lhasa when she went there in 1932. C. Suydam Cutting, naturalist, explorer, and collector for museums, was the first American in Lhasa in 1935, and two years later, in 1937 (the Tibetan Fire-Ox year; Cutting wrote a book using the name of the year as a title), Mrs. Cutting became the first American woman to visit the city.[4]

The third American in Lhasa was Theos Bernard from Arizona, who came to the city in 1937. Circumstances surrounding his life are mysterious and obscure. He appears to have been an eccentric and at one time enrolled himself in a Tibetan monastery, dressing and behaving like a Tibetan monk. He is reported to have died in 1947 in the Himalayas, perhaps killed in an avalanche, but his body was never found. Those of us inclined to mystery and romance might even conjecture that, like Conway, somewhere in the Tibetan snows and mountains, he, too, returned to his Shangri-La.

In 1942, Lieutenant-Colonel Ilia Tolstoy and Captain Brooke Dolan, United States army officers from the OSS (Office of Strategic Services), became the first and second Americans ever to have met a Dalai Lama in Tibet, when they had an audience with the present fourteenth Dalai Lama, His Holiness Tenzin Gyatso.

When I was born in Gyantse on June 5, 1931, my father was a clerk in the British Trade Agency there. I was the third son, the first having miscarried and the second having died when he was just over a year old, all in Gyantse. It is not through any arrogance or pride that I wish to clarify the title "Clerk" (or, in the Nepalese Indian language, *Babu*), by which many educated Tibetan and Sikkimese employees were designated. In British India, the term *Babu* was used in a derogatory or disparaging sense for Indian office clerical staff. It was not so in Tibet. It was a term of respect, much like the Tibetan *Kusho* or "Sir." We used to call our Yatung and Lhasa teachers *Guru Babu* ("Teacher Sir").

On account of the British, Nepalese, Sikkimese, and Indian influence, and because most of the junior staff in the British Trade Agencies were Tibetans of the Darjeeling district or Sikkimese educated in British-Indian schools in Kalimpong, Gangtok, or Darjeeling, there was in vogue hodgepodge of terms, expressions, and slang that gave verve, charm, and piquancy to their daily conversations and writings. Usually at these agencies, there was a British trade agent (abbreviated to BTA), akin to a minor deity, paid a handsome salary with enviable perquisites, and below him a "Head Clerk" (*Burra Babu*) and a "Junior Clerk" (*Chota Babu*)—*Burra* (big) and *Chota* (small) are familiar Anglo-Indian terms (viz. *Chota* and *Burra* pegs of whiskey). Needless to say, many *Chota Babus* were great consumers of *burra* pegs of whiskey, preferably Scotch. I think it would be more accurate to consider these *Chota* and *Burra* employees as third and second secretaries at consulates and embassies, because many of them rose to the ranks in Tibet of *Dzasas* (ministers) or *Rimshi Depöns* (equivalent to junior generals), finance and foreign secretaries, and in India they were given the high titles of *Rai Bahadur* and *Rai Sahib*, granted to civil officials during the British Raj. Sir Basil Gould calls the British Trade Agencies "more or less of the nature of Vice-Consulates, but [these] were called by another name in view of the indefiniteness of the political relations between China and Tibet."[5]

Gyantse, situated at an altitude of 13,000 feet, was halfway between Yatung in south Tibet and Lhasa. Younghusband had spent three months there during his expedition, and there had been fighting in Gyantse; Gyantse Dzong (center of civil administration) had been stormed by the British and an officer had been awarded a Victoria Cross during the battle. My father, in a letter dated March 9, 1954, from Gyantse, when I was a student in London, wrote, "Gyantse can claim to have the highest tennis court and football ground in the world –13,000 ft."[6] I have not consulted the Guinness Book of Records and so cannot substantiate his claims but quote them for the general interest of the reader. It gives me pride to have been born in a Tibetan town of superlatives! The Trade Agency had been established immediately after the Younghusband Expedition of 1904, and Captain (later Sir Frederick) O'Connor had been the first British trade agent. He had been secretary to Younghusband and the chief interpreter.

Gyantse was dry, with an annual rainfall not exceeding ten inches, whereas Lhasa, although still almost bone dry by Indian monsoon standards, had an average rainfall of about 14 inches in a year. Mrs. Margaret Williamson writes,

[L]ife at the Agency there was blighted in winter by regular dust-storms and bitter cold. From November until March, the double windows at the Agency were sealed and all the personnel donned heavy furs, lambswool underclothing, and Gilgit boots. Christmas was a keenly anticipated respite, but for the festivities, everything had to be hauled up from India over the Himalayas: the turkey, the fruit, and even the beer, which of necessity had to be thawed out because it invariably arrived frozen solid. Relief was found in games. Football, hockey and tennis were played and there was even a polo ground.[7]

I remember very well my father's Gilgit (a region in British India) boots, thickly padded and that reached to the groins, which could have easily substituted for a hockey goalkeeper's pads. Mrs. Williamson says that in 1933–1934 there was an escort of troops commanded by one or two British officers; a warrant officer of the Supply and Transport Corps of the Indian Army was in charge of the Commissariat department (we used to address him as *Kamseer Sahib*), and there were two British military telegraphists and a medical officer.[8] In 1931, Captain William Marshall of the 1/5 Maratha Light Infantry was in charge of the escort to the British trade agent. Between June 1931 and October 1933, he trained twenty-five men of the Dalai Lama's *kusung* (bodyguards) in the use of machine guns. Among the officer trainees was the young Jigme Taring, about whom I shall write when I arrive at my chapter on Lhasa. I came to know the Marathas later in Yatung and Gangtok: Indian soldiers from the south— lithe, sinewy men with oiled, glistening, wiry bodies twisting, contorting, acrobatic on the *malkhamb* (climbing pole) or prancing, striding, and dancing about to the hypnotic rhythm of their chains of bells and shouting their war cry, "Chatrapati Shivaji Maharaj ki jai!" The Marathas fought well against the Germans and Italians in Tobruk in 1942, and I wonder whether any of them served in Gyantse and Yatung and remembered the little boy soliciting them for *chappati* (Indian bread) and *dal* (lentil soup). The medical officer then was Captain David Tennant of the Indian Medical Service, who was designated acting surgeon. Later, when he came to Yatung, he became good friends with my father. I have seen some photographs of him: mustached, lean, necktie, rather dapper, long leather boots, tweed jacket, breeches, pocket handkerchief—I feel sure he was a jolly fine chap and a jolly good sport.

The agency had undergone some reconstruction before I was born, for Sir Basil Gould writes, "A large and genial sapper named Bartlett from India came to build new quarters for the Agency on a site a quarter of a mile from our present quarters . . . and the site was on alluvial ground in an angle between the Nyang Chu river and a tributary, liable to flood suddenly, which flowed in from the direction of the route to Lhasa."[9] Timber for the construction was brought from Yatung, as trees were scanty in Gyantse. Gould also recounts, in typical British fashion, that they played polo, "eight chukkas of ten minutes each. The ground was of hard-baked mud, about 100 yards by 50."[10] Talk of mad dogs and Englishmen—Gyantse is over 13,000 feet high!

Another letter from my father from Lhasa on January 7, 1954, before his transfer on promotion to Gyantse, says, "[T]he weather there is awful as Gyantse is over 13,000 ft. high and the winter season will go on to the end of April, whereas in Lhasa, we can be having fairly comfortable weather from the middle of February."[11]

There was a British cemetery in Gyantse with the graves of those who had died during the Younghusband Expedition. Mr. Frederick Williamson was buried there, having died in Lhasa on November 17, 1935. Mrs. Williamson brought a cross of granite, specially made for the grave, all the way from Aberdeen with "Far away yet among friends" inscribed upon it.[12]

Gyantse thus appears from all accounts to have been a fairly harsh and inhospitable place. I am sure my parents were delighted when news arrived that my father had been promoted to head clerk to the agency in Yatung, 130 miles south toward India. I was considered a lucky child, and my parents moved to Yatung, arriving there on August 3, 1931. The journey must have been very difficult, although mitigated by the fact that it was summer and that they were descending most of the time to Yatung, which, at 9,800 feet, is much lower than Gyantse. However, they had to cross the 15,200-foot Tang La pass, and so I can boast that at an age of less than two months, I encountered such a height (without oxygen, no less), but I am at present no Reinhold Messner, the German climber who was the first man to climb all the world's peaks above 8,000 meters and who was the first man to climb Mount Everest without oxygen (I met him in Bhutan in 1990). Nyima Wangmo, a Tibetan woman born in Gyantse in 1911, and who joined our household in Gyantse as a girl of seventeen, told me that I cried all the way to Yatung and that my mother had to stop frequently on the way and find some shelter to breastfeed me. I was carried on the back of a man named Chöphel, and later in Yatung my mother used to point this person out to me—a quiet man with a toothy smile always wearing a balaclava cap, a very popular headgear in Yatung.

My earliest memories are therefore of Yatung, and they are some of the most pleasant that I possess, having a charming, magical, dreamlike quality. Tibet at that time was independent, and her friends the British undisputed masters in India and ruling an empire on which the sun never set. For a boy in south Tibet, it was an idyllic place to grow up in, a time of bliss, in contrast to boys in Germany, Austria, Manchuria, and China. I was bossed by nobody, ordered around by nobody, bullied by nobody. I had no fears, no apprehensions, no oppressive burdens in the blue Tibetan sky above, the surrounding mountains, and absolute peace. At home, I recall total domestic bliss. Everything was in order and harmony. There were no doubts and tensions. Such a period of peace and tranquility is rare in one's life, especially when one thinks of the years 1931–1937. Little did I know of the sadness, misery, pain, agony, and degradation occurring in other parts of the world. Little could one visualize the cataclysmic world events about to engulf humanity within the next few years. There was no foreboding to disturb our serenity in Yatung.

I can feel the sunshine of Yatung, the soothing sighing of the wind among the pine trees, the tolling of the neck bells of mule trains heading southward to Sikkim and Kalimpong or northward to Phari, Gyantse, and Lhasa. Half the entire trade of Tibet to the outside world went through the Chumbi valley, of which Yatung was the chief town. There was peace in the surrounding pine-clad mountains, dotted with prayer flags, and in the air, always, the distant roar of the river that ran through the Chumbi valley and, after many geographical adventures, descended onto the plains of India, where, in the far distant future, I would cross it again and again in my journeys between Darjeeling and Bhutan.

There was the British Residency, with its gardens, where the British trade agent lived and the surrounding cluster of office buildings. People in Yatung called the residency *Gyaltengang*; a rough translation would be "Royal Ridge." Was it because the thirteenth Dalai Lama, while escaping to India in 1910, had spent a night there sharing a bedroom with David Macdonald? Mrs. Williamson, describing the residency, writes, "The bungalow itself was altogether delightful and had a garden where lupins and other flowers were growing, reminding me of an English garden."[13] Spencer-Chapman (whom I met in Britain in 1965) says,

> Agency . . . a lovely long low red-roofed bungalow with a glass verandah in front. It possesses a most heavenly garden, the drive bordered by riotous masses of nasturtiums, green lawns, and pergola of rambling roses in full bloom, a paved garden with huge pansies, lupins, antirrhinums, eschscholtsias, and petunias—all you could wish for. I should have liked to live there.[14]

When the British trade agent was not living there, the residency was a favorite place for us to visit and play in, and it also served as a colorful background for most photographs. Inside the bungalow there were the stuffed heads of antelopes, wild bison, mountain sheep, and bears, for the Yatung mountains had many bears. Some anonymous taxidermist had showered his skill on these trophies hanging on the walls and carpeting the floors, such as a bearskin rug with the paws and the head of the bear intact, its glassy eyes staring at you ferociously and its canines bared. However, there was a strange un-Tibetan smell about the whole place, a smell of varnish, of brass doorknobs assiduously polished with British polish, an air of European clinical cleanliness and an aura of the British Raj. There was the silent loneliness of empty hotel rooms. I had the feeling that the place was haunted, as if many *Sahibs* (masters) had left their unrequited dreams and passions, unfulfilled ambitions, twisted agonies within its walls in this corner of Tibet. Any *Sahib* who had stayed at the residency must have been unique and exceptional in many ways, perhaps an odd man out and eccentric, arriving at last in what he or she believed was "Mysterious Tibet" and "The Forbidden Land of the Lamas." Perhaps all of them left behind some of their dreams of Shangri-La at Yatung Residency.

If one went outside the bungalow and climbed over a small hillock, there was a path that led to our own bungalow, that of the head clerk or *Burra Babu*. *Bhalu* (the Hindi word for "bear"—shades of Rudyard Kipling), our Tibetan mastiff, who was huge, shaggy, and ferocious, yet gentle with children and had a deep resounding bark that would go on through the early hours of the morning, would greet us. Once he had found an enamel plate that had a bright floral pattern, which he placed at my feet, and thus the plate had become my own. There would be my grandmother, my mother, and Nyima Wangmo, our maidservant. Father would be away at his office, which he attended regularly and kept his office hours with clockwork British punctuality—something unknown among Tibetans, for in Tibet it is good manners to arrive a little late for all appointments, as Younghusband (who did not know our customs) found intolerably annoying. "These Tibetan blighters are invariably late!" he must have complained.

I would go off to see Nyima Wangmo milking our cows, for we sold the surplus milk to the Indian soldiers of the British escort. Nyima Wangmo once told me that if you lifted a newborn calf each day, then when it grew to be a cow, one could lift it just as easily. Off we would go with the milk, with the evening sun setting over the mountains, and sometimes if we were a bit early, we would hear in the distance the loud warning shouts of wood cutters as they rolled logs they had cut down, raising clouds of dust as they cascaded into the valley below. If it was getting dark, the

Indian buglers would sound the "Last Post" and lower the Union Jack from the flagpole.[15] Rarely, because one sleeps the deep soothing sleep of an undisturbed childhood, did I hear a "Reveille," but all my life when a bugler sounds "Reveille" or the "Last Post," I immediately think of Yatung evenings and of taking milk to the Indian soldiers.[16] The soldiers would give us their *chappatis* and *dal* and pat us on our heads. Those *chappatis*, made of whole meal wheat, had prevented beri-beri (Vitamin B deficiency) among the Indian sepoys in Gallipoli during the First World War when their *Sahib* officers eating ordinary bread had suffered from this nutritional disease.

The Indian soldiers were kind to us. They were dark, whiskered, and sharp featured, and they brought a foreign culture of rice, *dal, chappatis*, and their gods and goddesses from the Hindu pantheon of deities—strangers from hot sultry southern climes. They fraternized easily with the local Tibetans and the staff of the agency and took photographs of children sitting on their laps, many of the Sikhs turbaned, stalwart, and warlike. On rock faces high above Yatung, they carved the names of their regiments, some of them formed over a hundred years before, full of battle honors.

It would be dark when we arrived home. There were no streetlights in Yatung, no electricity or piped water anywhere. The kerosene lanterns had to be dismantled and cleaned, and Nyima Wangmo would show me how this was done; to this very day I do not think the structure of these lanterns have changed. I saw some at the Seventh Mile Fair in Milwaukee in 1992, and I am certain that Nyima Wangmo would have set to, dismantled, and cleaned them with consummate ease. I wonder why kerosene lanterns have not undergone any evolution in the last sixty years. Sometimes on special occasions, or when we had guests or threw a party or at Losar (Tibetan New Year), we would light the Tilley gas lamps.

Every morning, when I woke up, Nyima Wangmo would bring me a cup of milk. Before I drank the milk, my father would make me say in English, "Please bring me milk." Or sometimes it would be "Please open the door" and "Please shut the door." The reward was a cup of milk; my father was unknowingly a Pavlovian. One morning I found the milk to be contaminated with chili powder; I cried and complained, and my father hurled the cup of milk at Nyima Wangmo.

Occasionally my father would play the gramophone, His Master's Voice, hand-cranked for each record, seventy-eight revolutions per minute, needle changed after every two records and neatly deposited into a swiveling side pocket, record surface cleaned spotlessly with a brush with a velvet surface, monogrammed with the picture of a strange-looking dog of a breed I had never seen, and out would come my favorite songs. If I was seized with the mood and elan, I would bounce up and execute an appropriate dance. I still remember two of the songs: "It's a Long Way to Tipperary!" and "Shout for the Gallant Major." I visited Tipperary in 1952, but to this day I am mystified by the anonymity of the "Gallant Major." Who was he? What gallant deeds had he performed? Was he in charge of the Scots Greys at Waterloo, sabers flashing, on foaming steeds?

And now it was time to learn the English alphabet. My father was the one who taught me. He would cover up all the letters with an opaque piece of paper that had a tiny window cut into it and then manipulate the paper here and there at random and tell me to name the letter presented at the window. I learned the English and Hindi alphabets long before I learned Tibetan. At that time and season, the Tibetan language was of no use to the son of a head clerk of a British Trade Agency. It was English that held the golden key to a successful future. In a way, I am grateful to him for guiding me through the crucial revolutionary gate that would lead me to James Joyce, T. S. Elliot, Shakespeare, Charles Dickens, Bertrand Russell, Winston Churchill, and Ernest Hemingway.

The British Residency was built against a hill that rose above the Chumbi valley. At a little distance away were the rows of barracks of the military escort, and far across the valley was the Dak bungalow, a guest-house for those British who halted in Yatung and could not be accommodated at the residency.

In the valley was a playing field used for football, hockey, and polo. Nearby was an ice-skating rink (open air and primitive), a tennis court, a small hospital, and a school. Farther up the valley was a cemetery for the British, which used to fill us with awe and which we avoided because of its eerie atmosphere. The town of Yatung, with shingle-roofed houses and stones to keep down the shingles (much like Swiss chalets), was administered by the British and policed by a few *Bazaar Sirdars* appointed by the British. Far away up the valley was a road, and occasionally on weekends (for according to the British custom Saturday was a half day and Sunday a full holiday for the office staff, although in Tibet no government official ever worked to such a schedule), my parents would take us for picnics. The road forked, one path taking you to flowered meadows and thence to sulphurous health-giving hot springs, and the other to a crematorium, for in Yatung, unlike in Lhasa, the dead were cremated. (Throughout Tibet, no dead body was ever buried: they were either cremated or fed to the vultures.)

One path led to gaiety: picnics with *chang* (barley ale), Scotch whiskey, and cigarettes from tins for the adults; gramophone music, impromptu dancing to the throbbing of Indian drums, ankle bells, and the Indian harmonium; roast meat, chili pickle, Tibetan sweets, and fruits imported from India, Huntley and Palmer biscuits, Jacob's Golden Puffs, tea drunk from cups imprinted with Union Jacks and coronation commemoratives of the smiling King George VI and Queen Elizabeth—minor deities for us, who lived far away in Bilight or England (an Indian corruption of the British "Blighty"). For us, Great Britain was Bilight, where the King Emperor and the Queen Empress ruled perpetually, smiling kindly, benign, always robed in ermine, wearing their bejeweled crowns, and holding their scepters and orbs. We regarded British rule as benevolent, all powerful, and immutable, like the rising and the setting of the sun, all encompassing, everlasting.

The other path, led to death with all its immense complexities and intricacies created by the rich imagery of Tibetan Buddhism from a fabric of mysticism, mythology, and fables: to the crematorium, where the skeleton Durtrö Dakpo (owners of the crematorium) awaited the dead to lead them to the awesome hideous *Shinje*, Yama, the king of the dead and dispenser of judgement, and thence through the underworld of the *Bardo*, the interval between death and rebirth. But to us death was then far away. It was always the old who died, and I had not seen anybody dying or dead. Death did not happen to the young, although I knew about the deaths of my predecessors, both potential brothers if they had lived. But death was something that made you uncomfortable, and you couldn't quite drive it away from your mind. And one become aware of the first sounds of the mystic and the unknown, for who can avoid that in Tibet?

Above our house, half-hidden among the pine trees and brambles, was a decaying neglected *chorten*, a religious structure of a distinct shape, that stood in the boggy muddy ground, and a lazy stream meandered close to the base of the chorten, where I found some *tsa-tsas* (conical mud-cakes embossed with religious pictures and magic writing). Prayer flags, tattered and fading, surrounded the chorten and flapped in the wind. I picked up some of the *tsa-tsas* and crumbled them in my hand to examine their pulpy cores to see whether they contained anything, and my friends pushed me aside and warned me not to do that, for the *tsa-tsas* contained the ashes of the dead, and the chorten was the abode of a fierce, red-faced, vindictive local deity, a Tsekarn, who would wreak vengeance on anybody who touched the *tsa-tsas* of the dead. I left them alone; there in the darkness of the pine forest with murmurs of the flowing stream, I felt something eerie, mysterious, as if the place enshrined the secret melancholy enigma of death.

I enjoyed visiting my father in his office. Sometimes he and his friends would be standing near a chimney in front of a roaring wood fire, for there was plenty of wood in Yatung, unlike many other places in Tibet. The fire was kept ablaze with wood thrown in by tongs, and a British-style leather bellows would be used to liven up flagging flames. The office workers, almost all of them Sikkimese or Darjeeling District Tibetans (collectively known as Bhutias), wearing silk or serge Tibetan clothes, with their backs to the fire, would be in a merry, laughing mood and full of jokes, talking in a vivacious mixture of Tibetan, Sikkimese, Indian, Nepalese, and English. All of them were linguists. My father could read, write, and speak fluently Tibetan, Hindi, Nepalese, Sikkimese, and English; he also knew Urdu, as well as Sanskrit, the ancient classical language of India. Such fluency in so many languages gave rise to most picturesque expressive conversations full of humor and wit such as "Hezu ta mah-jong kehlera fungu tashi bhayu, bhai . . . dead broke, old chap, didn't have a sou on me when the game broke up" (Translation: *Hezu ta* = "yesterday" in Nepalese; *khelera* = "having played" in Nepalese; *bhai* = "Brother" in Hindi and Nepalese).

I took great delight in minutely examining my father's desk, containing the neat, tidy office paraphernalia of British-Indian bureaucracy, which drove the wheels of the British Raj: the table topped with green billiard cloth; the hemispherical glass paperweights, with flat frosted bases, filled with air bubbles (I used to wonder how the bubbles ever got into that impervious glass, what ingenuity); blotting papers, carbon paper (another source of endless delight, as you could produce so many copies by just writing on one sheet), thick pencils, half-blue and half-red, to underline, delete, and emphasize; paper clips, pincushions, inkstands with red and blue ink, fountain pens, rubber erasers, and files tied with white, blue and red tape—endless files that came and went carried by the office peons and *chaprassis* (Indian terms for office menial staff), files whose arcane contents I would never fathom. They wore brass badges, the British crown with the lion and the unicorn, with *Dieu et mon droit* and *Honi soit qui mal y pense* embossed on them. Tibetan pigtailed staff, with gnarled leathery faces, wore these badges of the British Raj with great pride; their salaries were good and the exchange rate of the Indian rupee into Tibetan *sangs* handsome, and their jobs carried prestige and status. And so they toiled hard and honestly, carrying their files back and forth from office to office, some of whom remembered the Younghusband Expedition vividly and as boys had been frightened and had hidden away from the British troops and Sikh sepoys.

Illness was something to be dreaded in Yatung in those days, where there was only a tiny hospital set up by the British. It could deal with simple illnesses and with basic surgical and obstetric conditions. I seldom went there, and I can only recall the smell of formaldehyde that pervaded the place. The doctor there was the Sikkimese Rai Sahib Dr. Tonyot Tsering, a man whom I was to know very well in the future. He was a great friend of the family—an ebullient live wire of a man; an extremely cheerful happy-go-lucky person whose loud, staccato, infectious laughter I shall never forget; full of Sikkimese charm and gaiety; skillful as a physician and an accoucheur, his conversations laced with a sparkling effervescent cocktail of Tibetan, Sikkimese, Nepalese, Indian, and English expressions and slang; non-smoking, chain betel-nut chewing; back slapping and shaking his patients and joking with them to cure them with reassurance, confidence, and good cheer. My grandmother had absolute faith in him. He carried a pocket watch on a chain and wore a Homburg hat, the brim tilted forward at a rakish angle. He was the life and soul of all parties, nattily dressed, a Sikkimese Balzes Boylan without the latter's wicked adulterous concupiscence. He was a dancer, singer, musician, but a terror to all ladies, high or low, for his bottom-slapping, bottom-pinching onslaughts. My mother told me that once she had mistakenly made me drink tincture of iodine thinking it was a cough mixture; I had become weak and sleepy, perhaps symptoms of halogen poisoning. Dr. Tonyot had forced me to eat flies to act as an emetic to make me vomit up the iodine. No comment! In those days, a qualified modern allopathic doctor who was an ethnic Tibetan or Sikkimese was a rarity, and Yatung was lucky to have the services of such a man as Dr. Tonyot Tsering.

In Tibet, there was a system of native medicine based on the Indian Ayurvedic system with medical schools in Lhasa. It was ancient, traditional, and empirical. Today it is fashionable in certain circles in Hollywood, Bombay, Delhi, and Europe, but when we were ill in Yatung, we never consulted native Tibetan doctors. They were considered anachronistic and backward, and all preferred the allopathic therapy dispensed in the Yatung British hospital, although, considered from present-day standards, what it had to offer was very little. Tibetan native physicians used herbs, branding, sucking of blood, and a form of acupuncture. In surgery and obstetrics, they had almost no remedies.

My father would become very anxious whenever any of his children fell ill. He would never forget the agony he had suffered when my brother died as an infant in Gyantse. Nyima Wangmo used to tell me how bright the little boy had been and how he would toddle to the door to welcome my father when he returned home from his office; how he had a sack full of British toys ordered specially for him by my father from Calcutta; and how, when he died of a chest infection, my parents had wept and become distraught. The death of a little child is the same everywhere in the world. "Your father gave away all the toys when your brother died," Nyima Wangmo told me. "That's when I started smoking," said my mother, "after your brother's death."

Home remedies and nursing by my parents is mostly what I remember. I did not regard illnesses as visitations from evil spirits or offended demons wreaking vengeance, as is the Tibetan belief, or the working out of *le gyudre* (*karma*), as my grandmother believed, but rather as natural phenomena, just something going wrong with the workings of the body, for that is what my father taught me. At home, there was aspirin for aches and pains, tincture of iodine for cuts (one winced and put on a stiff upper lip, as I was told that the more it stung, the more efficacious it was), Zambuk ointment for sores (still extant), Maclean's stomach powder, mixtures from the Yatung hospital (the doses indicated on the side by a paper label with serrated markings), Scott's emulsion cod-liver oil (with an intriguing picture of a straining fisherman with a trawlerman's cap carrying piggyback a giant fish larger than himself), glycerin for chapped hands and cracked lips (when mother made us use glycerin, we knew that the Yatung winter had arrived), worm medicines once a year to get rid of roundworms and hopefully tapeworms (which were common in Tibet), Eno's Fruit Salts to tone up digestion and the liver, and, best of all, "Peps" throat pastilles, which I called *men chiril* (medicine sweet), delicious and soothing, and wrapped like little chocolates in silver paper and on the bottle cover an alluring picture of a fir tree like the ones we saw in Yatung.

There was hydrogen peroxide for sores and ulcers, and its frothing bubbly action was reassuring to watch for both patient and amateur nurse; in addition, there was potassium permanganate—just a few grains colored a glass of water a deep purple, and it was fascinating watching the miniature purple snowflakes gently sinking in the glass jar and then disintegrating like exploding depth charges seen in a silent film. For a cut finger, the remedy was to urinate on it immediately; if the bleeding persisted, we would burn a little piece of wool and sprinkle the charred fragments on the surface of the cut. If one had a stomach colic, my mother would moisten her palms with mustard oil, warm them in front of a fire, and then gently apply them on our abdominal wall. If one suffered from an inflamed groin gland due to an infected toe, one drew a swastika with a piece of coal on the surface of a smooth flat stone and then, just before going to bed, pressed the magic diagram on the painful area, and in the morning the swelling would be gone. And, of course, there was quinine for all mysterious fevers, although there was no malaria in Tibet. I think quinine was favored because of its bitter taste, for Tibetans believed that the more horrible medicine tasted, the more efficacious it was. The bitter pill must be sweetened. An injection that did not cause pain was no good. "Mig tsum ne thung!" (Shut your eyes tight and drink!), my mother used to tell me when giving me the quinine. I was applauded and praised because I could swallow the most bitter pills and concoctions without wincing from an early age—a useful training from an early age to swallow life's bitter pills.

I can recall some evenings when my father would return from office and find me ill in bed; he would anxiously put his palm against my forehead, shake down a clinical thermometer, and put it in my mouth—to me something soothing, magical, therapeutic rather than diagnostic, the shining mercury column, the cool exotic glassy taste in my fevered mouth, Father accurately counting the minutes for the instrument to register, peering anxiously again and again to take the reading, and then shaking down the instrument. I could guess from studying the expression on his face how much fever I had.

If an illness was severe and protracted, then the monks would be consulted and the prescribed religious ceremonies performed. Nyima Wangmo told me that my mother went around to many households in Yatung, asking each to give her a little wool; from what she had collected, she wove a coat for me to wear whenever I was seriously ill. I have the coat with me still, moth-eaten and threadbare. I examined the stiches on the belt; perhaps my mother used a Tibetan thimble and cotton thread from India with "Made in England" embossed on the spool. There was dried snot and dirt on it, and it must be impregnated with her tears—a painful relic from the past for me. A child in Tibet at that time relied on his natural resistance and prayers and the prayers of the lamas to overcome illness.

When I had learned my English alphabet, it was time to go to the agency school; walking down the slope from our house, past the playing field, and then to the school building situated at the edge of the town of Yatung. It wasn't very far to go.

We were a mixture of boys and girls, mostly children of the agency staff. At that time hardly anybody went to school in Tibet, and even when they did, it was just for a few years to learn to read and to write, especially to write with an exquisite hand, for calligraphy was highly prized. The form, clarity, and legibility of the writing that were far more important than the substance of what one wrote. It was traditional for a Tibetan school to be harsh and disciplined, and severe corporal punishment (such as twanging cheeks with split bamboo sticks) was meted out for flimsy breaches of conduct or poor performance in lessons. But that was not so in our agency school. I spent some of the happiest years of my life in that school, and our teacher was the kindest of men. We had only one teacher, Mr. Migmar, who had been educated at the Scottish Universities Mission school in Kalimpong, ninety-five miles away from Yatung. He was thin and tall, bony faced, usually wearing European clothes, favoring checks, tweeds, and plus-fours. He was rather Japanese looking. Whatever he knew, he taught us well. I remember learning the Indian alphabet by forming the letters on the ground with pebbles. We had very few books. Once Mr. Migmar sprinkled some iron filings on a sheet of paper and then, with a magnet placed underneath the paper, made the filings march about like well-disciplined soldiers, much to our wonder and astonishment. Sometimes he took us for picnics up the valley, but when the weather was bad and kept us indoors, he made us play with balloons and miniature footballs.

One day he told us that some very important British *Sahibs* were com-ing to Yatung and we must dress in our best clothes, come early to school the next day, and greet the *Sahibs* when they arrived. I remember march-ing in line, carrying in our hands pretty little flags and waving them to the cavalcade of *Sahibs*. Spencer-Chapman records that day as follows. This was in 1936 when he traveled as Sir Basil Gould's private secretary to Lhasa. That morning he had breakfasted on "Porridge, tinned herrings, scrambled eggs, bacon, and potatoes"—a typical *Sahib*'s breakfast, and that, too, in Tibet![17] Captain Salomons, a Scotsman, was in charge of the agency escort, and the soldiers were the 2/7 Rajputs. He describes the fir-clad mountains of Yatung, and "then we inspected a group of tiny schoolboys, each holding a Union Jack."[18]

Returning home from school, we would be greeted by my mother and grandmother and given tea and something to put into our pockets to eat later, such as *sha kampo* (dried meat); dried sweetened or salted hard lumps of cheese, called *chura*; or dried beans or dried raisins from Bhu-tan. I had something called "beef jerkies" in Wisconsin in 1992, and they tasted just like our *sha kampo*. Occasionally we would have British tinned fruits, Tasmanian jam, Bovril soup, and Shippam's meat pastes smeared on Tibetan bread.

In the evenings, Father would give us a bath, place me on his lap, and cut my toenails. He might even make some stewed apples for us done in the English way. And afterward there were all my toys to play with: a selection of guns; the monkey that slid up and down a metal pole; the sol-dier kneeling, with rifle held at "high port" sliding here and there to the whirring noise of the motor; the drummer boy, shaking frenetically from side to side and madly drumming away; the toy cinema hand cranked and illuminated by a candle (but the image actually moved, unexplain-able magic!); and the lead race horses that slid down an incline. All these toys came from Britain to Calcutta, and then all the way to Yatung, carried over the 14,000-foot passes of Jelep La or Nathö La.

I might even be forced to eat some British corn flour, my father extol-ling its nutritious properties—corn flour made by Brown and Polson, in Esher, Surrey (and in the very far distant future how often I used to pass Esher while commuting from Waterloo to Woking). If I obeyed, I might be given some transfers to play with; wet the paper and rub it over the sur-face of another sheet of paper, and, lo and behold, there would be pictures of butterflies, bicycles, trams, cars, and airplanes. Butterflies I knew, but all the other things existed, my father assured me, outside Tibet.

Just before going to bed, my mother would spray Keating's flea pow-der on the bedclothes, for fleas and lice abounded in Yatung. Once a week she would make us take off all our clothes and hand them to her for inspection. We would lie naked in the fleecy snugness of our *tsuktruk* (woven blankets), watching her: the lice, slow, sluggish, and easy victims; the fleas, acrobatic, hunted with spit on pulp of index finger and thumb, trapped, rolled vigorously to and fro to paralyze them, and then, with the edge of thumbnail, squashed with a rupturing sound like the bursting of a miniature bubble, reminiscent of James Joyce's "Her shapely fingernails reddened by the blood of squashed lice from the children's shirts."[19]

Late at night, my father would be practicing on his violin or telling stories to my mother such as *Ali Baba and the Forty Thieves*. Sometimes he would be serious and silent, reading, for he studied hard to improve himself every way, to make up for the university education that Tashi Tsering deprived him of. Years later, I came across several of his books, all ordered from Calcuttta; in them his name, date of purchase, and price all penciled, underlining special passages and phrases that he fancied, making note of words whose meanings he did not know, and jotting the date where he had stopped reading for the day. All the books were in English: Goldsmith's *Vicar of Wakefield*, Kingsley's *Westward Ho!* (prophetic words for my future), and Dickens's *Oliver Twist*. He had the four-volume bulky Funk and Wagnall's dictionary (very expensive books, my mother once told me), a set of the British encyclopedia and a row of books that purported to contain extracts from the "world's best literature." He studied by the light of a hurricane lantern. He took a course of "Pelmanism" to improve his memory and powers of concentration, such as how to remember by association the names of all the presidents of the United States of America. One of the Pelman exercises required careful listening and noting down the things that one was hearing at the time, and my father assiduously wrote, "[G]randmother praying, wife knitting, the noise of the river, dogs barking, sepoys shouting."[20] All this while Tibet slept serenely and peacefully and in Europe Hitler was seizing absolute power.

Sometimes, before retiring, my father exercised with dumbbells following the instructions of the mustached, muscled Eugen Sandow's *Sandow's System*, for Eugen had also penetrated the southern bastions of mysterious Tibet.[21]

On a holiday, usually Sunday, my parents would take us for picnics into the surrounding mountains with their meadows, flowers, and fir trees, idyllic excursions searching for mushrooms and wild fruits: the horses saddled and quietly grazing, the forest floor speckled with filtered sunlight, like a frame from a Kurosawa film as samurai prepare for an ambush. However, they had menace; we had innocence.

Occasionally the military escort organized a theatrical show: Indian music, dancing, enacting Indian myths and legends to the accompaniment of bells, drums, cymbals, and the tinkling of percussion instruments.

I remember being carried home late one night after attending such a show and getting my leg burned by a hurricane lantern. I still have the scar.

Sometimes a *lama-mani* (wandering minstrel) would come to our house—a monk unrolling a *thanka*, or religious painting, and then with a metal rod pointing to the picture displayed and in a sonorous sing-song voice relating the story depicted in the painting while we sat entranced at his feet and absorbed the myths and legends of Tibet. Occasionally a beggar-minstrel would entertain us with Tibetan music from a wooden guitar or a fiddle, while his wife and little daughter danced. Very rarely, a troupe of Khampa dancers would come, having traveled all the way from eastern Tibet. Kham was the home of the warriors of Tibet, and Grandmother, whose home had been in Markham, would come out of the house and inquire where the dancers came from and whether they knew anybody from her district, for, in those days, there was no means of communication throughout Tibet except on the Yatung-Gyantse-Lhasa route. The Khampas would whirl and spin round and round, dance Cossack fashion on bended knees, and execute acrobatic somersaults; the women, too, danced vigorously, whirling and twisting, spinning their handheld drums. Grandmother would watch them intently and then applaud and sigh, remembering her own youth in Kham.

My father had, as his hobbies, fretwork and photography (utter darkness and sudden magnesium flares). Having photographs taken was a social occasion in Yatung, planned many days before like putting on a fashion show. When the actual day arrived, there was the careful rehearsing of many artistic poses before clicking the shutter. Out would come the His Master's Voice gramophone; jade cups placed on silver and gold saucers; the flower pots; the British table alarm clock; the Harrods thermos flask; the ladies in their finest silk dresses and brocades and adorned in all their jewelry, sitting on the special British cane chairs; the children too, all dressed up, some in British clothes from London, sailor suits and soldiers' uniforms and serge jackets, suitable attire for Kensington or Park Lane; the servants standing stiffly at attention like guardsmen on parade, proudly making sure that their "Honi soit qui mal y pense" emblems were not hidden by the noble children they were holding; and the maid-servants, also in their best dresses, sitting cross-legged on gorgeous colorful Tibetan rugs artistically patterned with dragons and phoenixes.

Readers may notice that at times there seems to be a confusion in my narrative of my use of the first-person singular and plural. That is, in a way, intentional because by then my sister Norzin was born, and then my brother Tsewang Norbu, followed by another girl, Norbu Dolma (abbreviated to Norden), all born in Yatung. They were all delivered smoothly and easily at home by relatives or local women experienced in the accoucheur's art, for there were no nurses throughout "Outer Tibet."

Left to right: Author's mother (Tsering Yangchen), Norzin (sister), author, author's father (Rai Sahib Pemba Tsering) (Yatung, Tibet, 1936). Courtesy of the author

In those days, a Caesarean section was not possible, and even a forceps delivery was a major undertaking. An obstructed labor was a death sentence for a Tibetan woman. All of us took the addition of another family member in our stride. Norden had a very severe eye infection soon after birth, and my mother had to clean her eyes every day, and I remember well the daily ritual, with cotton wool and warm water. My mother used to tell me that but for her care, Norden would have gone blind. Other relatives were my cousins (my mother's sister's children), Migmar and Thubten, both of them a few years older than myself. Migmar had a very checkered and adventurous career, serving in the Second World War in the first battalion of the 10th Gurkha Rifles (the famous "Fush-ten"). Thubten became a monk at the Dungkar ("white conch") monastery in Yatung at the age of six.

My grandmother, born in 1868, was in her sixties when I was in Yatung, and she was extremely fond of us. She was a great storyteller, and often in the evenings we would sit at her bedside while she related stories of Gesar, the legendary Tibetan hero who is believed to be from eastern Tibet. She told us of incidents during her girlhood days in Kham, where turbulence, banditry, and vendettas were common. Once she had hidden herself in a chest storing grain while outside two rival clans clashed and fought each other with swords, and when all the men of one clan had been killed, their women had come out to take up their challenge. Then the Chinese Amban (Chinese government representative in Central Tibet during the Manchus) had intervened, dispensing justice, and the main culprits had been publicly beheaded, and Grandmother had watched the beheadings. She explained to us that earthquakes were caused by the shakings and contortions of a giant tortoise on which the earth rested. She said that the earth was flat and that the sun orbited around it.

During earthquakes in Yatung, we used to pray earnestly to Ugyen Rinpoche, the Indian Tantric-Buddhist teacher who founded the first monastery in Tibet in the eighth century AD in Samye; this was because Ugyen Rinpoche was subduing the evil spirits of the underworld, and, presumably, the tortoise was also in his domain. Granny believed that lunar eclipses were caused by the demon Sao Wokrey/Rahula (Violent Deities) swallowing the moon. The demon is believed to have a hole in his gullet, and if one shouts and frightens him, the swallowed moon is regurgitated through this hole. Hence during such eclipses, she encouraged us to go out, beat on the tins and utensils, and make as much bedlam as we could create. Needless to say, we hardly required such exhortations. Tibetans are very superstitious about lunar and solar eclipses, especially the latter, and about the appearance of comets. These phenomena forbade evil and some terrible harm that would befall the country or the Dalai Lama. My grandmother was also the first to give me a glimmer of the religion of Tibet, one of the most fascinating, complex, and fabulous religions in the world.

Losar (the Tibetan New Year) was the most exciting time for us children in Yatung. Months before the event, we would discuss it and make our plans. New clothes and shoes would be bought. All of us led by *Lata* ("idiot" in Nepalese) Bu Tsering would prepare for the *Seng-ge* (Lion Dance), which is traditionally performed at Losar. *Lata* was a very unkind sobriquet because he was the kindest and gentlest of companions and a most resourceful young boy. It was his slow nasal speech that made him appear backward. The lion was made of papier-mâché, and two boys performed the dance. Another boy, wearing a mask and bells around his chest in bandolier fashion, tamed the lion. The dance was executed to the throbbing of drums, and we used to practice this drumming every evening until it became too dark to see. After Losar, the *Seng-ge* was ritually burned and the charred fragments distributed as talismans.

We would run off to the Yatung *bazaar* (another Indian-Nepalese word creeping into the Tibetan spoken in Yatung) to buy parts for the *Seng-ge* and would find the town busy and crowded with people bringing merchandise from various neighboring regions to sell at Losar. There were tough, close-cropped Bhutanese (the Bhutan border was close to Yatung), with their clothes hitched above their knees, sharp daggers tucked into their voluminous waists, continuously chewing betel nut, and with legs more muscular than I have ever seen. They sold dry raisins, rice, walnuts, roasted rice, maize, chilies, and baskets made from bamboo. Little did I realize how much of my future life was destined to be spent in Bhutan and how close my links and connections would be with that kingdom. There were tall, swaggering Khampa muleteers with swords carried horizontally at their waists and long pigtails intertwined with red ribbon. There were Indians, soldiers and Marwari traders, Nepalese, Sherpas, Sikkimese and tall fierce-looking Amdos from northeast Tibet, little knowing that in their land would be born the fourteenth Dalai Lama. The Amdos, with smooth, hairless, bony faces, carried long deadly swords trailing at their sides, and they were tonsured like warriors serving a medieval shogun or samurai from a Kurosawa film.

In Yatung our favorite shop was that of Babu Injung, who was a relative of our teacher, Mr. Migmar. Just before each Losar, this enterprising tradesman would journey to Kalimpong and bring back commodities specially in demand in Losar. We would feast our boyish eyes on his shop: toys, fireworks, shoes, sweets, chocolates, and all kinds of novelties from the bright, modern world of Kalimpong that lay beyond the mountains. The walls of his shop were decorated with most interesting pictures: prancing plumed circus horses and performing bears, monkeys riding bicycles, trapeze artists, lions and tigers tamed by a top-hatted man with a trailing whip; Chiang Kai-shek surrounded by his generals, and in the foreground his infantry, helmeted, carrying automatic weapons; tanks, motorcycles, and, in the air, wave after wave of his squadrons. Little did we know that these were Chiang Kai-shek's propaganda pictures, for he would be beaten and on his knees by the onslaught of the Japanese within a few years.

Losar was in the air. In our large smoky kitchen, with meat hanging from the rafters, a man had been hired especially to make noodles. I remember the piles of dough kneaded by mixing water and eggs with the flour and his strong muscular arms flattening the dough with a "rolling pin" almost six feet long and heavy enough to fell an ox (in fact, a bandit had been once demolished by such an instrument in the woods of Yatung). He sang as he worked, a melodious Losar song, and gave me bits of dough, out of which I fashioned birds and beasts. Then he used a *tsayto* (Chinese chopper) to deftly machine-like slice the flattened dough, and I would wince, expecting him to slice a bit of his fingertip during the rapid rhythmic process.

And now a yak had to be slaughtered. We used to have a saying: "If you have a yak, slaughter it at Losar." In Tibet, where the taking of any form of life is considered a sin, somebody must do the slaughtering, for no Tibetan, be he incarnate lama or beggar, can do without meat. My grandmother always kept a chunk of roasted meat cooked in Khampa style in the house, and she ate it liberally the whole day and encouraged us to do the same. She taught me to eat the meat holding a piece in the mouth and then cutting off a portion with a sharp knife. She cautioned me to be careful, saying jokingly that I was liable to cut off the end of my nose if I was inordinately enthusiastic. Interestingly, I once saw a documentary about Bantus in the Kalahari Desert, and adults and children ate meat in the same fashion. The man hired to do the slaughtering was Shao Tashi, a Khampa, and we used to sing a song in Nepalese which went like this:

> *Shao Tashi ayo*
> *Gora ma charey ra*
> *Sabai zana hasnu lagew*
> *Shao Tashi dekhera*
>
> [Here comes Lame Tashi
> Riding on a pony
> Everybody burst out in laughter
> On seeing Lame Tashi]

In contradiction to the words of the song, Shao Tashi was too poor to ride and none of us would have dreamed of laughing in his presence, as he had a most malevolent demeanor and appearance. The Khampa butcher had a sinister Richard III limp; matador-like, he would step in to fell the yak with a lethal stab to the heart. The animal was dismembered, its limbs and torso hung in our kitchen storeroom, with blood and *tsampa* (roasted milled barley flour, the staple diet of Tibet) sausages made from the intestines, and its bladder provided us with a balloon to play with. With childish curiosity, and perhaps pity and sadness, I examined the huge, decapitated head of the yak: mute, immobile, its fixed jellied eyes now insensate; yet yesterday it stood tethered at one end of our apple orchard, fierce, menacing, alive, with stamping feet and snorting with flared steaming nostrils. Now it was dead. But as boys, we never thought of life and death.

On the night of the twenty-ninth day of the twelfth Tibetan month, we drank the *guthug* ("nine-gruel"), made of vegetables and little dough balls. The traditional saying went, "Guthug thung ne nane na; guthug thungne shine shi" ("Having drunk the guthu, what does it matter if one falls ill; having drunk the *guthug*, it does not matter if one even dies"). This could be literally interpreted, because one was expected to down nine bowls of the *guthug* (*gu* meaning "nine" in Tibetan). If one refused to comply, the gruel was "served" down your neck! In the *guthug* were bigger dough balls fashioned to represent a sun and a moon (signifying virtue), a woman carrying a child (pregnancy or another addition to the family), a book (devoted to religion), a piece of charcoal (an evil mind), wool (new clothes), garlic (flatulent fellow), paper (a drifter and a lazy-no-good like a bit of paper drifting in the wind), and above all "Sema Rango," an unmistakable image that one tried at all costs to avoid, for it symbolized buffoonery, evil, ill luck. Any adult drawing "Sema Rango" in his or her bowl was fined by being forced to drink, and any children getting it had to clown and sing.

The *guthug* was stirred, poured, and distributed by a blindfolded person. After collecting all the large dough balls, each person received a separate lump of dough, which you rubbed all over your body to take away ills of the past and to ensure good health in the coming year. You spat into this lump and embedded some hair or frayed bits of clothes that you were wearing and placed the dough in a common container to throw away later with the *Barmo* (witch), a repulsive image with matted hair and pendulous breasts. Then crackers of the Chinese type would be exploded, and my father would bring out his double-barreled "Made in England" shotgun and fire cartridges into the clear starry night, shots that would burst like flares and scatter into a hundred flashing stars—the only household in Yatung to possess this novelty on *nyishu-gu* (twenty-nine). Nyima Wangmo would light up rolls of straw, somebody would carry the *Barmo* and all the large dough balls, and then, shouting defiance into the night air—"*Barmo dön-shog ma!*" (Come on out, witch!) and screaming fierce

"*Kyi! Kyi!*" (Tibetan war cries)—they would rush out to hurl everything at the junction of three roads. On returning, they would sing a traditional song blessing our house and would be allowed to enter after passing in a white stone in exchange for a black. After this, pandemonium would break out and there would be great excitement as everybody threw *tsampa* flour at each other, a hilarious riotous free-for-all, followed by singing and dancing, and the adults would drink *chang* or Scotch whiskey, saved especially for Losar.

The next day, *namgang* (Losar Eve), the house was cleaned and our new clothes put out. The kitchen would be decorated with Losar emblems, and there would be stacks of *khabseys* (Tibetan cookies), long pieces of bread called *bong gü amcho* (which translates as "donkey's ears" because of their shape), and intricately designed biscuits with *khadas* (ceremonial scarves) draped on them.

On Losar day we got up very early and put on our new clothes, standing in front of the chimneys with roaring log-fires. Our parents would give us money, and all of us wished each other "*Tashi Delek Phünsum Tso*" (Good luck and the heaping of the Three Graces). Hordes of excited Yatung children would come from dawn, all attired in new clothes, to wish us "*Tashi Delek*," and they would be given presents of money. Later friends and officials would call and be given tea and drinks. There was much exchanging of ceremonial scarves. We would all play, burst crackers, and go to the bazaar to meet friends and to buy toys from Babu Injung's shop.

A few days after Losar, prayer flags, thirty to forty feet in length, would be erected outside our house, the local people coming to help, and there would be much shouting, laughter, merrymaking, and drinking, followed by more drinking, dancing, Losar songs (the same ones I had heard our noodle maker sing), the stamping of feet, whirling bodies, and laughing faces. Tibetans were a very merry people, happy, full of fun, humor, and laughter, and they loved singing, dancing, dicing, and joking. There followed a series of parties given turn by turn by the agency staff, lasting the whole day and going on for weeks. They played cards, *mah-jong, bahg* (Tibetan dominoes), and *sho* (a dice game), while ladies sang songs, gossiped, told jokes, admired each other's jewelry, or played pranks on the men. It was some of the happiest days for Yatung, and all who lived there during those years never ceased to talk of the fun, laughter, and gaiety of the 1930s and treasured those memories all their lives.

I found a Letts 1933 diary, printed in Shaftesbury Avenue, London (more familiar to me later than even Yatung), which belonged to my father. My father made very terse entries, but I think a few quotations from his diary illuminates the Yatung of those days. I shall comment in brackets where pertinent:

January 1, Fine day. Went down to Pipithang to see Depon, new TTA. Presented him with a tea-set and vegetables. [Pipithang was three miles away from Yatung, where my grandmother had a house. *Depön* is a Tibetan rank. "TTA" is "Tibet Trade Agent." My father, at that time being in charge of the British Trade Agency, appears keen to foster good Anglo-Tibetan relations with the TTA.]

January 2: Ice-skated for the first time. Needs good practice. Mr. L.D. Lama was conferred title of Rai Sahib. First Hillman to get it in the Post and Telegraph Department. Sepoys paraded. ["Hillman" refers to Tibetan, Sikkimese, or Nepalese living in the Himalayan regions of Sikkim and the Darjeeling district, in contradistinction to "plainsman" or Indians generally. There was an unspoken suspicion that "hillmen" were regarded with some condescension by "plainsmen" as being intellectually inferior and backward. The British, however, tended to pamper "hillmen," and if you happened to be a Tibetan, you could get away with most things. My father too, before Indian Independence in 1947, received the title of "Rai Sahib" from the British Raj. "Sepoys" refers to the agency escort.]

January 3: No skating. Thin ice. [My father apparently did not believe in skating on thin ice.]

January 4: Apples pruned.

January 15: Played hockey. [Fancy playing hockey in the bitter Yatung winter!]

January 27: Earthquake at 2 A.M. [We must have prayed fervently to Ugyen Rinpoche for protection and intercession.]

January 31: Planted daffodil bulbs.

February 6: Dr. Tennant and Captain Rerrie arrived. [Captain Dr. David Tennant of the Indian Medical Service was acting surgeon at Gyantse. I have already said something about him. Captain Rerrie was in the Marathas, and many years later I met him in Darjeeling, where he was working for the Indian tea industry.]

February 11: Cow delivered calf at 6 P.M.

February 13: Gloomy day. Snowfall the whole day.

February 16: Went out to Chubithang for shooting with Captain Rerrie and Dr. Tennant. [Chubithang is the first halt when one travels from Yatung to Gangtok.]

March 5: Snow about nine inches in the morning.

March 16: Everest Expedition first party arrived.

March 18: Everest Expedition party left for Gautsa. [Gautsa is the first halting station on the way to Lhasa from Yatung.]

April 14: Good Friday. Still snowing. Captain Morris held up at Chubithang owing to heavy snow. [I cannot trace who Captain Morris was.]

May 14: Mr. Ludlow and Captain Sherriff arrived. [References to Mr. Ludlow will be made later in this book. Captain (later Major) Sherriff I got to know very well in Britain when I was a student. He became a farmer and settled in Angus.]

May 19: Rained in the afternoon. Jemadar shot a wild boar weighing 210 pounds the preceding night. A record. ["Jemadar" is a sergeant in the Indian army.]

May 20: Marathas preparing a theatrical performance. We Babus also preparing one.

May 25: Fine day. Mrs. Prince presented me a pencil. Captain and Mrs Roddick arrived. [I have the silver pencil still in 1992. Who Mrs. Prince or the Captain and wife were, I have no idea.]

May 27: Tennis court fences completed. Whooping cough epidemic prevailing here. [It must have been an anxious time for my father in case I should catch the illness. The clinical thermometer must have been produced frequently. Regarding tennis, he was very fond of the game. When I was in London, one thing my father envied was that I was able to watch tennis at the Centre Court at Wimbledon. It was the era of Gorgeous Gussie Moran. My father wrote saying that before he died, he must visit Wimbledon. Alas, he never did.]

June 3: King George V born in 1865. The political officer gave us lunch. [Mr. Frederick Williamson was the British political officer. Mrs. Williamson, in her book, records the occasion as follows: "We were thirteen to lunch that day, all Tibetans save for two Nepalese, Derrick and myself."]

July 22: Played tennis. Wife fell ill (labour). Delivered a daughter at 2.15 P.M. [There might be some confusion here, as my sister Norzin was born on July 23. However, like Drake at his bowls in Plymouth, I hope Norzin's advent did not disturb his tennis.]

August 28: 2/7 Rajputs arrive. [They were to replace the Marathas.]

October 22: Dr. Tonyot returned here. [I do not know where Dr. Tonyot Tsering had gone, but his return must have produced a sigh of relief from my mother and grandmother.][22]

It was in Yatung that I met Tashi Tsering, my grand-uncle, for the first time. Pola (grandfather), as I used to call him, was then in his late forties, undergoing enforced retirement on an "invalid's pension" in Gangtok, where his wife—a large, handsome, domineering woman—had opened a shop and become rich. Tashi Tsering spent most of his time "chewing the cud," as he put it, and indulging in his favorite occupation: the pursuit of English literature. They came to Yatung for a holiday, usually visiting the Khambu hotsprings, which were a little distance away from Yatung. They had no children and used to pamper the grandnieces and grandnephews. I remember him as a jolly man who made paper footballs and played games with us. In the evenings I used to entertain him with songs and dances, my pièce de résistance being a song about Khampa innkeeperesses in Banashöl, the district in Lhasa where Khampas congregated. The song had rather irreverent words: "Innkeeperess of Banashöl, do you have any chang to sell? If you don't, then do you have wenches to sell?"

In Yatung I seldom looked at the sky except when there was a lunar eclipse or on *nyishu-gu* before Losar when my father fired his cartridges into the Tibetan night sky. I never looked at the stars or the Milky Way, though they must have been there and the Tibetan night sky in its stark high-altitude clarity must have been breathtaking and spectacular. I took the moon, sun, and stars for granted like the trees, stones, mountains, and streams. They offered no philosophical or ontological enigmas or challenges. We were close to the warmth and snugness of the earth and forgot that the rest of the universe existed.

My mother was an amateur pawnbroker, although quite unlike the repulsive old lady Raskolnikov murdered in Dostoevsky's *Crime and Punishment*.[23] My father had a good salary, paid in silver coins, Indian rupees with King George V's head on them, regal, mantled, crowned, bearded; he was Rex Imperator, fidelis defender and emperor of India. They rang each coin on a stone on pay day outside the agency office before disbursing the salaries. My mother had never been to school, but after her marriage she began to learn Tibetan, English, and Nepalese and later became fairly proficient in them. The head clerk's wife had Indian rupees, and these had the same aura as the present-day United States dollar. Indian rupees were legal tender throughout Tibet. Families in Yatung pawned their corrals, gold, *zhis* (patterned necklace beads made from an agate-like stone, much valued in Tibet, Sikkim, and Bhutan), and my mother wrapped the pawned goods carefully, sealed them, and labeled the dates when they were to be redeemed. Eventually she had a collection of unredeemed jewelry that was the envy of all ladies in Yatung.

The first Europeans I ever saw in my life were in Yatung. They were invariably British. They were *Sahibs* to us, beings from another world: tall, gaunt, aseptic, clean with their daily all-weather baths; blue-eyed, yellowhaired; rulers, administrators, and masters, closer to Lhayul or the land of the gods than us Tibetans. It was not a question of feeling inferior but of being, oh, so different! We were worlds apart. Of course, to us all *Sahibs* who came to Yatung were important—British officials, their wives (*Memsahibs*) and their children (*Babas*). I remember the occasion very well when I saw my first *Sahib* family. It was at the British Residency, and I stared at them for some time with great curiosity and interest: a tall red-faced man wearing breeches and a tweed coat, the woman just as tall but wearing skirts and a hat, and with them a most adorable little girl with blonde ringlets and blue eyes, exactly like the dolls that my sister Norzin used to play with. The girl was wearing a long grey coat, and she appeared friendly. They were accompanied by some Tibetan officials and members of the agency staff. What an encounter! I couldn't get over it for days. Perhaps my father might have welcomed such people to Yatung because when the official British trade agent was not at his post in Yatung, my father was in charge. Mrs. Margaret Williamson has written about such a reception when she came to Yatung in 1933: "As we approached Yatung, we were met by a small reception committee composed of . . . Mr. Pemba, the Chief Clerk, and several others."[24]

In 1987, I received a very strange and thrilling letter. It was from Mrs. Verena Rybicki, who was then living in Lexington, Massachusetts. She said she was the daughter of Dr. William Morgan, about whom I shall write later. She said she was in Yatung in the 1930s as a little girl and that she had come across a little boy and girl playing near a stream close to the residency and her father had told her that they were the children of a member of the agency staff. She had wanted to play with the children but had been whisked away. It could very well have been my sister and myself, and perhaps I had stared at Verena too and studied her exotic features.

My father left Yatung for Lhasa in the middle of 1936 with Sir Basil Gould on his mission to Lhasa, when Spencer-Chapman went as Gould's private secretary. Many months later, my mother one day told me that we, too, would be going to Lhasa. My grandmother told me how interesting and wonderful I would find Lhasa, a city she had visited as a young girl. She reminded me particularly to look out for a goat that was growing out miraculously from a rock inside the Jokhang temple. When she was in Lhasa, the head of the goat had been visible. She told me that when the goat was fully grown, the monastery of Samye, south of Lhasa, and the oldest monastery in Tibet, would be enshrouded by a sandstorm, and the great image of the Jowo (Buddha) in Lhasa, Tibet's holiest idol, would be carried down to the swirling depths of a celestial ocean, and the world would come to an end. These were not very reassuring words for a young boy eager to see the new world of Lhasa, but I did promise to grandmother that I would keep a special lookout for the divine goat growing out of the rock and report its exact details when I returned to Yatung. But I did not know when I would return to Yatung, and it was a very sad day when I bid good-bye to her and left for Lhasa.

## NOTES

1. Kenneth W. Thompson, *Winston Churchill's World View. Statesmanship and Power* (Baton Rouge: Louisiana State University Press, 1983), 106.

2. Frederick Spencer-Chapman, *Lhasa: The Holy City* (London: Chatto and Windus, 1940), 2.

3. Charles Bell, "A Year in Lhasa," *Geographical Journal* 63, no. 2 (February 1924): 85.

4. C. Sudyam Cutting, *The Fire Ox and Other Years* (N.p.: Collins), 1947.

5. Gould, *The Jewel in the Lotus*, 17.

6. Pemba Tsering, letter to the author, March 9, 1954.

7. Williamson and Snelling, *Memoirs of a Political Officer's Wife*, 38–39.

8. Ibid., 38.

9. Gould, *The Jewel in the Lotus*, 21–22.

10. Ibid., 23.

11. Pemba Tsering, letter to the author, January 7, 1954.

12. Williamson and Snelling, *Memoirs of a Political Officer's Wife*, 226.

13. Ibid., 78.

14. Spencer-Chapman, *Lhasa*, 28.

15. Adjutant-General's Office, *The Queen's Regulations and Orders for the Army* (London: The Superintendence of Her Majesty's Stationary Office, 1868), 178.

16. "A Wartime Musical Hit," My Learning, accessed January 22, 2022, https://www.mylearning.org/stories/its-a-long-way-to-tipperary/764.

17. Spencer-Chapman, *Lhasa*, 24.

18. Ibid., 28.

19. James Joyce, *Ulysses*, ed. Hans Walter Gabler (New York: Vintage Books, 1986), 9.

20. Pemba Tsering's Notebook, n.d.

21. Eugen Sandow, *Sandow's System: Sandow on Physical Training*, ed. G. Mercer Adam (New York: J. Selwin & Sons, 1894).

22. Pemba Tsering's Diary, 1933.

23. Fyodor Dostoevsky, *Crime and Punishment*, trans. Richard Pevear and Larissa Volokhonsky (New York: Vintage Books, 1993), 76.

24. Williamson and Snelling, *Memoirs of a Political Officer's Wife*, 64.

# 4

~

# Journey to Lhasa

We traveled to Lhasa with the second wife of Rai Bahadur Dzasa Norbu Dhondup, a Darjeeling Tibetan, stationed in Lhasa with the British Mission. In those days, it was foolhardy and reckless to undertake the long journey to Lhasa from Yatung on one's own. My mother took with her all her children—I myself was almost seven years old; Norzin at four and half; Norbu, my brother, who was two and a half; and the youngest, my sister Norden, only eight months old. My father was in Lhasa when Norden was born in Yatung, and he had not seen her yet. It would be no mean feat of endurance for one as young as Norden to travel all the way to Lhasa. It was sometime in November 1937 when we left Yatung. Being children, we were callous, thoughtless, and inconsiderate, never imagining the immense difficulties of that journey for my mother, taking with her four little children. It was for her, truly, a "Long March," and it was a journey that changed the course of all our lives.

I rode on horseback, sitting in the lap of a servant, but when the weather was inclement, I sat huddled in a box, the size and shape of a tea chest, sharing it cramped up with my sister Norzin. We traveled at dawn at *chakey dangpo* (first cockcrow) so as to arrive at our destination as early as possible to avoid the duststorms of the afternoon.

We first came to the plain of Lingmathang, with clear streams and a river flowing through it where Nepalese who lived in Yatung went fishing. Tibetans seldom fished, considering it a sin. Although Tibetans ate fish, my grandmother used to tell me that eating fish was one of the greatest sins because fishes died in a cruel way with hooks in their mouths. Early impressions last because even now I have an aversion for fish, although in Lhasa we ate tinned British sardines, herrings, and salmon. Perhaps my subconscious reasoned that British fish were not caught with hooks. From Lingmathang we could see the monastery of Dungkar above us, my cousin Thubten's monastery, although he was not there at the time (as we shall see later). Our first halt was at Gau or Gautsa, fifteen miles from Yatung and at an altitude of 12,400 feet. We had ascended almost three thousand feet on our first day.

The next day we continued to climb, and when we passed near Dotha, between Gau and Phari, my mother pointed out to me a small monastery in the distance, lonely and isolated in barren surroundings, telling me that my cousin was there with his teacher, Gen Jinpa. Later in life Thubten, who is three years my senior, told me that the name of the monastery was Pema Chöling, and his teacher was the monk in charge of the place. My cousin, who had become a monk at the age of six, said that there were only four other monks at the little monastery, and he remembered the place as being intensely cold most of the year. Once my parents had visited him there, and my mother had broken down and wept because Thubten had been looking terribly thin and his monk's clothes had been filthy with dirt, and he was spending most of the day collecting dried dung to use as fuel for the monastery. My mother had remonstrated with Gen Jinpa and told him that if Thubten was not looking cleaner the next time she visited him, she would withdraw him from the monastery and forget about him ever becoming a monk if all he did the whole day was collect manure. Perhaps conditions improved because Thubten is still a monk and now lives at his monastery of Samten Chöling in Darjeeling.

Spencer-Chapman writes that above Gautsa there was "the wildest and most formidably beautiful valley that I have ever seen,"[1] but we, being children, were immune to such charms. Instead, we sang our Yatung songs and talked about the friends we had left behind, and the tough, hardy servant on whose lap I rode regaled me with stories and amusing anecdotes all the way. To him, each obstacle on the road was something to be challenged and overtaken with contempt and aplomb, and nothing was so difficult that one couldn't treat it as a joke. He was inveterately cheerful, sang songs, scowled fiercely at the mountains and crags with tongue-in-cheek, and whispered dirty jokes in my ear.

Traveling in Tibet was great fun. Sometimes I was lulled into sleep by the shaking, nodding mane of the horse and the voice of my servant saying prayers, for the Tibetan character is ambivalent and switches easily from crude ribaldry to solemn prayers; there were also the monotonous never-ending rows and rows of telegraph poles erected after the Younghusband Expedition, going all the way to Lhasa and cared for by Nepalese linemen. I learned so much about the traditions and folklore of Tibet while traveling in Tibet, for to break the boredom of the journey

*Left to right: Attendant Rinchen carrying Norden (author's youngest sister), author, Norzin (author's younger sister) in front of author's mother, who is standing behind, and Tsewang Norbu (author's younger brother) (Dekyi Lingkha, Lhasa, Tibet, 1939). Courtesy of the author*

everybody conversed and all were expert raconteurs, and each prominent landmark in the journey prompted its own flood of stories, and heated but pleasant discussions arose. Perhaps Chaucer's pilgrims on their way to Canterbury did the same to pass the day. Sometimes, if anybody possessed a good voice, he sang a song. There were, however, intervals when, as if awed by the magnificence, grandeur, and immensity of the surroundings, everybody prayed in unison, the favorite prayer being to the Goddess Jetsun Dölma, beloved and adored by all Tibetans and protectress and savior of all lonely travelers. At dawn, when the cavalcade set out on its long journey, everybody prayed, for one did not know what the day would bring; jokes and merriment only came in the afternoons or toward the end of the road.

In the late evening, we arrived at Phari, which, situated at an altitude of about 14,500 feet, was higher than the Nathö La pass, forming the boundary between Tibet and Sikkim, and the highest point on the road between Yatung and Gangtok. In Tibet, there were valleys and plains that stood more than 16,000 feet above sea level. Phari was about twenty-five miles from Gautsa, negligible in miles, but the horses climbed at about four miles an hour, and even that was considered a good speed at certain sections of the road. The town was aptly named, for Phari in Tibetan means "the hill of the pig," and even Tibetans spoke of it as being extremely filthy, refuse heaps accumulating in the streets and encroaching to the first floor of houses. The British described it as the highest and dirtiest town in the world.[2] But the town was a very important trade center, and at that time most of Bhutan's trade was carried out through this town, rice and rice products being the chief Bhutanese exports, for rice does not grow in Tibet.

All the way from Yatung to Gyantse, we stayed at the dak bungalows or rest houses built by the British after the Younghusband Expedition. From Gyantse to Lhasa, there were none, and we had to billet at the homes of local villagers. These dak bungalows were very comfortable, and each was in charge of a Tibetan *chowkidar* (Indian word for a caretaker) employed by the British Trade Agencies. The *chowkidar* would come out to receive the cavalcade, doff his cap, and lead the horses in. He would give presents of fodder for the horses, dry meat (Phari was famous for this, and it is reported that a British officer once said of the place, "Dirt, dirt everywhere but good mutton!"), eggs, and the inevitable biscuits (Huntley and Palmer or Jacob's).[3] In Tibet, it was the custom to give each other presents on many occasions, and biscuits, or "bissy-cutti" (as Tibetans pronounced the word), were the most common and acceptable gifts.

These dak bungalows always welcomed travelers with a roaring fire. There were tongs and all the other paraphernalia that one sees in British homes in front of their fireplaces during the winter, and the flames were fanned by British hand bellows. There were English chairs and tables, beds with mattresses, and even footmats. In the bathrooms there were wash bowls and towel racks and, of course, the "thunder-box" toilets with enamel and aluminum receptacles, cleared away by the *jamadars* (sweepers) who were low-caste Indians, for Nepalese and Tibetans considered it inferior to clean toilets. Water was hauled in buckets usually by the *jamadars* or by our own servants. There would be a shelf of magazines—*Illustrated London News*, *Wide World*, *Blackwood's*, and of course *Punch*—and a rack of novels and other books left behind by British travelers who had used these bungalows. I used to rummage and leaf through these magazines, riffling the pages to stop at some interesting picture. In those days, *Punch* had an easily recognizable cover, the outer zone ringed by a chain of fairy figures conical capped (much like the Tibetan hats of the Gelukpa or Yellow Hat School of monks), Punch riding and holding what my servant would snigger at—a giant phallus.

At Phari, there was not much time to glance through British magazines, for I had an agonizing headache and put my head in my mother's lap, inhaling the woolly aroma of her Tibetan *pangden* (apron), worn by all married women in Tibet. My mother gave me no sympathy, for when I come to think of it, I was a bit of a hypochondriac in those days. She warned me that if my headache was no better the next day, then I was going to be sent back immediately to Yatung. I was too young to plead altitude sickness, for at 14,500 feet even a hypochondriac was entitled to a little sympathy. However, the warning worked like a charm, for the next day I was "right as rain."

Before we reached Gyantse, which took about five days from Phari, there were some interesting places that we traveled through, most of them connected with the Younghusband Expedition and the battles the Tibetans had fought with the British. There was Red Idol Gorge, which Spencer-Chapman says is "certainly the most marvellous place for an ambush," describing the region surrounding it as "an awesome and forbidding place, wilder that Glencoe or Killiecrankie."[4] Years later, I, too, visited Glencoe, but I saw it through the windows of a comfortable British coach. The gorge is so named, probably by the British, because there is a very large image of the Buddha carved on a rock face and painted in red.

There was the plain of Guru, where the Tibetans suffered most casualties. Lieutenant-Colonel F. M. Bailey was a young lieutenant at the battle. We had a Tibetan servant in the caravan who as a boy of thirteen had been recruited to guard some of the passes into Tibet and keep a look out for Younghusband's soldiers. It was the custom to select boys aged thirteen owing to a superstitious belief in this number being evil, the same in Tibet as in the rest of the world. He said that they were armed only with slings and that they had been frightened at the sight of Sikhs of the Indian army (possibly Bailey's men of the 32nd Sikh Pioneers). At Guru, the British opened fire with their modern weapons on Tibetans armed with matchlocks, muzzle-loaders, swords, and slings but confident in their amulets and talismans given to them by their lamas to render them bulletproof. The Guru battle arose probably from an unfortunate misunderstanding, and there are many versions as to how it started; Lieutenant-Colonel Bailey gave me details of those who fought there, the parleying between Tibetan officials and the British, and who fired the first shots. Speaking of Glencoe in a previous paragraph, ironically, this time the British were commanded by a General Macdonald, and those who were massacred were the Tibetans. There are tales of Tibetans smearing themselves with blood and pretending to be dead and of Tibetan village women with baskets on their backs scavenging among the dead in the middle of the night; one Lhasa aristocrat had his bejeweled fingers nearly lopped off when a woman couldn't get the rings off and the man had to remove the rings himself. This led to a discussion of the Tibetan methods of bulletproofing and whether they really worked. Many became skeptical and mentioned the Guru battle. Some said that amulets given by very holy lamas who had rendered them magical with *mantras* (secret verbal formulae) were said to really work. However, the most infallible method was to burn some pages from the sacred text, the *Dorje Choepa*, and to swallow the ashes. Doing so made the chest wall black in color, and one became completely bulletproof, but it was a most hideous sin and the perpetrator had to spend many *kalpas* (eons) in hell as atonement.

On the road close to Gyantse, we were told about the giant image of the Gyalwa Jamba, or "Victorious Affection" Maitreya Buddha, who will follow the present Shakyamuni Buddha. This idol was built by the sixth Panchen Rinpoche, who was a contemporary of the thirteenth Dalai Lama and, in a political dispute with the latter, had fled to China in 1923. I was told that an adult could fit into one nostril of the idol, and if one wore a hat and leaned backward to look at the crown of the image, your hat would fall off. It has now (at the time of writing this book) been confirmed that the statue is indeed the biggest in the world, 26.2 meters high when compared with the Vairochana Buddha of Japan, which measures 21.5 meters. In the making of the image, over 115 tons of red copper and 150 kilograms of gold were used.

It is strange that I do not recall very much about Gyantse, although my mother must have met some friends there and they must have remarked on the number of her children. She had left Gyantse seven years before and had not been there since; she had left with only me and the memory of a dead one, and now she had three more, all born in Yatung.

From Gyantse to Lhasa was the most difficult part of our journey. In those days, traveling from Yatung to Gyantse was considered a pleasant vacation, like a jaunt through a summer meadow. Now there were no more dak bungalows after we left Gyantse, no bathrooms with "thunder boxes," no mattressed beds, no *Illustrated London News* and *Punch* to glance through.

At Ralung, at an altitude of 14,800 feet, like coming across a CAT scan machine in a primitive hospital, was a cast-iron British stove. I don't know how it ever got there. Ralung was famous as a place where the Drukpa Kagyü School of Tibetan Buddhism had its origin, and this school would become very familiar to me in the future, as it is the predominant one in the Kingdom of Bhutan. Ralung also has probably the biggest nunnery in Tibet, and the nuns with shaven heads and wearing a peculiar wooly headgear could be seen in many parts of Tibet. They have a way of clapping their hands in unison to the chanting of prayers. We used to call them Ralung Anis.

Then there was Dzara, situated at an altitude of 15,700 feet, close to Ralung; it was a bleak, bitterly cold, inhospitable place, possibly the most inhospitable that I have ever seen, where all the inhabitants were in league with bandits and robbers, where the caravans were large and well armed. The people carried out a brisk trade and rented out rooms for the night; if small, weak groups sought shelter, they would signal to the surrounding mountains, and the innocent travelers would be robbed and slaughtered without mercy. That was one of the reasons why caravans in Tibet always traveled in large groups. All our men carried swords, daggers, pistols, and rifles. The favorite weapon was the Mauser pistol (manufactured by Waffenfabrik Mauser in Germany), which, by sliding into slotted groove on the wooden case, could be converted into a rifle. The Mauser was called a *Sissylhendu* by Tibetans, and it gave kudos to anybody owing one. British .303 rifles and Russian rifles with long barrels called *pamaley* were also much in favor.

A rifle, a pistol, a good sword or dagger (Bhutanese ones were highly prized), and a strong reliable horse or mule were things one took pride in owing in Tibet. In some regions, mules, because of their surefootedness and stamina, were more in demand than horses—except in Kham, where they loved speedy horses. Only in some areas of Tibet were yaks ridden, contrary to the mistaken Western belief that everybody rode yaks in Tibet. Donkeys certainly vied with mules and horses as pack animals, but one seldom rode a donkey, as this was done only by country yokels. The boatmen in Lhasa employed sheep to carry their belongings upstream, and my father told me that in western Tibet they used sheep to carry loads of salt. My mother, when traveling in Tibet (and especially in places like Dzara), carried a toy pistol in a real holster. She could have done just as well if she had stuffed the holster with toilet paper, emulating the Italian army doctor in Hemingway's *A Farewell to Arms*.[5]

The highest altitude that we traveled on the route from Gyantse to Lhasa was at Karo La pass, 16,800 feet high, between Ralung and Dzara. The British, during the Younghusband Expedition, encamped at the base of the Karo La, and I cannot imagine a more forbidding palace to pitch hundreds of tents. "Mad dogs and Englishmen" may go out in the midday sun, but surely it is madder still to camp at the foot of Karo La.[6] Hugh Richardson, living in Scotland at the time of my writing this book (1992), and Spencer-Chapman climbed the mountains surrounding Dzara, which the latter said "in this weather is the bleakest and most unfriendly place, delphinium with sticky foliage and a nauseous smell of cheap scent and sweat; we are going to call it *Aconitum barma idiae*."[7]

We crossed Gampa La, the pass famous in many songs of Tibet, and notorious for bandits. This was the occasion to tease the Tsangpas in our caravan, those who came from the U-Tsang (Pure) province of Tibet, which includes Shigatse and Gyantse. I, too, was a Tsangpa! U-Tsang people are teased as being fainthearted. A regiment of U-Tsang soldiers on their way to Lhasa stopped at the foot of Gampa La and, in great trepidation, asked some travelers who were coming down, "We are five hundred soldiers from U-Tsang, are there any robbers at Gampa La?" And there is also a romantic song of the young man who looks back from the top of Gampa La toward Lhasa, where he has left his loved one behind, and laments that he will not see her again.

We rode along the shore of the Yardrok Tso (lake) on the higher pastures, the lake nearly fifty miles in length, and at an altitude of 14,500 feet, higher than the summit of the Nathö La pass. It freezes in winter, and caravans of horses and donkeys pass over its frozen surface. The Yardrok area is famous for its *sha kampo* (dried meat); perhaps it is the purity of the cold air of the lake that gives the meat its taste and texture. The lake is considered sacred by Tibetans, and the British of the Younghusband Expedition did not realize how they offended Tibetan sentiments by their sacrilegious behavior in shooting teal there, boating, and fishing. Far away, on the shore of the Yardrok, could be seen the monastery of Samding. This monastery was unique in Tibet for being an institution for monks but ruled by a nun. She was perhaps the only high-ranking female incarnate lama in Tibet and the only female to be blessed by the hands of the Dalai Lama. She was the Samding Dorje (supreme of stones or diamond) Phamo (sow). Legend has it that once, when Muslim invaders attacked her monastery, she transformed herself and the inmates of the monastery into pigs, confounding and disgusting the Muslims. Subsequent incarnations claimed they grew bristles on their backs. I once examined in Bhutan a sick young girl claiming to be an incarnation of the Dorje Phagmo, but I'm afraid I cannot confirm that I saw bristles. The thirteenth Dalai Lama stayed at Samding when he fled from the Chinese in 1910, and it was from there that he sent a message to Sir Basil Gould requesting British asylum.

One memorable day, we arrived at Chaksam Drukha (Iron Bridge ferry), the ferry across the Tsangpo River that eventually becomes the Brahmaputra of northeastern India and flows into the Bay of Bengal close to Calcutta (now Kolkatta). Some of the horses were tied together and swam across. We crossed in Tibetan coracles, made of hide stretched across a framework of wood. It was the first time in my life that I had been in a boat. Our baggage was loaded into a huge wooden boat with prayer flags stuck in it and a carved horse's head at one end, much like a Viking ship.

Chaksam Drukha had been so named because of the iron suspension bridge that existed there, built by an eccentric wandering ascetic of the fifteenth century named Thangtong-Gyalpo, his name meaning "King of the Empty Plains." When questioned about where he came from, he would reply "where my back faces," and where he was going, "where my chest faces." He must have meant literally what he said because one finds he is ubiquitous, and even in relatively far-away Bhutan in the south in Paro, where I worked as a doctor for three years, there is *chorten* and a small temple, both said to have been built by him.

After the fun of the ferry crossing, we headed toward Chushül, where we were met by our father, who had come from Lhasa, two days away, to greet us. He smiled at all of us and peered with pleasure at Norden, swathed in blankets, carried on a servant's back, whom he was seeing for the first time. At Chushül, he opened a tin of peaches for us and gave us roasted meat. I had not seen my father for over a year.

We were now approaching Lhasa, and before I describe our entry into that city, there are some remarks that I wish to make about our journey so far. I remember seeing *kiangs* (wild asses), striped like zebras, on the wide plains that seemed to be stretched on. We saw many marmots that darted here and there on seeing us; vultures feeding on dead donkeys, mules, horses, and dogs—exposed entrails, hollowed thoraces, the birds hopping away at the approach of the caravan—but because nobody ate vultures, they did not fear human beings. They must have, however, viewed us as prospective items on the menu of vulturine cuisine.

I remember a scene of bare somber rocky mountains and a flat plain strewn with pebbles and boulders, denuded of all vegetation, and a track across it, and our cavalcade of horses, stalwarts in the front, rifles slung across their shoulders, wearing Gurkha slouch hats, with whips and swords, and the ladies wearing bright Tibetan dresses, their faces shielded against the wind with scarves and mufflers. At the end of the day, we children knew immediately that we were arriving at our destination; one servant would gallop ahead bearing the Tibetan government's *Lam-yik* (road letter), the permit that forced the local people to provide fodder and lodgings, corvee labor, arrange young women to bring dried dung for fires (as wood was scarce), and draw water for the kitchens. The best rooms would be provided free of charge, fresh horses for the next day's journey supplied, and porters arranged. Some of the servants were bossy, harsh, oppressive, and they flaunted the *Lam-yik* and took advantage of the servant girls when the day's work was over and their masters and mistresses all asleep, tired after a day's journey across the Tibetan mountains and snows.

Near Dzara, I can still remember the distant lonely snowclad mountains, a freezing, biting, whipping wind, the evening's last rays on a dilapidated Tibetan mud-brick wall, pale yellow in the fading light, with particles of sand and silica glinting and shining.

From Chushül we went to Nyethang, passing caves where robbers were said to live. I did not know then that Nyethang had the mausoleum of Jowoje Palden Atisha, the famous Indian teacher who had come to Tibet at the age of fifty-nine in the eleventh century AD, to bring about a revival of Buddhism after its decline in the previous century. The

Kadampas (Binders of the Word of the Buddha) had been the first school to branch off from the original strain of Buddhism introduced into Tibet in the eighth century AD, and they owed their inception to a disciple of Atisha. From this new school arose later the Gelukpas, who, under the Dalai Lamas, took over the spiritual and secular domains of Tibet.

Nyethang, at an altitude of 11,600 feet, is 200 feet lower than Lhasa, and yet only sixteen miles away. We rode at a leisurely pace, and everybody was in a pleasant mood, as on that day they would arrive in Lhasa, the journey over at last. Then somebody said excitedly that he could see Lhasa. For me, there was nothing dramatic at my first sight of Lhasa or, more correctly, the top of the Potala. Many European travelers have mentioned this first vision of the city with the Potala dominating everything as something ethereal, breathtaking, and awesome. Heinrich Harrer has this to say: "We turned a corner and saw gleaming in the distance, the golden roofs of the Potala, the winter residence of the Dalai Lama and the most famous landmark of Lhasa. This moment compensated us for much. We felt inclined to go down on our knees like the pilgrims and touch the ground with our foreheads."[8] All I can remember is the relief and the excitement of arrival at our destination, of horses galloping helter-skelter in every direction, and many people coming out to greet our caravan. And thus began my life in Lhasa.

## NOTES

1. Spencer-Chapman, *Lhasa*, 30.

2. Walter Buchanan, "A Recent Trip into the Chumbi Valley, Tibet," *Geographical Journal* 53, no. 6 (June 1919), 408.

3. Edmund Candler, *The Unveiling of Lhasa* (London: Edward Arnold, 1905), 71.

4. Spencer-Chapman, *Lhasa*, 46; Candler, *The Unveiling of Lhasa*, 47.

5. Ernest Hemingway, *A Farewell to Arms* (London: Vintage Books, 2005), 27–28.

6. Noel Coward, "Mad Dogs and Englishmen," Traditional Music, accessed January 10, 2022, http://www.traditionalmusic.co.uk/folk-song-lyrics/Mad_Dogs_and_Englishmen.htm.

7. Spencer-Chapman, *Lhasa*, 60.

8. Harrer, *Seven Years in Tibet*, 111.

# 5

~

# Forbidden Bastion
# or Open City

## A Portrait of Lhasa

I was in Lhasa from the end of 1937 until the beginning of 1941, and my account of the city is of what I heard and saw during those years. Momentous events for Tibet took place during that time. The Panchen Rinpoche—Tibet's second greatest incarnate lama, who ruled in the U-Tsang Province—died in November 1937, the Sino-Japanese war intensified, and the Second World War began in 1939. The present (fourteenth) Dalai Lama was discovered and installed on his throne in 1940, his predecessor having passed into the Fields of Bliss in 1933.

Legend has it that originally there was a lake where the city of Lhasa stood. Princess Wencheng Kungcho, daughter of the Chinese emperor Tai-tsung, of the Tang dynasty, whom Songtsen Gampo, thirty-third in line and the greatest king in Tibetan history, had married in 641 AD, threw a magic ring into the lake and prayed to Tibet's patron deity, the Bodhisattva Chenresig; the lake miraculously dried up, and on it the city of Lhasa was built. During the building of the capital, a celestial goat played no small part in carrying sand and stone, and this goat was now reincarnating from a rock in the Jokhang temple of Lhasa, the very goat that my grandmother had mentioned and instructed me to keep a special lookout for. It is therefore said that the city was at one time called *Rasa*, meaning "the place of the goat," but later changed to Lhasa, the "abode of the gods." That was the reason why there were no earthquakes in Lhasa—the old lakebed cushioned the city against seismic tremors.

The city stands at an altitude of nearly 12,000 feet on a wide valley on the right bank of the Kyichu River, which joins the Tsangpo at Chushül, nearly thirty miles downstream to the west, where my father had come to

*Left to right: Maid carrying child, Ghanki la, Nyima Wangmo, Rinchen; on horse the author's mother (Lhasa, Tibet, 1949). Courtesy of the author*

meet us on our way to Lhasa. The annual rainfall in Lhasa was only about 40 centimeters, and wood was scarce, the willow and poplar groves of the city being carefully guarded by *Lingsungas* (park caretakers) employed by the government. Lhasa is surrounded by a ring of mostly bare and rocky mountains, none exceeding 19,000 feet in height.

The population of Lhasa at the time of my account was about fifty or sixty thousand, but this number was greatly exceeded by the influx of monks, pilgrims, and traders during festival times.

Dominating the city and its surroundings, and a landmark seen from every direction, was the Potala. Magnificent, detailed descriptions of this building, considered by many as one of the wonders of the world, can be read in any of the numerous books on Tibet and the recent travel guides and tourist brochures provided by the Chinese, for, alas, for all "dreamers of dreams" even the Potala now figures in slick glossy handbooks on Tibet. None disagree about its stupendous size, its breathtaking architecture possessed of an almost supernatural otherworldly form and symmetry and the sheer magnificence of its setting. I peruse these brochures as one who has spent a lifetime in Los Angeles or London reads the descriptions of his city and learns much and is suitably enlightened.

During my time, the Potala housed monks, had a school for training priest secretaries, contained important government offices, was a place for worship and a place to hold ceremonies and ritual monastic dances, had the fabulous treasury of Tibet, and enshrined the mausolea of several Dalai Lamas. In it was a palace for the Dalai Lama, used mostly in the winter. The Potala is therefore not synonymous with "the winter palace of the Dalai Lama," as is so often written in books. The name *Potala* is not Tibetan but Indian, and I am told that it is derived from the name of a rock at Cape Comorin in south India believed to be the abode of the Bodhisattva Chenresig. For those intrigued by exact statistical data, I am told that the structure measures 900 feet in length and 440 feet in height, but I know of nobody who actually carried out these measurements. The building stands on a hill rising from the Lhasa plain, and it was originally begun by King Songtsen Gampo but much enlarged, attaining its present architecture and proportions during the rule of the fifth Dalai Lama and his chief minister, and completed by 1695 AD.

I personally remember it as an immense structure, easily visible from everywhere in Lhasa, and it was full of steps and dotted with innumerable windows. Speaking of windows, there is an amusing story told of a villager riding on a donkey and driving a team of donkeys to Lhasa, who, while passing through Shway (groups of houses lying at the base of the Potala), decided to count the windows of the immense building and was so engrossed in this form of higher mathematics that after a while, when he started to count his own team of donkeys to see whether any had strayed while he was thus engaged, he was terribly upset, as one donkey appeared to be always missing, no matter how often he counted; the man's head had become so befuddled by the numberless windows of the Potala that he had forgotten to count the donkey that he was riding. I am not aware that anybody else has emulated his performance.

Concerning the treasures of the Potala, it must indeed be fabulous, perhaps as great as those of the Tsargor (the monarchs of ancient kingdoms); all the gifts from kings and emperors to the Dalai Lamas of Tibet, all the priceless offerings made by thousands of pilgrims and devotees visiting the Holy City of Lhasa, were poured into the treasures of this unique building. I remember talking to a very good Lhasa aristocrat friend of mine who at one time, in an official position, was allowed to visit the vaults and chambers, and he said it was indescribable and defied audit; there were staircases paved with gold bricks.

Rivalling the Potala in height is a nearby hill called Chakphori ("Iron Hill"), which rises some 700 feet above the valley. In the past, there might have been buildings on the hill that served as palaces for the queens and relatives of the Tibetan kings. When I was in Lhasa, Chakphori was a famous medical school for the form of native Tibetan medicine that I have mentioned before, the other medical school in Lhasa being Mentsikhang (House of Medicine and Astronomy), and medical graduates or *Emchis* from these two institutions were famous throughout Tibet and the neighboring regions of Bhutan, Sikkim, and Ladakh. I know several Tibetan and Ladakhi physicians who graduated from these two medical schools, which were active and flourishing when I was in Lhasa. The Dalai Lama and most incarnate lamas had their own native physicians, and almost all Tibetans consulted these *Emchis* for their illnesses, unlike in Yatung.

The only Western-style hospital at that time was in Dekyi Lingkha, the residence of the British Mission, where we lived. Religion influenced, guided, and dominated the lives of all Tibetans, and the center of their religion was in Lhasa. The city was its heart and soul, and pilgrims from every corner of Tibet and outlying regions that believed in Tibetan Buddhism flocked to the city. Near Lhasa were two of the largest monasteries in the world, Drepung (Rice Heap) and Sera ("Hail" or perhaps even "Rose Fence"); Ganden (Tushita, Six Heavenly Realms), the third largest, with more than 3,300 monks and older than the other two, being founded by Tsongkhapa himself in 1409, lay about thirty miles beyond Lhasa. All three monasteries had been founded more than seventy years before Columbus landed in America: Drepung in 1410, having 7,700 monks on its official rolls (but always exceeded unofficially), five miles away from Lhasa, and Sera in 1419 with 5,500 monks, three miles away from Lhasa. Both Drepung and Sera were built by disciples of Tsongkhapa.

These monasteries were gigantic, more like self-sufficient towns, and were a law unto themselves. Since the Lhasa Uprising of 1959 and the destruction and emptying of these monasteries by the Chinese Communists, monasteries with the same names and disciplines have come into existence in India, the land from which Buddhism was imported into Tibet in the seventh century AD. Recently, while traveling from the United States to Britain in a United Airlines plane, I opened the flight magazine and, with a pleasant surprise, saw the smiling, happy faces of several yellow-hatted Tibetan monks in an advertisement for an Apple word processor proclaiming the "Tradition of Drepung Loseling," Loseling being one of the four colleges (*Dratshang*) of Drepung. The religion of Tibet continues to flourish with renewed vigor in exotic climes and lands.

If Lhasa was the soul of the religion of Tibet, then the Jokhang (House of Lord Buddha) was its very core. This temple, standing in the middle of the city, was Tibet's first temple and built by King Songtsen Gampo in the seventh century AD. It was for Tibetans what the Kaaba in Mecca is for Muslims and Jerusalem for Christians and Jews. Hundreds of pilgrims prostrate themselves outside its entrance. Inside is the image of the Jowo Rinpoche, said to represent the Buddha Shakyamuni as a boy. The image came originally from India to China and was then brought by Princess Wencheng Kungcho as a dowry when she married Songtsen Gampo. It is gilded with gold, but its ornaments are made of pure gold and it is crowned with a dazzling jeweled headdress encrusted with pearls, diamonds, rare gems, corals, turquoise, and the offerings of Lhasa aristocrats and rich devotees over the centuries. In front of the idol, butter lamps in giant chalices made of gold and silver burn throughout the day and night unceasingly. Strangely, in a passage leading to the shrine, there hangs a bell left behind by Christian missionaries, perhaps Capuchins, who set up unsuccessful proselytizing missions in Lhasa in the eighteenth century. Inscribed on the bell are the words *Te deum laudamus* (God in You we Praise).

The Jokhang was dark and slippery, and there was the all-pervading smell of butter lamps flickering from every nook and corner, each shrine with its caretaker monk, to whom money was presented to say special prayers for the supplicant or to light more butter lamps. There were the images of Songtsen Gampo, turbaned and dressed as a king of ancient Tibet, long before the coming of the Dalai Lamas, and his two queens (one from China and the other from Nepal, although he had Tibetan wives too). Then I came across a large stone, and if one put one's ears to it, I was told that one could hear the sound of geese on the Yardrok Lake. And I found the rock slab, curtained, and there was a distinct image of a goat, the very one that my grandmother had mentioned, and half of its body appeared to be in view, as if it was growing out of the rock. I lingered at that particular shrine for a long time until my mother pulled me away to make way for other worshippers behind us, crowding, praying, and pushing, all wanting to see the goat deity. I surmised that the end of the world was not far off, seeing that most of the goat had emerged miraculously out of the rock surface. Did the goat forebode an atomic cataclysm in the future that would engulf the whole world?

On the roof of the Jokhang was the temple of Palden Lhamo, said to be the same as the Indian goddess Kali; when I bowed down and touched the foot of the image with my head in an act of worship and devotion, I shivered, because hundreds of tiny mice ran over the goddess. They were said to be her servants, and when any mouse died, its body was preserved and used in ointments and liniments and was considered highly efficacious for wounds, burns, and blisters. We were told that the mice never damaged the rich brocades or the ornaments of the goddess. But the mice were not used for myomancy. At many of the shrines in the Jokhang, we prostrated thrice and then went up to the caretaker, who blessed us with a silver jar of holy water adorned with peacock feathers before pouring a little of the water into our cupped palms, from which we sipped the holy water and rubbed the wet palm on our heads, as was the custom. We came out of the darkness of the Jokhang temple into the bright sunshine of the street outside happy in the knowledge that we had visited the oldest and most sacred temple in the whole of Tibet and that we had prostrated ourselves in front of the idol of Jowo Rinpoche, the most holy in Tibetan Buddhism.

Around the city of Lhasa ran the *Lingkor* (outer circumambulation), a path about five miles long, circumambulated in a clockwise direction by pilgrims in order to gain merit and to be absolved from their sins. Women sold delicious turnips along the way, for which the Lingkor was famous. I remember a vertical rockface full of carvings of the various Buddhas and deities and festooned with prayer flags in the colors denoting the five Tibetan elements that made up the material world (blue for sky; white for clouds; red for fire; green for water; yellow for earth). On the rockface was a hole. I was told to close my eyes, stand at a distance, and then walk toward the hole and aim to put my index finger in the hole; if successful, it meant that you would meet friends and relatives again in the next world, or, if you were parted from a loved one for some time, you would meet that person again soon. There was also an inclined slab of rock; if you walked under it and rubbed your back against the slab, all backaches would be cured.

Hundreds of beggars lined the Lingkor, sticking out their tongues, making clucking sucking noises, scratching their heads, making thumbs-up gestures with both hands—all Tibetan acts of respect, humility, and utter abnegation. Hundreds of devout pilgrims from all over Tibet, some of whom had traveled months to reach the holy city of Lhasa—the realization of a lifetime's dream—were prostrating all the way round the Lingkor, their bodies and faces begrimed by the dust of many feet, some even prostrating sideways to make their tasks more rigorous in order to earn extra merit and to atone for grievous sins. Probably very few people anywhere in the world display as intense a religious devotion as do Tibetans.

In Lhasa, an unceasing round of pageantry, ceremony, and religious and civil festivals took place the whole year round, and there was hardly a day when there wasn't something spectacular or entertaining to watch.

On the twenty-fifth day of the tenth Tibetan month was Ganden Ngamchö, the death anniversary of Tsongkhapa (1358–1419 AD), religious reformer, teacher, Buddhist theoretician, mystic, and founder of the Gelukpa or "Yellow Hat School," to which belong the Dalai Lamas of Tibet. At night, like the Indian festival of Diwali, oil lamps are lit everywhere, and special prayers are said to honor the saint, revered by Gelukpas as much as the Buddha himself. My mother used to light such lamps in our house, make us carry sticks of incense, and then march about reciting and chanting prayers. It is traditional to drink the same kind of dough ball gruel that night as is done at Losar on the night of *nyishu-gu*, which I have mentioned. But no pranks that night; instead, there is solemnity and the chanting of prayers in the flickering lights of hundreds of oil lamps to the memory of the man who changed Tibetan Buddhism as no one has ever done again. The festival also marks the official beginning of the Tibetan winter, and Lhasa noblemen may from that night don their winter furs when they attend office. The winter officially ends next year on the eighth day of the third month, so that winter in Lhasa is recognized to last for almost five months.

Preparations are made at the end of the old year to celebrate the New Year auspiciously and without a hitch, for superstition and omens rule the lives of all Tibetans, and nothing must go amiss during the performance of these ceremonies. On the twenty-ninth day of the twelfth month, there is a monastic dance at the Potala and also stylized dances by old retainers wearing battle dresses that must have been used in ancient battles when Tibet was a highly feared military nation with extensive conquests in Central Asia. There is the burning of dough images and the casting out of devils. On the third day of the first month, the oracle of Nechung (Tibet's national and most famous oracle) goes into a trance and makes his secret predictions and prophecies for the new year, the occasion being attended with anxiety and apprehension by the highest in the land. In the afternoon there is an archery competition on the outskirts of Lhasa; I remember the cold windy afternoon, the crowds muffled up against the swirling dust and wind, and the archers shooting into the sky, straining their bows against the wind, with the one to shoot an arrow the farthest rewarded with the prize.

At the start of the new year, I witnessed several ceremonies and sporting events sponsored by the government or the monasteries. They were all connected with ancient Tibetan history, and one saw in the costumes and titles of the participants the decisive role played in Tibetan history by Mongol arms and martial prowess. There were footraces and horse racing without riders when a pack of horses were driven by a single rider, servants placed at strategic points on the route favoring the teams of Lhasa aristocratic houses. There was wrestling in which each individual wrestler did not know until the last minute who his opponent was, causing much hilarity and buffoonery when a pair were utterly mismatched. The wrestlers entered the ring spraying barley flour into the air and praying for victory and pranced about displaying their strength and agility; they wrestled holding each other by the shoulders, and when one sustained a fall in which any part of the torso touched the ground, trumpeters with feathered headdresses and wicker armor blared forth, signaling the end of the bout. There was a spectacular race performed by young government officials, usually aristocrats, who galloped at full speed down a lane, shooting at several targets one after the other with a flintlock or bow and arrow, exhibiting equestrian skills that made the crowds gasp and hold their breath.

On the night of the fifteenth day of the first month was Chönga Chöpa, or "Religious Offerings of the Fifteenth," when the Lhasa streets were so packed that, as children, we were not allowed to go out for fear of being trampled to death, as had occurred on several occasions. Each aristocrat in the streets of Lhasa constructed on a scaffolding of wood and leather intricate delicate designs in butter with moving puppet-like figures as religious emblems, and the streets were lit with oil lamps so that Lhasa took on the appearance of a flood-lit city. The only people able to make any headway in the dense crowded streets and granted a free passage were traditionally the villagers of Gyang, situated opposite our house on the other side of the Kyichu river. These men and women, holding hands, merrily sang a Gyang song and executed a shuffling dance before each butter structure, and then the appreciative crowd made a way for them, allowing them to go on to the next structure. The next day, before the sun rose, regretfully, each offering had to be dismantled before the sun melted the butter. Tibetans therefore have a witticism, administered to any braggart who is scared to prove his mettle: "*Chönga chöpa shebo yöna nyime gungla dönshog*" (Butter offerings of the fifteenth, if you've any guts, come on out in the midday sun).

The ceremony that overshadowed everything at this time of the year was that of *Monlam* (Prayers). It was instituted by Tsongkhapa and later expanded and modified by the fifth Dalai Lama (1617–80 AD), one of the greatest among the Dalai Lamas. The Monlam is to offer prayers for the coming Buddha, who will usher in a new eon when that of the present Shakyamuni is over. He is Gyalwa Jampa or the Maitreya. During his time, mankind will be found in a degenerate wretched state, each human being stunted and deformed, no taller than a cubit (possibly mutants following a thermonuclear disaster); the Gyalwa Jamba will heal them, renew and restore them, and there will flower forth a new era of love, compassion, and affection far exceeding the present *kalpa* or eon of the Shakyamuni Buddha.

Strangely, as if to anticipate a European avatar or incarnation, the Gyalwa Jampa, unlike any other Tibetan Bodhisattva, is depicted sitting in a European fashion, as in a chair, and his eyes are blue. But it was not with such benevolent sentiments that Monlams were held in Lhasa then. Some Tibetans complained that, unlike in Gyantse and Yatung, the Losar or New Year in Lhasa was spoiled by the harsh realities of the Monlam festival. There was no time to celebrate, throw parties, and have a good time. In fact, it was the opposite. Monlam for most of us ushered in a time of gloom and apprehension, during which Lhasa fell into the grip of an iron monkish discipline. Starting from the third day of the first month, droves of monks streamed into Lhasa from Drepung, Sera, Ganden, and other places. There might be as many as thirty thousand monks in Lhasa.

The entire city was placed under the jurisdiction of the monks for a duration of about three weeks and ruled by two of the senior *She-ngos* (disciplinators) of the monastery of Drepung. What they said was law without exception. They would give an arrogant, formal, bragging speech when they took over the city, saying that from that day forth there was only the Dalai Lama above them and nobody else. All must bow down to their dictates. They had their own monk guards, tough stalwarts, with swords at their waists, and they carried whips and long staves to belabor the public. As symbols of authority, they carried fasces-like objects of great weight, which they struck onto the ground to emphasize their words. When they rode forth into the Lhasa streets, their guards would go in front, shouting abuse at the populace, scattering them about, beating a way through, and all who came across the two *She-ngos* had to dismount, even cabinet ministers.

During Monlam, men and women had to keep their hair in certain specified ways, and they were forbidden to wear certain types of clothes. Any trifling misdemeanor was disproportionately punished. People went about in terror of the *She-ngos*, and there were many floggings, mostly in public. An aristocrat friend of mine from Lhasa who deplored the rule of the *She-ngos* told me that when these priest-magistrates demanded sums of money as punishment, they wouldn't name any exact figure but would point to the top of a table and say this much or that much of the table to be covered with cash. Many Lhasa dwellers heaved sighs of relief when Monlam came to an end and the hordes of monks headed back to their monasteries. It is no wonder that pilgrims from the wild Chang Thang ("Northern Plains") who had trekked across desolate wastes for months to come to worship during Monlam lamented, *"Drepung tsogchen Shengo, go la tarka matey, losum chöra drim ney ne, phayül chola lodro"* (Drepung's great assembly She-ngos, pray do not give us walnut [size bumps] on our heads; once we have completed studying in monastic enclosures for three years, we shall return to our fatherland).

When I was in Lhasa, the incarnate lama of Radreng (also called Reting) Rinpoche (meaning "most precious," a title usually given to incarnate lamas) was the Gyaltsab, or regent, of Tibet, and he ruled the country. His name was Thubten Jamphel Yishey Tenpa Gyaltsen, and he had been appointed regent in 1934 at the age of twenty-three years. Normally, after the death of a Dalai Lama, until his discovery and attainment of majority at the age of eighteen, a regent is appointed by the unanimous agreement of the monasteries of Drepung, Sera, Ganden, and the Tibetan Cabinet, consisting usually of three lay *Shabpe*s (ministers) and one monk *Shabpe* as well as the Tsongdu (National Assembly) composed of ecclesiastical and civil officials. Sometimes a regent was selected from the heads of the smaller, richer, more exclusive, and elite monasteries in Lhasa or its vicinity. Radreng was such a monastery, founded in 1057 AD (nine years before William of Normandy invaded England) by a disciple of Atisha and situated sixty miles north of Lhasa.

Radreng Rinpoche was a thin, young, shy, emaciated priest, a deity in Lhasa, with the whole of Tibet in the palm of his hand. Many Tibetans speak of the Radreng era as being one of the happiest in the history of Tibet, particularly the years when I was in Lhasa. Tibet was then de facto independent, as China was engaged in a life-or-death struggle with the Japanese, paying scant attention to Tibetan affairs; trade flourished as never before, and merchandise was brought from India, transported through Lhasa and thence to eastern Tibet and to China. This became one of the main supply routes for the beleaguered nation cut off completely at sea by the Japanese. It was a boom period and money flowed freely, and everybody became rich—traders, muleteers, innkeepers, and prostitutes. Radreng's rule was not strict or disciplined; on the contrary, he tended to be fun loving, fascinated by modern gadgets and instruments and toys, eager to modernize Tibet, encouraging fashions and modern customs, serving as a patron of songs, dances, music, and operas. Some may even say that he was secular, rather frivolous, and a hedonist. But I remember those Lhasa days as happy, full of fun and laughter, and people seemed to sing all the time.

In Lhasa, Radreng Rinpoche had his residence at his monastery of Shide, and often I went there with my parents to watch *Ache Lhamo* (operas) during those pleasant summer months. I can still recall vividly the singing, the dancing, the beating of drums and cymbals, eating Chinese Haw sweets, drinking endless cups of tea, eating fruits and nuts, and teasing the pretty young girls. There was one night that was unforgettable. We went to Shide to see a special performance of a dragon dance by a Chinese troupe: the dense surging night crowds, the dark cobbled courtyard, the unceasing blaring of trumpets, the long undulating gaudy cloth-dragon, the shaking twisting fanged dragon's head chasing frantically, obsessively, a magic fireball held by a weaving dancer running in front. No doubt Radreng Rinpoche must have been watching, shaking his head with laughter, clapping his hands in delight, drinking Tibetan tea from jade cups on golden stands, surrounded by his sycophantic retinue of servants and beautiful young monks, some holding his favorite British-gifted dachshund puppies in their laps.

In Lhasa we sang a song about Radreng that had a lilting Chinese Kuomintang tune, and my mother used to make me sing it sometimes: *"Shide nyomchung gyalway ka rey Shide gyalway ka rey"* (It is the command of the victorious one of Shide, it is). One verse exhorted you to buy slick shoes if you had the money and torn ones if you didn't, but whichever shoes you bought, have fun, for it was the command of the

Victorious One at Shide. And fun we certainly had, all of us in Lhasa; we had fun.

Lhasa was certainly the heart of the religion of Tibet, but there was another aspect to the city. It was a light-hearted city full of fun and gaiety, and many came to the city for its pleasures. It was the avant-garde center of fashion and song, and it had the most beautiful and uninhibited girls in the whole of Tibet. The Lhasa dialect was the most musical, expressive, and refined, and its accent the most imitated. In a country with such a diversity of dialects, that of Lhasa was the most widely understood.

In the streets of Lhasa could be found goods from every part of the world, and it was a city of shops. Tibetans tended to favor a particular brand of goods and then stuck loyally to that brand. Marwari business-men used to confess to me how easy it was to do business in Tibet, as you only had to buy one brand. The merchandise most in favor when I was in Lhasa were Homburg hats, worn by both men and women, from Italy; Philips radios; gold flake, W. D. and H. O. Wills cigarettes; Huntley and Palmer biscuits; His Master's Voice gramophones; Leica cameras; Tiger Balm from Singapore for headaches; Chinese Haw-flakes sweets; and last, but not least, White Horse Scotch whiskey, each sheathed bottle accom-panied by a miniature brooch-like plastic white horse—in Tibet during those carefree days, the Gurkha expression *sheto gora charnu* (riding the white horse) came to have an eyebrow-raising connotation.

Tibet, as I have stated often, was dominated and controlled by the monks, half a million or more in a land with a population of about four million, and Lhasa was no exception, but in Lhasa there was another dominant force, that of the *kudraks* (superiors or aristocrats). They had their houses inside the town and on the outskirts amid poplar and wil-low groves: luxurious mansions full of jade, rich paintings, rare porcelain. Many of the aristocratic families were very ancient and descended from relatives of past Dalai Lamas. We have a saying: *"Lhasa, Lhasa kyipa; deley Lhalu kyipa"* (Lhasa, Lhasa is indeed pleasant; but pleasanter still is Lhalu). Lhalu was a famous aristocratic estate where Younghusband had stayed when he was in Lhasa in 1904.

There were dozens of aristocratic houses in Lhasa with hereditary titles, lands, and wealth, and almost all the important government posts were held by them, many obtained by subtle bribery or through nepotism.

Tibet was a land of iron-tight class and social distinctions, and it was easy to make out the rank of a person by the way their hair was kept, the kind of earrings worn (especially in the case of the men), the kind of dresses and shoes worn, and the tasseled pendants hanging from the necks of the mounts—two for the highest officials, and one for their wives and for junior officials. Some of the senior aristocrat officials kept their hair in a distinct style, and they had to summon special hairdressers every so often to fix their hair; this was called the *pachok* style, in which a turquoise and gold ornament was braided into the hair and kept in place with red ribbon, which created the British quip that in Tibet senior officials had red tape even in their hair! The aristocrats had hordes of servants and maidservants, and the servants also had their special uniforms.

The aristocrats owned vast areas of land, for which they paid no taxes. Many of these *shikhas* (estates) lay outside Lhasa, and they left these in the hands of family caretakers. Very few books on Tibet mention the existence of serfdom in the country, and many British authors ignore the subject completely or gloss over it, euphemistically calling it "tenantry." But Tibetan aristocratic houses owed a large part of their wealth to the system of serfdom then prevalent in Tibet. A serf could not run away from his estate, could not attend a school unless permission was granted, and serfs were the source of servants for an aristocratic household. Corvee labor was rampant in Tibet, and one serf told me that at the end of the day, while carrying loads for the government, the last thing he expected was payment for his labors; he was only too glad to get away if his load, on inspection by a harsh overseer, was pronounced intact and he escaped a whipping. Even such an authoritative and prolific writer on Tibet as Sir Charles Bell calls the system of serfdom "tenantry."[1] But in the next sentence he mentions that such tenants were liable to have their hands cut off or be whipped by their landlords if they failed to carry out their obligations.[2] If a tenant in an apartment in Los Angeles or London was subjected to such punishment by his landlord, would he still be called a "tenant"?

However, it would be wrong to think of the aristocrats as ogres or slave owners. Among them was to be found a high degree of taste and culture. Who could be more refined and cultured than a Lhasa aristocrat? Who could be more suave, sophisticated, elegant, tactful, courteous, diplomatic? They were the true Mandarins, which even China did not possess at that time. They favored the arts; many of them were accomplished musicians and singers, playing the *dranyen* (guitar), *lingbu* (flute), *piwang* (fiddle), and *yanggyin* (Chinese xylophone-like instrument), and they sang with vibrant voices the *namthar* songs of the *Ache Lhamo* operas, whose season began in Lhasa in the seventh Tibetan month. The Lhasa aristocrats conversed with a delicate refined accent, and their exquisite courtesy, tact, and graceful gestures bespoke beings of the highest breeding and civilization. True indeed it was that in Lhasa then there was almost nothing technical or modern such as sanitation, plumbing, electricity, telephones, and everything labeled "modern conveniences," but in manners, courtesy, cuisine, behavior, taste and culture, it was a civilization attained by very few in the world. Lord Curzon would have felt quite at home in the mansion of a Lhasa aristocrat.

There was no sanitation in the city of Lhasa, which was extremely filthy, its inhabitants (with typical Tibetan lack of inhibitions) defecating and urinating where they stood. It would have required a Hercules to clean the Augean dirt of the Lhasa streets. In spite of this issue, the streets swarmed with a variety of people: monks, traders, villagers, aristocratic lords, and ladies; tall, muscular, hard-faced Khampas from eastern Tibet; Amdos such as the ones we saw in the streets of Yatung, both men and women wearing colorful clothes and headdresses; wild nomads from the inhospitable Chang Thang, bringing meat, cheese, and butter to sell, dressed in fleece-lined leather clothes, their arms bare to the shoulders, staring in wonder at the exotic merchandise of the Lhasa shops, many owned by Tibetan Muslims in Tibetan clothes but wearing fez caps and the heads of their women covered with shawls, descendants of Muslims who had entered Tibet in the past or had come from Ladakh in northwest India, whose language and culture have Tibetan affinities. There were very few Bhutanese, Nepalese, Sikkimese, or Indians, and an European face was so rare as to make the populace gape, attracting an inquisitive giggling crowd, pointing fingers childishly at the *Chilingpas* (outsiders), as all Europeans were called.

And, of course, there were the beggars. Tibet had a whole segment of the population dedicated to this profession—men, women, and children, both the young and the old, deformed or healthy. What was the reason? It was surprising to find so many beggars in a land exceptional for Asia in being scantily populated. Perhaps the Tibetan belief in the giving of alms to accumulate merit to obtain a higher rebirth attracted the poor to the beggar's profession. They would be everywhere: whining, pestering, supplicating in a pitiful, mourning singsong voice. They used to migrate from one part of Tibet to another, and many came down to Sikkim. I remember in Sikkim during the winter months having a container specially kept in our house containing "beggar's rice," the cheapest in the market, to give away as alms. No wonder the Nepalese used to say in a derogatory fashion to Tibetans, "*Bhotay mangney*," and the Sikkimese, "*Bhop changlo*," both of them picturesque abusive expletives meaning "Tibetan beggar."

There was no law or order in the streets of Lhasa, and sometimes brawls broke out in which swords, daggers, and stones would be used in a free-for-all, for most Tibetan youths and men carried daggers. There was supposed to be a police force in Lhasa, but this was a Gilbert and Sullivan affair, for there were very few of them, and whenever a fight took place, they made sure they weren't in the vicinity. They invariably appeared impoverished to me; when unoccupied, they sat in their sentry boxes making soles for Tibetan boots either for personal use or to enhance a meager salary. Why every Lhasa policeman I saw spent his time making soles and nothing but soles, I could never understand.

There were no cars, carriages, motorcycles, or any wheeled vehicles in the streets of Lhasa or, for that matter, anywhere in "Outer Tibet" at that time. Europeans have commented with amazement on this highly civilized nation spurning anything "wheeled" in its daily life except for the *mani* (the prayer wheel) or the milling stones. In Tibet, it is true that anything wheeled or revolving has a religious connotation, such as *chö kyi khorlo* ("wheel of religion") to signify the Tibetan religion, *sibai khorlo* ("wheel of being"), and so on. It could be that Tibetans feel it is sacrilegious to ride or to sit on something that revolves.

Soccer football was played in Lhasa during those days and became very popular during the rule of the Radreng regent, who did not discourage it, but his successor to the regency (the change of regency was a matter of political controversy and later led to much bitterness, animosity, and a minor civil war), Takdrak Rinpoche, a tutor to the present fourteenth Dalai Lama, and a stern Cromwellian puritanical man—an exact antithesis of the Radreng—suppressed football. Sir Basil Gould, who had left Lhasa some months before my arrival, writes, "After we left, competition became so keen and spectators so many that the Tibetan government was forced to the conclusion that more money was being spent on uniforms for teams and more man days of labour were being lost than the country could afford. So, the game was suppressed."[3] I couldn't see the logic! After all, how much money can one spend on football uniforms? And far more money was spent by the people on kites during the kite season than was ever spent on football uniforms. As for many days of labor, that was the last thing a Tibetan government would bother about, because if Tibet did have anything, it was time.

Nobody worked to the clock. Some of the rich wore watches, and some very expensive makes too, Omega, Rolex, and West-End being the favorites, but many did not know how to tell the time and did not even trouble to wind their watches. Watches were for ornamentation and decoration, for kudos rather than chronology, and what Tibetan does not love an ornament or an expensive pen, clock, or watch? Everybody had time. In fact, it was rude to be punctual, and a person of good breeding always came a little late to an appointment. Times of journeys were vaguely indicated. If there was one commodity that Tibet possessed (sadly, exasperatingly lacking in the modern techno-democracies), it was time. There was ample time for everything. People went by cockcrow, by the rising and setting of the sun; the ticking of the clock or the strident tones of the alarm did not tyrannize and enslave our lives.

I think football was stopped because it was a modern innovation, the thin end of the wedge that could permeate Tibet with scientific-technocratic ideas and undermine her religion; it was a form of *luksö sarpa* (new custom), *chigyal kyi tsemo* (an outsider's game). A fire must be put out when it is a tiny flame, so goes a Tibetan saying—not when it is a raging conflagration. To give an "imprimatur" to their orders, the monks circulated the rumor that kicking a football was symbolic of kicking the *chö kyi khorlo* (wheel of religion). One wheeled vehicle that one might see in the Lhasa streets, and that too rarely, was a bicycle, usually ridden by a pampered, effeminate, silk-costumed aristocratic Lothario, trying to keep his balance on the machine and aided with care and concern by a cohort of laughing sycophantic servants. If a Nepalese, who enjoyed much-resented extra-territorial rights in Lhasa, rode a bicycle, there would be no objection. A similar sentiment might also apply to the advanced, modernized Indian-educated Tibetans and Sikkimese working for the British Trade Agencies, but no Tibetan civilian was allowed to ride a bicycle or a motorcycle in Lhasa at that time. I think one enterprising officer from the British Mission rode a motorcycle, but this sight so frightened horses that he was requested to desist.

Tibetans are very fond of gambling, and in Lhasa *mah-jong*, cards, Tibetan dominoes, and dicing were popular. They loved music, and there was a band much in demand (about which I shall write in the next chapter). Lhasa also had its courtesans, coquettes, and prostitutes, the latter having special "brand" names given by their clientele. For those so inclined, girls were easily available, as Tibetans tend to have an exuberant unprejudiced approach to sexual matters and are somewhat amoral in this respect.

Of foreign legations and representatives, there was the British Mission, well ensconced at Dekyi Lingkha and favored by the Tibetans; the Nepalese, with an escort of soldiers, many of whom had Lhasa mistresses; a Ladakhi contingent; a Bhutanese trade agent; and a Chinese Mission, much dwindled in power and prestige and with hardly any say in Tibetan affairs. China was locked in combat with the *Ribin*, as the Japanese were called (and greatly liked by the Tibetans, as they were the adversaries of the Chinese). There was a general feeling that China would be defeated. Russia or *Urusu* was far away to the north and meant nothing to the Tibetans. We were told that they were a weak nation addicted to horse flesh. Tibet was getting rich and strategically important. She was for the first time indisputably independent. But again, all she wanted was to be left alone. The aristocrats and the ruling powers utilized the good times to gain their own individual ends and to accumulate wealth with lucrative trade and privileges. The traders and the middle class were interested in nothing but money; the poor continued in their ancient ways; the clergy and the vast town-like monasteries consolidated their secular powers and tightened their grip on their dues and rights, jealously guarding their religion and their absolute rule over the theocratic nation, and averse to and adamantly opposing any and every move to change or modernize

Tibet and refusing to converse and fraternize with other nations of the "Outer Circle."

## NOTES

1. Charles Alfred Bell, *The People of Tibet* (Oxford: Clarendon Press, 1968), 86.
2. Ibid.
3. Gould, *The Jewel in the Lotus*, 207.

# 6

~

# Three Years in Lhasa

The British Mission was situated at Dekyi Lingkha (Park of Happiness), half a mile away from the city of Lhasa and close to the hill of Chakphori. We were not very far away from Norbu Lingkha (Jewel Park), the pleasant park with several summer palaces of the Dalai Lama. From Dekyi Lingkha, we could see the top of the Potala and in the distance the monastery of Drepung, the largest in the world, nestling at the base of a rocky mountain. A stream ran near the mission, and a little farther away was the Kyichu river. There were groves of weeping willows and poplar trees. The main buildings where the British resident lived and where there was a radio station (code AC4YN) had at one time been the summer residence of the incarnate lama of Kundeling monastery, a former regent of Tibet like the Radreng Rinpoche. Sir Charles Bell notes that "the regent had never lived in this house during the winter, and it was feared that we might find it cold then, but it was chosen because it was clean."[1]

My father's house, the place where l was to spend three and a half years of my life, was within walking distance of the main buildings. Inside was a stone-flagged courtyard with two peach trees, a long verandah curtained to serve as a kitchen and servants' quarters, a shuttered office, and a large room used as a living room, in which was erected a British mountaineering tent to be used as a bedroom (the pockets inside the tent served as drawers). In this tent, father, mother, and we four children slept. There was no plumbing in the house; for that matter, Tibet had none in any houses then, water for the kitchen and for washing being drawn from the nearby stream and then stored in large bronze cauldrons. There was no toilet; for such purposes, we used the back of the house. When I think of it, the whole accommodation for a family with four children was ludicrous in the extreme and most primitive, especially that tent inside a room, but for me it was home.

When I first arrived in Lhasa, the Norbu Lingkha was empty because the fourteenth Dalai Lama had not yet been discovered and the regent, Radreng Rinpoche, stayed at his monastery of Shide. Norbu Lingkha, the summer palace of the Dalai Lama, was built by the seventh Dalai Lama in 1783 and was about a mile from the Potala, where he had his winter palace. It was surrounded by a square wall, each side about a mile long. We used to go there sometimes, watching Tibetan soldiers drilling. In those days, Tibet had a standing army of perhaps ten thousand men. The Dalai Lama's *kusung* (bodyguard) wore Western uniforms and Wolseley helmets and marched smartly to a fife, drums, and bagpipes, with tall drummers wearing leopard-skin ponchos, playing such tunes as "God Save the King," "Cock of the North," "Highland Laddie," "Marching through Georgia," and "Auld Lang Syne."

The top brass Tibetan troops were stationed at Drabchi, a little distance away from Lhasa, where there was an arsenal and a mint; these troops wore khaki Tibetan uniforms with knee-length boots and kept their hair in pigtails and wore earrings. They were said to be dour fighters who had kept the Chinese at bay in Kham in the 1920s. The *kusung* blew bugles, signaled with hand flags in semaphore, and gave British Aldershot commands in quaint Tibetan accents and intonations: "Ber thar rite, queek mach!" "Eeslope amms!" "Thundey ees!" What a British Guards regimental sergeant major or a United States Marine Corps trainer at boot camp would have made of all this is a matter of conjecture. The heaviest arms the Tibetan army possessed were mountain howitzers and Lewis guns. Many years before, when Tibetans had been fighting the Chinese in Lhasa in 1911–1912, innovative Tibetans had produced homemade cannons, but these killed more Tibetan gunners than Chinese and had been dubbed *megyo kukpa* (fool cannons) by the populace, which made Lhasa folks comment, "*Megyo kukpa che chay, gyabngey kukpa nyey chay; trön pe nang gyi beba, kepa chaney ehadu!*" (First a fool cannon, and then second a fool gunner; a shot has broken the back of a frog in a well!). Tibetans love making fun of themselves.

The man in charge of the British Mission then was Rai Bahadur Dzasa Norbu Dhondup, a Darjeeling Tibetan, with whose wife we had traveled from Yatung. When he was at school, he had been recruited by Captain (later Sir) Frederick O'Connor as secretary to and chief interpreter for Younghusband. Norbu had seen the battles at Guru, Red Idol Gorge, and Gyantse. Since then, he had served the British faithfully and with distinction and had held the post of British trade agent at Yatung and Gyantse. He dressed, spoke, and behaved like a member of the Tibetan aristocracy.

His official designation was "confidential adviser" to the British political officer for Tibet, Bhutan, and Sikkim.

The radio operator was Reginald Fox, a Londoner with an adventurous history behind him. When I was in Lhasa, he was in his late thirties. He had served in the First World War as a teenager and had been a dispatch rider in France. Later he had been to the Middle East and then finally served in the British army in India, from which point he had gravitated, out of all outlandish places, to Lhasa. I remember him as a breezy, cheerful, red-faced, whistling *Sahib* who chain smoked. He was always kind to me. It was in his bedroom that I saw my first crucifix, my first encounter with the Christian God, a man hanging by his hands with head bowed and legs crossed. Something simple and clinical seemed to me the religion of Christianity when compared to the profusion of gods seen in any Tibetan temple.

The mission building was surrounded by high walls enclosing a garden full of British flowers and vegetables, much of the seeds supplied by Carter's of London. Many Lhasa aristocrats took the same seeds and duplicated such gardens in their estates. At that time tomatoes, cauliflower, and cabbage were rare in Lhasa.

The mission had a small hospital at one time run by Dr. William Morgan, a Welshman who is described by Sir Basil Gould as "rugger playing."[2] His daughter, Verena Rybicki of Lexington in Massachusetts, is the lady I wrote about in a previous chapter. There was no space or facilities to take in any inpatients, and such had to camp out in tents. There was a large room used as an operating theater with a skylight, and my friends and I used to climb up there, hide, and surreptitiously watch the surgery being performed below. I remember watching a gangrenous hand being amputated. Dr. Morgan also carried out many cataract operations, and soon he became famous in Lhasa for this service, as cataracts were a common cause of blindness in Tibet. Patients with cataracts flocked to Dr. Morgan from all parts of Tibet, and many of them, after being cured and their sight restored, used to prostrate toward the hospital as if it were a sacred Tibetan shrine.

Dr. Morgan was a tall, genial man who had the reputation of being the only man in Lhasa able to swim across the Kyichu River when it was in full flood during the summer months. I was intrigued by something he did and could never make out what he was trying to do. He would pick up a stone, run, and then throw the stone in a peculiar whirling over-arm motion at a Dekyi Lingkha poplar or willow trunk. He, like his compatriot Fox, chain smoked, favoring cork-tipped De Reszke cigarettes from flat tin cases, the only cork-tipped cigarettes I ever saw in Lhasa. We used to line up whenever Dr. Morgan came toward us, smoking, and then greet him with a deep bow and an Indian *salaam*, and he would flick the butts at us; we scrambled for the butts and smoked them, cork tip and all.

Just beyond our house was a small stream that was a tributary of the Kyichu River that flowed a little distance away. Between the stream and the river was land covered with fine sand and dotted with bushes. This was our favorite playground. In the summer, I tried to swim with two football bladders tucked under my armpits to keep me afloat. There were little fishes in the stream, and I used to steal pins from my father's office pincushions, fashion them into hooks, and fish—a Tibetan Tom Sawyer, sitting on the little wooden bridge that spanned the stream, the warm grainy surface of the bridge soothing against the insides of my bare knees, my feet dangling, staring at the waters that flowed toward Nyethang, the tiny darting fishes, and the undulating weeds.

Sometimes I saw coracles on the Kyichu with boatmen straining against their oars, whistling or singing. Sometimes a flock of cranes alighted on a sandbank and stood there upraised, immobile on one leg. Close to the edge of the stream were bushes populated with whirring dragonflies and copulating insects, an ooze on your fingertips as you drew them apart from their ecstatic embrace. We used to lure a little girl nicknamed Ani (nun) because of her close-cropped hair and discover undisturbed what little girls are made like. Afterward we would rush off and play ducks-and-drakes on the placid surface of a small lake, and somebody would shout a warning that an octopus-like demoness called a "Päl lhamo" dwelled in the lake, who would appear suddenly and seize us and drag us into its depths, and we would run away with fright to play somewhere else.

Once Rinchen, our servant, took my father's double-barreled gun (the same with which he shot the flares in the Yatung night), and the two of us went duck shooting and nobody challenged us, although we were close to Norbu Lingkha. It was a bad thing to do, shooting so close to the precincts of the Dalai Lama's summer palace. Sir Charles Bell says that he forbade all shooting, hunting, and fishing by his mission staff in Lhasa in order not to hurt Tibetan religious sentiments, which abhor the taking of any form of life.[3] But even Rai Bahadur Norbu Dhondup, one evening, took some of his servants with him to shoot at targets near the place where we played and afterward discussed marksmanship, and I trailed behind, engrossed in the conversation. In the evenings in winter, we hunted ducks with catapults, the rubber straps made from stolen stethoscopes from Dr. Morgan's stores. And in the winter the stream was ideal for our form of Tibetan skating, taking a run on hobnailed boots and sliding on the crystal clear surface of the ice.

We were luckier than some of the village boys, who had to spend their time spearing every bit of dung they could lay their eyes on and dropping them deftly into baskets that they carried, for dung was the chief fuel in Lhasa. We often came across donkeys from Gyang, a village across the Kyichu, wading across the shallow parts of the river, carrying loads of dung to sell in the Lhasa markets. Gyang itself was denuded of every vegetation, and the other villages along the river and Ramagang were just as bare—hence the indecent verse we used to recite: "*Gyang, Gyang, Chushül, Ramagang, tula musu mindu, mar cher cher!*" (No pubic hair on the vulva, looking so pink, pink).

Spencer-Chapman and Hugh Richardson narrate how they walked along the same banks of the Kyichu River, where we boys and girls had Spartan-like wrestled and frolicked naked in the sand and experienced our first sexual contacts and where we had fled away in fright from the octopus-like demoness of the lake.[4] But they were amateur British ornithologists, *Sahibs* of the "Outer Circle," worlds apart from us Tibetan urchins. The two of them went birdwatching and describe seeing Brahminy ducks, mallards, goosander, gadwall, and ruddy sheldrake, cataloging each genus and species with erudite scientific names, a whole world of birdsong undetected by our boyish rustic ears.[5] Sir Charles Bell, too, walking one afternoon along the same path, met his friend the thirteenth Dalai Lama taking a walk accompanied by a single attendant.[6]

One of the office workers was Mr. Gyatso Topden from Yatung, who had been educated in Kalimpong. He was one of the *rara avis* among Tibetans of those days and a figure of envy for my father, a Tibetan with a college degree, although he was only an I.A. (Intermediate Arts). He was a good-looking man, something of a lothario; was fond of music, archery, *mah-jong*, and dancing; and had a debonair air about him. He would set off Lhasa after the day's office work was done, riding a gaily caparisoned horse, British-saddled, a revolver in his pocket and a tasseled Chinese Kuomintang dagger hanging from his waist. He was a very good footballer; the matches were played in a park outside Lhasa, the other teams being an aristocratic club and the Lhasa Muslims. Gyatso wore an unmistakable yellow jersey and played wing, a dashing Tibetan Stanley Matthews, and a terror for the opposing goalkeeper, the Ladakhi who kept goal, insisting on wearing even during play his red fez, conical and tasseled. In Port Said, nobody would have looked at him twice. Mr. Gyatso, my father once told me, could type without looking at the keyboard, and I used to stand in awe at his office door watching him perform this feat.

Lhasa was a city of shops, with most of the stalls in the open air under bright awnings. In those days, goods with "Made in U.S.A.," "Made in England," and "Made in Germany" were favored by the customers. Something marked "Made in Japan" drew contempt, for the cheapest and most shoddy goods were Japanese. How times have changed! And what were the things we bought? Chinese Haw-flake sweets; a kaleido-scope, with each shake a blaze of symmetrical patterns; some Japanese slides with a viewer (geisha women, teahouses, and samurai); a wallet with numerous pockets; chocolates brought all the way from India (the first one I ate made me so sick that I was put off chocolates for years); a penknife with a multitude of blades. My favorite shop was Beijing Tsong-khang ("Beijing Shop"). It was clean, airy but still—very few customers visited this shop because things were so expensive there—and in a desk at one corner of the shop would sit a lone Chinese shopkeeper, a studious serious young man ignoring my stares. There were rolls of silks and bro-cades, cloisonné, ceramics, flowered porcelain vases, rare jades, but what caught my eye was a bicycle, shining and alluring. How often I looked at that bicycle, unattainable and beyond my means. It was a *shelgö nang gi momo* (dumplings inside a glass-case), beyond reach, only to be admired from a distance. I was to discover in the future how many of the things in life are *shelgö nang gi momo*.

In Lhasa we took the supernatural and the miraculous for granted. It was all part of the Tibetan milieu that we lived in. Scattered around Lhasa, high up on the mountains or built into crags, were hermitages and the meditation cells of mystics, recluses, and ascetics. I was told that they meditated for years and some for life. Some immured themselves in caves, shut off completely from the outer world, and one never saw them again. Some could render themselves so tiny that they could travel through keyholes and crevices. Others practiced the magic art of *tummo*, the yogic exercise by which body heat was generated; in the middle of a Tibetan winter, they could, with their naked bodies, melt slabs of ice. Some called *lung-gom* could induce a trance during which they could run at great speeds over immense distances without stopping. And then there were those secret adepts who, after many years of esoteric training, could perform *Phowa drongjuk*, through which they could transfer their psyches into the bodies of animals or into corpses. We talked of such feats and believed in them without question, and I met some who said they had seen some of these things with their own eyes.

And what of Shangri-La? Readers of James Hilton's 1933 novel *Lost Horizon* will recall that enthralling prologue to the book that begins, "Cigars had burnt low, and we were beginning to sample the disillusion-ment," and the ensuing discussion about whether Conway found his way back to Shangri-La.[7] Nobody in Tibet has ever heard of Shangri-La, nor did it ever enter our conversations. Somebody has suggested that Hilton might have based it on the Tibetan legend of *Jang Shambala* (North Shambala), a mythical kingdom to the north of Tibet that had disap-peared mysteriously, Atlantis-like, many centuries ago and that would emerge one day to come to the salvation of Tibet in her hour of need. I was ignorant even about Shambala until many years later. When I was in Lhasa, nobody talked about *Jang Shambala.*

I think one reason why Tibetans do not fancy and hunger after an earthly Shangri-La where nobody grows old or dies is that they are too concerned with the afterlife. They know for certain that they will die one day and that they will be reborn again, and that this process will continue for a very long time, and that every rebirth will depend entirely on the merits accumulated in the past lives, such merit being acquired by practicing their religion and avoiding sin. All Tibetan religious practices among the majority of the people are aimed at acquiring merit in order to obtain a better rebirth. They are interested in moving up the ladder of phenomenal existence until, in the end, Nirvana is attained. They have no wish to linger in a Shangri-La. However, since immediate release from the round of existence is unattainable for most of us, Tibetans pray that they may be born in *Dewa chen kyi shing kham* (Fields of Bliss), a paradise from which Nirvana is easier to reach and not very different from the Shangri-La that Hilton envisaged.

It was in Lhasa that I saw my first *Dob-dob.* The etymology of the word *Dob-dob* is debatable, and several authorities say that it has no logical meaning but indicates somebody who is a "rough-and-tough." The *Dob-dob*, found almost exclusively in the Gelukpa school of Tibetan Buddhism (to which the Dalai Lama belongs) were the "warrior-monks" of Tibet. In Lhasa they were found in the monasteries of Drepung and Sera and constituted a formidable force to be reckoned with in any political or social disputes. These monks, the dull-witted backward ones of the monasteries, gifted with brawn rather than brain, carried water, cooked, hewed wood, and fought the monastery's battles. They were tough, arrogant, fanatical monks whom even the soldiers of the crack Drabchi regiment seldom challenged. These monks had a distinct appearance, their faces painted with streaks of black, their heads shaved except for sinister-looking tufts of hair above their ears, a scarf wrapped around their right upper arm. Their weapons were a key, a *kheu* (a curved razor-sharp blade, like that of an axe), knives, swords, and sometimes a revolver hidden in the folds of their robes. Their clothes were begrimed with dirt and grease, and they took pride in wearing dirty clothes, like modern youths with slashed jeans. Readers may wonder how a key could be used as a weapon, but some Tibetan keys, with jagged irregular edges, weighed many pounds. A leather thong was tied to the key and then used as a flail, generating enough force to crack a skull.

*Dob-dob* exercised themselves and trained by running, swimming, and long jumping. Sera and Drepung competed with each other in such sporting events, and bloody disputes would break out on such occasions. *Dob-dob* roamed in gangs, and often such gangs challenged each other to duels. Many of these *Dob-dob* were homosexuals, and individuals fought for the favors of a pretty novice monk. *Dob-dob* were hired by aristocratic houses to work for them and to carry out important errands requiring some show of brute force; they were even known to murder officials who refused to pay taxes on monastic land.

Although there was no capital punishment in Tibet when I was in Lhasa, in the old days criminals were executed by being sewn into a leather bag and drowned in the Kyichu River or else thrown from a cliff. Penalties were harsh and barbaric for a land steeped in the tenets of Buddhism: whipping, hundreds of lashes administered on bare buttocks; amputations of arms and legs, with the stumps immediately immersed in boiling oil to staunch the bleeding; leg and arm fetters; stocks on arms and legs; and the cangue, a heavy square board placed as a collar around the neck. There were dungeons at Shway below the Potala, which I remember seeing from the parapets of a house, the criminals sitting below with long matted hair, filthy clothes, and stocks on their wrists and ankles. Compassionate folk threw down momos or dumplings into their laps like crowds feeding animals in a zoo. A government official or an aristocrat found guilty of civil crimes (rivalry, jockeying for power, bribery, corruption, nepotism, sneaking, intrigue, and blackmail were all found in Tibet, and especially in Lhasa, the seat of ecclesiastical and civil government and the homes of most aristocrats) could have all his lands forfeited, his mansions locked and sealed (*godey gyabpa*, or "door locked," as it was called), and everything he owned confiscated and he himself banished (*gyangpey tangpa*, or "banished far away"), riding ignominiously a bullock or a donkey in a reverse way, wearing white homespun clothes and his face smeared with *tsampa*.

In Dekyi Lingkha, we often talked of *Tsiba* (Finance Secretary) Lungshar, the aristocrat, as if he was the devil incarnate, horns and all. He had lived during the rule of the thirteenth Dalai Lama. Indulging in the extreme form of sacrilege and insolence, he went about with photographs of the Dalai Lama inside his boots. He kept two scorpions, or *dikpa rajas* (monarchs of sin), a white and a black one, and made them fight each other every morning; if the white (good) won, he would be angry and depressed the whole day. Tibetans have a morbid fear of scorpions. One day he was caught red-handed, confessed haughtily to his crimes, and poured insults on the government. His punishment was blinding. In this process, a necklace of *upjus* (sheep's knucklebones, with which we used to play in Lhasa, the painted bones thrown into the air and the positions in which they fell counted, much like the game of *dibs* played by British children at one time) strung on a wet leather thong was placed around his forehead and then tightened with a stick to squeeze out the eyeballs; when they protruded, they were cut out, followed by burning oil being poured into the sockets. I was told that Lungshar neither winced nor cried out in pain but scolded the men who were doing it with haughty words: "Heh, you serfs, just take it easy."

*Tsiba* Lungshar and the punishment that he suffered, like the biblical Samson—eyeless in Gaza, at the mill—never went away from my mind.[8] In Lhasa everybody believed in the version I have related. Lungshar was the Tibetan official in charge of the four boys who went to England with Sir Basil Gould in 1913, about which I shall have something to say later. On June 26, 1913, he and the Tibetan boys had an audience with King George V and the queen at Buckingham Palace. In England, he was suspected of intriguing with the Chinese and of being anti-British. Mrs. Williamson, writing of the 1933–1934 Tibet, says he was "malevolent" and "while he was in England with the boys who went to Rugby, our agents had to keep a close watch on him for he was up to all kinds of underhand tricks, making secret overtures not only to the Chinese but to the Russians as well."[9] He had an incurable propensity for political intrigue, which later came out very forcibly, and was altogether a proud, arrogant, and highly ruthless man.

Lungshar, on his return from England, rose high in the political world of Tibet. At one time, he was the main power in the National Assembly and commander-in-chief of the Tibetan army from 1929 until 1933. He was accused of intriguing against the Tibetan government after the death of the thirteenth Dalai Lama in 1933 and was blinded on May 20, 1934, and kept in the Shway dungeons until 1935; at the time that I was in Lhasa.

Today many Tibetans hold a different view. They say that Lungshar was a very intelligent man—ambitious, certainly, but progressive-minded—a man out of step and ahead of his times, who wanted to make Tibet into a strong, united, independent country with a compact, well-trained army, finances for which were to be obtained by making all aristocrats pay taxes on their hitherto untaxed vast wealth and estates, introducing into Tibet a form of taxation similar to the British system, which Lungshar must have studied during his sojourn in that country. On all counts, it was Lungshar's innovative ideas on taxation and modernization of Tibet that caused uneasy aristocrats to band together in intrigue to bring about his downfall rather than the black and white scorpions and the pictures of the Dalai Lama in his boots. Tibet, too, is no exception to instances of miscarried justice.

I never knew his name, but we used to call him *Cho Dakpa* (Brother Postman), and I don't know why we called him that because I never saw him carry mail. He was an employee of the British Mission, and he went daily to Lhasa on various errands. A postal service had been started from Lhasa to India after the Younghusband Expedition. At some parts of the

route were relays of horses traveling nonstop, but some mail was also carried by runners armed with a spear with warning bells at one end.

*Cho Dakpa* was a thin old man, a serf who had obtained permission
from his aristocratic landlord to work at the mission. He had bleary,
watery eyes, and his nose was always powdered with snuff, which he carried in a horn, tapping the snuff onto the surface of a thumbnail couched
against the curled inside of the index finger and then vigorously inhaling
the snuff into each nostril with deep satisfaction. That was the way Tibetans took snuff, and I learned from him how to do it (and sneezed incessantly in the process). He told me that he had fought against the Manchu
Chinese in Lhasa in 1911 and how the Chinese bullets always seemed
to make two sounds when they struck: "*Tak-dum!*" He told me how the
monastery of Sera had been besieged and the Chinese tried to set fire to its
walls and how the monks armed with Tibetan slings in David and Goliath
fashion had driven them back.

Being a retainer, *Cho Dakpa* had to take part for his master's *shiga*
(landed estate) in the annual dances held in the Potala on the twenty-
ninth day of the last month of the year. He would demonstrate to me his
dance, enacting the martial deeds of the Tibetan kings of the seventh and
eighth centuries AD when Tibetan arms had reigned supreme in Central
Asia: prancing about on nimble feet, igniting an ancient matchlock, and
then suddenly, with a flourish, turning away from an imagined explosion and executing a defiant triumphant war dance. Whenever I wanted
something from the shops of Lhasa, *Cho Dakpa* would bring it for me. He
taught me how to use a *wurdu* or Tibetan sling (he said it was better than
a gun because you never ran out of ammunition) and how to crack it like
Zorro's whip. Slings were still used by shepherds and muleteers in Tibet.

A long jump pitch and a summer afternoon. The Tibetan style of long
jumping, much practiced by the *Dob-dob*, was to run up a long incline
of piled turf slabs and then leap. We were jumping one day when Dr.
Morgan came to watch us. "Too high, too high," he commented to me in
English, pointing to the takeoff. Years later, I had a letter from him from
Australia in which he wrote, "I remember you pottering about the Dekyi
Lingkha. You were good in long jump."[10]

Most young men in Lhasa carried daggers, and occasionally there were
brawls in the streets of the city, as when some *Dob-dob* challenged soldiers
from the Drabchi barracks. We were instructed that the ideal place to stab
was in the buttocks, so that your opponent was incapacitated without
inflicting a lethal wound that might have dire consequences for yourself such as whipping, stocks and fetters, or a cangue around your neck
(unless you paid a heavy bribe). Women fought by pulling each other by
the hair and striking at the breasts, as it was believed that a breast blow
was as agonizing as a kick in the testicles for a man. I remember hearing

about a fight between Dekyi Lingkha servants and their wives and some ruffians, in which the women gathered stones in their aprons to provide ammunition for their menfolk. During such fights, even in broad daylight, it was not unusual for women to taunt their adversaries with a display of bare buttocks, but a full-frontal offering accompanied by a jeering "*Dhi sahl Dhi sahl*" (eat this, eat this) was reserved only to express utter defiance and contempt.

A man's masculinity was indicated by the number of pleats or *kupsoes* in his dress, which looked like a kilt. It was like a peacock showing off its feathers. Somebody once pointed out a man to me in the neighborhood of Kundeling monastery who was reputed to have the greatest number of pleats in Lhasa—eighteen, I think it was—and I saw him swaggering about surrounded by a retinue of young bloods.

Once we got into a fight with some young monks who came from Zara, a village close to Dekyi Lingkha, and one of them threw a stone that hit my brother Norbu on his head (unfortunately, my mother had only a few days before shaved off all his hair); he still has the scar. I wonder whether the animosity shown by the monks was due to the extreme conservatism and antagonism preached by the clergy to anything foreign and modern, a threat to their way of life. Tibetan monks still abhorred any relations with outsiders, and the xenophobia and fanatic desire to be a reclusive hermetic nation that had brought about the Younghusband Expedition of 1904 was still very much alive four decades later.

On the fifteenth day of the fourth Tibetan month, the four *Shabpe*s (cabinet ministers), accompanied by other government officials, made a round of the *Lingkor* (sacred walk). This probably was the longest distance any of them walked the whole year. In the afternoon they attended the ceremony at the Zonggyab Lukhang (the house of amphibian and serpent deities behind the Potala), and I remember those occasions: summer; cool breezes; merry crowds; the women dressed in colorful silks and satins, carrying parasols; everywhere groups of men, women, and children picnicking, singing, dancing. The sixth Dalai Lama, Tsangyang Gyatso (Pure Melody Ocean), from his Fields of Bliss, would indeed have smiled in approval.

There was a lovely, serene lake, its surface touched by the bending branches of weeping willows, and in the center of the lake an exquisite temple dedicated to the amphibian and serpent deities said to dwell within the lake's depths. I was told that in ancient times the festival at Zonggyab Lukhang (back side of Potala Palace) was more solemn, and a sacrificial drowning of a thirteen-year-old youth and maiden was made to propitiate the deities. But just then it was quite different: leather coracles filled with laughing, joking aristocrats in rich brocades and ornate hats, as well as ladies displaying the latest fashions, heavily rouged and powdered with cosmetics from Paris, London, and New York. They circled the lake, mixing with the ordinary people of Lhasa, in similar coracles and also flaunting their summer clothes and singing in unison to the swish of the oar blades as they skipped on the glinting surface of the placid waters of the lake. The temple in the middle of the lake was built by the sixth Dalai Lama, unique among all Dalai Lamas in being a poet, aesthete, patron of the arts, and a lover of song and music; it was here that he secretly summoned the maidens of his choice, dallied with them, and composed his romantic poems.

An aristocrat who frequently came to the parties at Dekyi Lingkha was the head of the Tsarong House, Tsarong *Shabpe*. He was stout, jovial, and hearty and at that time about fifty years old. He was an Anglophile, and one saw him back-slapping British officers or moving about with his arm linked in theirs. He would have been happy to know that several of his future descendants would have British blood in them.

Tsarong was of humble beginnings and had accompanied the Dalai Lama during his exile to Mongolia and China in 1904. In 1910, when the Dalai Lama fled to India, Tsarong had fought a rearguard action at Chaksam ferry that allowed the Dalai Lama to get safely away. Later Tsarong had sought shelter at the British Residency in Yatung and then crossed into India disguised as a mail runner. After the Dalai Lama returned to Tibet in 1912, Tsarong rose rapidly in the ranks and became a cabinet minister and also a commander-in-chief of the Tibetan army. Sometime before the death of the Dalai Lama in 1933, Tsarong fell out of favor, but despite this, in the late 1930s he was a man of great wealth, influence, and power. One of his sons was in an English school in India.

Tibetans were beginning to appreciate a modern education for their children, and several boys and girls from the aristocratic families were in British schools in India. Rai Bahadur Norbu had his son Charles (English names were also becoming fashionable, such as "George," "Daisy," "Betty," "Peggy," and so on) in a Jesuit school in Darjeeling. I remember meeting Charles when he came up once to Lhasa for his holidays, talking and behaving very British. My father had taught me the answers to such standard questions as "How are you?" and "What is your name?" (the stereotyped reply to the first being "I am quite well, thank you"). But when Charles Norbu breezily greeted me with a "How do you do?" I was rooted to the spot, and, to my father's utter chagrin, I was dumbfounded and did not understand the question and stood there speechless and embarrassed.

I remember visiting Tsarong House with my father: the altar-like rooms, the floors polished spotlessly by servants sliding about in felt slippers, the walls covered with precious paintings and *thankas* (Tibetan religious paintings), with priceless cloisonné, ceramics, porcelain, and jade in the cupboards. Many of his windows had glass panes (glass being uncommon and costly then in Lhasa), and there were British-style chairs and tables in many of the rooms, lying side by side with richly carved, Tibetan furniture.

Then there was Mr. Jigme Taring, the son of the brother of the Maharajah of Sikkim, who had lived in Tibet and become an aristocrat. He was one of the very few Tibetan aristocrats who had been educated in India, having studied in St. Paul's School, Darjeeling. He had been an officer in the Tibetan army, but at the time I was in Lhasa he was a government official—a tall, good-looking man who was about thirty-one. His wife, Rinchen Dolma Taring (called "Mary" by her friends and author of the book *Daughter of Tibet*) had also been educated in an English school in Darjeeling, and she was at that time the only aristocratic lady able to speak fluent English. My mother always envied her facility in English. I once spent a few days in the Lhasa mansion of the Tarings, for my parents were friendly with them.

One day, when I was talking to Taring Lhechamkusho (equivalent to "noble lady"), I answered her questions with the non-honorific *Hon* (meaning yes) and *Men* (meaning no), in place of the honorific *La hon* and *La men*. My mother, who was present, was very upset. "You must always add the honorific 'La' whenever you reply," she scolded me afterward in annoyance. "How ill mannered you are!" In Lhasa, speaking in the correct form was extremely important, and the Tibetan language abounds in honorifics: "Come!" could be *Sho!* or *Fey!* or *Chibgyur nang!* depending on whom you were addressing. Years later, whenever we met Mrs. Taring in Gangtok, she used to give us large sums of money as presents, which delighted us.

Rai Sahib Dr. Tonyot Tsering, the Sikkimese doctor, was also in Lhasa when I was there. He was just as cheerful, jaunty, and colorful as ever, still the life and soul of all parties. At every party he slapped the buttocks of ladies and pinched them, not discriminating between married and unmarried women, widows or nuns, prime minister's noble wife or a local Dekyi Lingkha girl. He was more assiduous and persistent than any Italian paparazzi in pursuing Scandinavian blondes. Immense hilarity was created by him, and everybody took it in fun, for Tibetans love getting up to such "jolly japes" and "high cockalorum." One evening, at a special riotous party at a Lhasa nobleman's mansion, the ladies could stand it no more and planned a sudden preemptive onslaught on him to denude him of all his clothes and to pinch him black and blue. This action, executed with all the finesse and timing of a military task force, in no way deterred him from his chosen ways.

Dr. Tonyot lived at Zara, a little village a stone's throw away from Dekyi Lingkha, where he took his afternoon siesta, an un-Sikkimese habit that he kept throughout his life. Zara was famous for its curds. It was also, interestingly enough, the place where Mr. and Mrs. Suydam Cutting, the first Americans ever to visit Lhasa, lived in 1935 and 1937. In my time, there was a villager of Zara, a poor man, almost a serf, who had the absolute temerity in the oligarchic theocratic society that Tibetans then lived in to say that all men are the same when stripped naked! The old man taught us our first lessons in *liberté*, *égalite*, and *fraternité*, which was rare in feudal Tibet. A decade later, another form of *égalite*—more sinister, all pervading, and tyrannical—would appear from the east and engulf Lhasa.

From Zara, in the evenings a pretty young milkmaid ("my face is my fortune, sir," she said) with a flawless complexion (even Jenner would have admired her) brought our milk, for alas in Dekyi Lingkha, unlike in Yatung, keeping cows was out of the question. We used to tease her amorously and make obscene suggestions, and she appeared to enjoy our teasing, for what milkmaid does not secretly appreciate a compliment or a wolf whistle, but she made sulking back-chat at the adults who joined in and favored us with smiles.

Mr. Shakabpa, who later became a *tsipon* (finance minister) in the Tibetan government and, as an émigré following the Communist take-over of Tibet, wrote a well-documented book called *A Political History of Tibet*, was a very good friend of my father. My father used to teach him English, and one of his sons later told me that he could always tell when my father was at his house by looking at the English saddles on the tethered horses outside his house. Mr. Shakabpa, born in 1907, was the leader of the Tibetan Trade Mission (Tibetans, too, were learning fast the disguised nomenclature and subtleties of diplomatic language taught by the British) that visited in 1948 many places in the world, including the United States of America, in a fruitless, desperate, and all-too-late effort to obtain recognition for Tibet as an independent country, with Mao Tse-tung already promising irrevocably to "liberate" Tibet and bring her back into the Han Motherland from which she had been enticed away by impe-rialists. Mr. Shakabpa died in the United States, and several of his chil-dren have emigrated there and become successful in modern professions.

In Lhasa, there were only Tibetan native schools of the type I have mentioned before, along with a school for monk officials in the Potala. Of course, in the innumerable monasteries and nunneries they learned to read and write, but their education was perforce all religious. The Tibetan Muslims educated their children in Urdu and taught them to read and write Arabic so that they could recite the Koran. At first, for me at Dekyi Lingkha, there was no school teaching modern subjects. My father was my private tutor, and he was a strict disciplinarian, teaching me English, Hindi, and arithmetic. However, in 1938, the Radreng Rinpoche requested that the British start a school for some boys specially selected by the regent's officials, and this became my second school after my first one in Yatung. Almost no books on Tibet mention this school, and it could be because there were only about a dozen boys in it and there were no classrooms, studies being held in the open air in the courtyard in front of my father's office.

Our teacher was Mr. Tseten Wangdi, a Tibetan from Yatung who had been educated in the Scottish Universities Mission school in Kalimpong. He was thirty-one years old, a smiling rosy-cheeked athletic man, a footballer, with (surprising and exceptional for a Tibetan) curly close-cropped hair and a small Hitler moustache (the Führer was then at his zenith and about to launch World War II within a year). In fact, I thought he had a striking resemblance to Himmler (if only he had stuck to his chicken farming and not become the chief of the SS!). This resemblance was enhanced by Mr. Tseten's steel-rimmed spectacles. However, he was the least Nazi of men. He played the harmonica with stirring verve, and his favorite tune was "Marching through Georgia."

He stayed with Mr. Dongjesur, the Nepalese dentist friend of my father, who lived in the city and had become very rich fixing dentures and gold teeth, much in fashion in Lhasa society then among both sexes. I think Dongjesur was the only dentist in the whole of Lhasa at that time. Actually, "Dongjesur" was the name of the area of Lhasa where the Nepalese lived, but he was known to everybody as "Dongjesur Babu." Mr. Tseten rode to work on his bicycle, perhaps the only man in the whole of Lhasa to do so, and it took him ten minutes to reach Dekyi Lingkha. One of our students was also the son of the Nepalese representative in Lhasa, and he used to come riding on a pony escorted by a Nepalese soldier.

Mr. Tseten taught us English, Hindi, and arithmetic, and sometimes we drilled outside near the willow trees and played games. "This is the queen," "This is the king," and "The cat sat on the mat" (and, for the more intellectual, a complicated version: "A big fat cat sat on the mat") were the standard sentences in English that we tried to master. There was also "This is a fig," showing an exotic fruit I never saw in Tibet and did not encounter until I came across it in Delhi in 1981. No Tibetan language was taught, as, sadly, in the milieu of those days, any knowledge of Tibetan was considered a waste of time.

One day, Migmar, the biggest boy in our lot, was summoned to read from his English textbook by Sir Basil Gould. He was told to read "A cat sat on the mat"; Migmar pronounced "A" as "A" in the English alphabet, but Sir Basil had looked displeased and had insisted that it should be pronounced "Er," which flabbergasted Migmar, and he returned crestfallen to our class and described his ordeal unable to make out why "A" should be pronounced in two different ways. No doubt Bertrand Russell would have made much of this incident and would have been delighted, intrigued by this semantic puzzle occurring in the heart of mysterious Tibet in the holy Forbidden City.

Tseten Wangdi advised me that when I went down to India for schooling, I must go to an English medium school, which, although meant for the children of *Sahibs*, would eventually benefit me immeasurably. He told me not to go to the Kalimpong school, where he had been and where the teaching was in an Indian language. He said that I should aim to become a lawyer, as they made the most money. He also told us of a game called "boxing" and said that boxers could fell an ox with a blow; this was perhaps a reference to Joe Louis, whose pugilistic sun was then rising. I remember particularly an evening walking home with Mr. Tseten and going through some dunes near Sera monastery, where we had gone to see a ceremony, and the sun was setting, casting a golden glow over the sand, and he again reminded me to insist with my father that he send me to an "English" school.

One of my good friends at our school was Gendün, a few years older than myself. He came from the household of the head of the Kundeling monastery, which had about a hundred monks and was close to Dekyi Lingkha. In fact, he was the student who composed the famous "There are many cocks at Bagmari" sentence (to which I shall refer later). One day he produced a thick red book, looking like the account books that some crafty businessmen in India maintain, it is rumored, to flummox officials of the Indian Internal Revenue—no mean feat. Gendün told me that the book held the key to the English language and that anybody reading it from cover to cover would master that language. This idea intrigued me considerably because mastering English was something I always wanted to do. But to this day I have no idea which book it was, this magic compendium!

Gendün and I often went to that part of the *Lingkor* (the sacred path for pilgrims that I have described), close to Dekyi Lingkha, where, with eyes shut, one tried to put one's fingertip in a hole in the rock. Once, just before I left Lhasa, we went there, and I succeeded in performing the feat; Gendün was delighted and assured me that we would certainly meet sometime in the future. He gave me an image of the Buddha Tsepagme (Buddha of Infinite Life), taught me to say prayers to him, and said that this Buddha was my guardian. Some years after I left Lhasa, my mother told me that he had become a minor government official and that his sister Sedon had become a nun. In the turmoil following the entry of the Chinese Communists into Tibet in 1950, Gendün's family became scattered and could not be traced. I heard rumors that he had immigrated to Canada as a refugee. Perhaps if he should read these pages, he might wish to contact me and make the prophecy of the rock wall of the Lingkor in Lhasa when we were boys come true.

*On the fifteenth day of the fourth Tibetan month, the cabinet ministers visit the Lukhang (Serpent Palace) behind the Potala Palace (Lhasa, ca. 1949). Photo by author's father, Rai Sahib Pemba Tsering*

In Lhasa, everybody threw parties, especially in the summer months, and the British Mission at Dekyi Lingkha was no exception. In fact, the place was famous for its parties and probably gave the best. These lasted the whole day and the guests departed late at night. Almost all those invited—men, women and children, monks and nuns—were members of the aristocracy. A Dekyi Lingkha invitation was very seldom declined. They all came—cabinet ministers and the chief abbots of the monasteries of Drepung and Sera; little incarnate lamas, almost toddlers; officials and noble ladies; and of course the hordes of servants and maidservants of the dignitaries, for a cabinet minister and his lady might have at least six servants accompanying them, including the grooms. Sometimes the parties were only for children, such as at Christmas, with a fully costumed masked Santa Claus distributing gifts and balloons and cutting a Christmas cake brought all the way from elite confectioneries in Calcutta.

At these parties, Tibetan, Chinese, and English dishes would be served, and tinned British fruits and food were considered a delicacy. There would be the popular much-sought-after Lhasa band in attendance, booked weeks in advance. They played Tibetan tunes. *Achu* (Brother) Namgyal, the blind, pigtailed dark-goggled guitarist, was the head of the band, a dignified middle-aged man, a darling of the young aristocrats, who spent much of their time indulging in aestheticism and gambling, and who were obsessed with music and in playing an elegant game of *mah-jong* with scintillating finesse. The red fez-capped Lhasa Muslim played the flute or fiddle, while another Tibetan played the *yanggyin* (a Chinese xylophone-like instrument), which Tibetans claim originated in Tibet.

The music was accompanied by dancing and singing by four ladies richly and fashionably dressed, tapping their feet on wooden boards, delicate, dainty, graceful movements to the swirling of colorful silk blouses, and giving demure coquettish smiles and glances to an admiring audience of portly cabinet ministers, austere dignified abbots, and young officials. The dancers had nicknames such as *Shimey lamba* ("Cat brand," for she had kittenish features), *Pore lamba* ("Crow brand," as she was dark skinned and had a hawked nose), *Showgwey metok* ("Paper-flower brand," for she was as delicate and beautiful as a bunch of paper flowers). *Lamba* was the way Tibetans pronounced the English word "number," which was used as a synonym for "brand" or "trademark." The women were mostly rather matronly and not exactly what Hollywood fans imagine eastern "dancing girls" to be like, but what entranced the crowd were their lovely voices and the grace of their dancing. They weren't exactly call girls, but I was told that they could be tactfully propositioned.

The pièce de résistance of all parties held at the Dekyi Lingkha was the silent cinema. Tibetans marveled at and loved the cinema, and the British Mission in Lhasa was the only place in the city where one could see a film. We would all crowd into the large room in the lower part of the mission building; aristocrats and their ladies, young noblemen, incarnate and ordinary monks, and excited children of the nobility. Every available space was taken up, and the servants would likewise crowd into the front and sit on the floor. There was only one projector powered by an electric generator, and after each reel we would break forth into chatter, discussing the reel we had just seen and anticipating the events to be depicted in the next, rubbing our eyes in the glare and impatiently waiting for the whirring unwinding of the old reel to stop, the fresh reel inserted, and the projector to begin again.

The films they showed were *Trooping the Colour*, *Balmoral Castle*, *Mickey Mouse*, *Rin Tin Tin*, and Charlie Chaplin movies like *Easy Street*, *The Waiter*, *The Crook*, *One O'Clock in the Morning*, and *Shanghaied*. Chaplin was without doubt the most popular, vociferously in demand again and again, and dubbed *kuma* ("thief") after one of his most hilarious roles as an escaped convict. What a wonderful new world the cinema opened for us! In the last show before I left Lhasa (and, to my utter disappointment, I was unable to see the full reel because of an electric failure), there were

Chinese Kuomintang troops fighting against the Japanese, quilt-padded, fur-hatted infantry climbing a tree used as an observation post. During the cinema shows, Rai Bahadur Norbu was the commentator, excitedly telling the crowds how tall the bush-hatted British Guardsmen were, he himself being diminutive. Even the highest in the land were not immune to the charms of the Dekyi Lingkha cinema, because the Radreng regent Rinpoche demanded a private show for himself and his entourage in his chapel at Shide, and all the equipment had to be carried down for the show.

When it became dark, the hissing kerosene gas lamps would be lit, and some of the obsessive *mah-jong* and card-playing guests might be persuaded to come to the large room from where the cinema equipment had just been vacated to join in English dancing. *Mah-jong* was played even by some of the monks, and they, too, would stand in groups and enjoy the English dancing when they could be drawn away from the music and dancing of the Lhasa band. The most popular numbers in the English dancing were "Boomps-a-Daisy" and the "Palais Glide." There would be much bonhomie, consumption of Scotch White Horse whiskey, port wine, creme de menthe, sherry, Benedictine, and cigarettes were passed around, Wills' gold flake in tins being the favorite. I recall clearly that the soda for the whiskey came from siphon bottles with crisscrossed metallic jackets and loaded like a gun with soda cartridges. But I do not remember Drambuie being consumed. Readers may remember that television advertisement that went something like this: "Drambuie is drunk all over the world except in Tibet where the natives prefer fermented yak's milk. Today the world, tomorrow Tibet." As a native, I would like to inform the manufacturers of Drambuie that we didn't drink fermented yak's milk either. I don't know where they got that from.

The elder Tsarong would be the life and soul of such parties, dancing with abandon with the British representatives and encouraging the others to drop their shyness and join in the fun; Jigme and Mary Taring would teach some of the novices the steps, and there would be Dr. Tonyot in his element, on the prowl, and all the young ladies, giggling, laughing, fleeing from his attention.

While their masters watched Charlie Chaplin, danced the "Palais Glide," drank creme de menthe, played *mah-jong,* or discussed Chiang Kai-shek's chances against the Japanese Kwangtung army, the servants sat on the cobbled courtyard and played cards, the horses tethered to the willow trees outside. They smoked, and each showed me their packs, telling me to read the English captions and pronounce how good the cigarettes were. I would read, "These cigarettes are the goods of . . ." and as soon as the word "good" leaped into my sight, I would tell them that the cigarette was "excellent," to their great satisfaction. None of them seemed to realize that all of them apparently smoked "good" cigarettes.

*On right: Author kneeling in front with folded hands with the rest of the cast for the play* Harish Chandra *hosted by the British Mission in Lhasa, Tibet. Fifth from the left is the author's father, who played Harish Chandra. Rai Bhadur Norbhu is seated (Lhasa, Tibet, 1940). Photo by author's father, Rai Sahib Pemba Tsering*

When the party was over and the guests had departed, I would look around—the half-empty glasses with a cherry speared at the end of a stick immersed in it, the cigarette stubs, and the soda syphon bottles. I loved tinned fruits, and my father would give me a large helping, getting annoyed if I refused through good Tibetan manners. My mother had taught me never to ask for a second helping and always to leave something behind in the plate, for such were the signs of good breeding. Respect for your elders, restrained behavior, proper manners, courtesy, the exact honorific, precocity, and behaving older than your years were all so important in the social world of Tibet.

I would stare at the posters on the walls of the room showing scenes from *Gyakar* (white expanse from the white clothes of Indians), as India was called by Tibetans, a country I had never seen lying far away in the south: Benaras, Budh Gaya, exotic stone temples, serene golden Buddhas, and a river scene with tall dusky maidens with nose rings and ankle bracelets, carrying huge shining pots on their heads, a blazing orangeness in the landscape, a hot sun and warm sands.

The staff of the British Mission decided to put on a theatrical show for their friends in Lhasa. Rai Sahib Dr. Tonyot Tsering was put in charge, and he selected the Indian play *King Harish Chandra* about a Buddhist king addicted to giving alms, so much so that he even donates his own eyes to a blind man. My father had to take the part of a wild-haired, bearded saffron-robed *Sadhu* (holy man) telling sandalwood beads but capable of murdering the son of the king. I was chosen to play the prince but also did several dance numbers. I had to carry a bow and arrow, and while out hunting, the *Sadhu* would stab me to death. My father found a plumed brooch in the wardrobe and thought I should wear it pinned to my crown. He read the label "Made in Czecho-Slovakia" on the brooch and commented, "This country is no more" (thanks to Hitler). Dongjesur, the Nepalese dentist, was the king, and a relative of his, Man Bahadur, one of the "dancing girls." The droopy-mustached, Mexican-looking compounder of the hospital dressed as a clown, and Norbu Lhendup, Rai Bahadur Norbu's favorite servant, was a police officer wearing Jigme Taring's British officer's uniform complete with *solar topee* (pith helmet), Sam Browne belt, breeches, and sword. There was music from drums, flutes, violins, and a harmonium. Reginald Fox had contrived a lifelike snake with blazing eyes.

During the interval, entertainment was provided by Fox and Dr. Tonyot tap dancing, the first time that anybody had ever tap danced in the Forbidden City, with scarves tied around their heads, samurai style, and cummerbunds at their waists. The British radio operator from the East End of London with a Bhutanese-Tibetan wife, paired with a Sikkimese doctor, a tap-dancing duo in front of the house that had once belonged to a monk regent of Tibet. The audience, aristocrats and their retinues in silk robes, earrings, ornaments in their hair, as exotic and surrealistic a scene as any in the world. But such reveries were soon shattered by the angry shouts and abuse of monks from the surrounding monasteries who had gate-crashed because they had not been invited. Stones were hurled at the curtain that had hastily been dropped to protect the players on the stage.

Spencer-Chapman reports a similar incident in 1936 when monks forced their way in, on that occasion, to a cinema show featuring Charlie Chaplin, and Dr. Morgan had to employ "rugger" tactics to expel the clergy.[11] Tibetan monks are not the gentle creatures of Shangri-La. Norbu Lhendup had to go out to face the angry monkish mob, Sam Browne belt and breeches, all but holding a real gun, and Mr. Gyatso Topden, the remarkable typist, always courageous and up to the front in such situations, brought out his revolver and threatened the priests, one of whom was heard to shout defiantly, "Charge them! You've nothing to fear . . . he can kill only six of us!" (a reference, no doubt, to Mr. Gyatso's six-chambered revolver). Eventually, peace was restored; I think it was with the assurance that a special show would be put on for the monks. Looking back, I don't think Broadway or Covent Garden could have upstaged us, especially the dramatic, uninvited, unrehearsed entry of the stone-throwing Tibetan monks.

In Lhasa, the public composed songs and sang them everywhere; nobody could criticize or censor them. Not even the highest in the land were safe from their verses. Many of these compositions dealt with politics, bribery, nepotism, or scandal. These songs became a podium for public opinion in a land where open criticism was forbidden and suppressed. There was such a song about Dekyi Lingkha:

> *Dekyi Lingkha lamai chosra marey*
> *Emji Sayo chawey lama marey*
> *Lhasa fumu kachoe shungay marey*
> *Enji gormo thusen shungay rey.*

> [Dekyi Lingkha is not a religious enclosure for monks
> *Emji* (doctor) Sahib is not a chief lama
> The girls are not there to seek sermons
> They are there to receive gifts of English rupees.]

It was outside the hospital that I first came across death. There was a tent, and inside I learned was a very sick patient; in a few days, I heard that he was dead. I stood outside the tent watching a lone priest sitting cross-legged, wearing a conical hat, rattling a tiny hand-held *damaru* (small drum), which he rotated to and fro, and he chanted, drumming in unison, an eerie monotonous chant that had the sadness, loneliness, smell, and mystery of death in it. In front of him was a table of offerings and some oil lamps burning. I stood there for a long time, watching and listening, perplexed as to why we are born and why we die. After a day, some *Ragyabas* came and carried the corpse away tied in a sack with *khadas* (ceremonial scarves) wrapped around it. The *Ragyabas* were a class of people who lived on the outskirts of the city in houses built of animal horns cemented with mud. They were the lowest of the low, lower even than blacksmiths and butchers in the Tibetan hierarchy of social distinctions. Their tasks were to clear the Lhasa streets of dead dogs and other animals and to dispose the human dead. The corpses were taken to special places far away from the city on the mountainsides and then fed to the vultures, the *Ragyabas* hacking them to bits on stone slabs, crushing the bones, mixing them with *tsamba* to make palatable dough balls for the carnivorous birds but keeping the eyeballs to the last, hidden away. I was told that the vultures regarded the eyeballs as delicacies, and if one fed them with these at the beginning of the feast, they might become fussy and disdain the rest of the menu.

*Sebey* (measles) was dreaded by Tibetans in Lhasa, as it took a heavy toll on the children. I used to see the corpses of infants floating in rivers and streams where they had been thrown, as dead children need not be fed to the vultures. During fevers, the accepted treatment was to pile on more and more blankets to sweat out the evil spirits, and the sick were kept dehydrated, while meat was forbidden in the diet. Patients who dozed during the day were kept awake in case demons might entice them away in their sleep. Such perverse measures resulted in a terribly high infant mortality rate. All four children in our family contracted measles but recovered uneventfully because my father nursed us by giving us plenty of fluids and fresh air and keeping us cool. He thought our Tibetan method of nursing those with fevers was stupid and the reason why so many children died.

Syphilis and gonorrhea were extremely common in Lhasa, as Tibetans were lax about sexual matters and the city was full of pretty lascivious girls. Our Mexican-looking compounder, the one who acted as a clown in our theatrical shows, would be busy giving injections of acetylarsan, the only remedy for syphilis in those days. He would be smelling of *chang* (barley ale), or perhaps it was Dr. Morgan's absolute alcohol or methylated spirits, which must have added an exotic touch to his daily intake, variety being the spice of life. He would entertain us with lurid accounts of the operations that Dr. Morgan performed and sometimes, beckoning to us with a conspiratorial air, would show us amputated specimens of limbs, looking pale and waxen. It took a great deal of persuasion before Tibetan patients agreed to an amputation because, in Tibet, criminals were punished in this manner, and they could be ostracized by the public. We hunted for ampoulesaws in the rubbish dump at the back of the hospital and examined the discarded phials. Coquettish Lhasa courtesans, their Hamburg hats tilted, with rouged cheeks, beauty spots on their chins, and melodious whispering voices, would demurely roll up their silken sleeves and expose their arms for injections while their devoted pimps shaded them with gaily colored parasols to protect their lovely, delicate complexions from the sun. We used to tease mercilessly the male sufferers of venereal diseases and shout *"Chebu kupcho!"* at them. They got this name from their awkward painful gait, as they walked with parted legs taking halting shuffling steps. It meant "libidinous crooked-bottoms" or "randy crooked-arses."

Despite the horrible punishments meted out for theft and robbery in Lhasa, such crimes were common. One heard of thieves breaking down a brick wall and putting in a stick with a cloth hanging at one end to see whether there was anybody in the house. One woman thus awakened had stood to one side, unsheathed a sword, and decapitated an unsuspecting thief. She must have been a formidable Amazon.

One night I woke to find my father sitting up in our tent-bedroom looking quite distraught. He told me that our horses had been stolen. There was one particular dappled grey that I was very fond of. A stolen horse in Lhasa is like an automobile lost in Los Angeles. My father's horses were Siling ones coming from far-away Gansu, a Chinese-Muslim province 800 miles to the northeast of Lhasa. Siling horses were considered the best, and often I used to watch them being tested before a sale, with the prospective buyers forcibly opening the mouths of the horses to see what *na* (age) they were, a one-year-old having six and a five-year-old twelve pairs of incisors. When the surfaces of the lower teeth were worn smooth, the animal was thought to be at least eight years old.

The next day, my servants went off to consult an astrologer, who did a *mo* (divination) and indicated the direction in which the thieves had fled with the horses; the servants came away looking sheepish and apprehensive. My father was furious and, seizing one of the bubbles-entrapped glass paperweights, hurled it at Trasi. My father could have made it easily in any U.S. major league as a pitcher. I don't think we ever recovered the horses, but I remembered my father's temper, of which there was another instance. One day he came to beat me with the tripod of his camera (still pursuing his Yatung hobby in Lhasa), and I ran to the roof of our house and threatened to bungee jump without ankle straps from the parapets onto the stone-flagged courtyard below (scene of many incidents in this book) if he did not forgive me. My father promptly did so, telling me not to be silly and to come down immediately. But, in all fairness to him, I must confess that I was not an easy child in Lhasa.

Some of the most charming of beggars in Lhasa were the young boys and girls who pursued relentlessly society and aristocratic ladies singing:

> *Achala gvi sherey diney yagala*
> *Gyabney tena gyabsoe diney yagala*
> *Dunney tena dunsoe diney yagala*
> *Achala gyi sherey diney karala . . .*

> [Lady, your countenance is so pleasant
> From the back your back-view is so nice
> From the front your front-view is so nice
> Lady, your complexion is so white . . .]

More and more verses would be sung praising every aspect of the lady, especially how light and generous her hands were that were heading straight to her wallet, until the beggar had been given some money and told to go away.

Every so often, our menservants Trasi and Rinchen polished my father's saddles in the shade of the willow trees, and I would sit and watch them and smell the polish. British saddles were highly prized, and since the ones in Lhasa had the picture of an ape as a trademark, they were called

*Pew lamba* (monkey trademark). Only years later, in 1985, did I discover what the name of the polish was, and it was a Marcel Proust experience. It was "Propert's Leather and Saddle Soap," showing a foxhunter like English gentleman riding, carrying a whip, and clearing a country gate. The label on the tin read, "Savon pour cuir. Leder und Sattelseife. The best leather cleanser and softener known. Made in Hull." I treasured the discovery, for the smell of that polish under the willow trees of Lhasa had haunted me for many years.

Autumn was the season for flying kites, and Tibetans of every age and class, as well as monks, indulged in the pastime. The kites were not very big, rectangular in shape, and made of Tibetan parchment. The kite string—the best being *Langchen lamba* (Elephant Brand) because of the picture of an elephant on the spool—was rolled onto a holder, and the string was made razor sharp by smearing it with a special glue mixed with powdered glass. Kite fliers challenged each other to duels, and it required considerable skill to maneuver the kites to make them dive, climb, turn, and give the coup de grâce to a lagging kite by climbing high above him and then coming down like a dive bomber. As soon as a kite was cut, you shouted a triumphant *"Tang nga yoeta,"* which means "I've sliced you!" Many boys fell off the roofs of houses watching such engrossing kite fights, especially when several were knotted together. I used to ask Cho Dakpa, the old postman, to buy me kites and smeared kite strings from the Lhasa market, and I would wait anxiously in the evening when he returned hiding a kite behind his back, pretending he had forgotten, and then prancing and doing his war dance and suddenly producing with a flourish a beautiful brand-new kite.

The Sino-Japanese war had begun in 1937, Nanking being captured in 1938, and on the August 23, 1939, the Soviet-German Non-Aggression Pact had been signed. All these developments caused much discussion in Dekyi Lingkha, and I used to eavesdrop and listen to the conversations of the many Tibetan officials who came to my father's office to talk politics and discuss world affairs. Tibetans were happy that the Japanese onslaught had cut China down to her knees. It was the best thing that could have happened to Tibet, for then China would leave her alone. Tibet could do just as she wished. Trade with enormous profits flourished for businessmen selling goods to China brought up from India, for Chinese sea routes had been cut by the Japanese. Tibetans wondered what Soviet Russia was getting up to, and the few who knew studied with interest the Nazi expansions into Austria, Czecho-Slovakia, and the Danzig Corridor.

In the early mornings, we would sit in the chill of the courtyard of our house under the peach trees, eating our breakfast of Tibetan butter tea and *tsamba* kneaded in our wooden bowls of birch and maple, the grain and texture of the wood pleasant to feel and inside a shell of lacquer. I would be wearing a *maksha* (military hat) of fox fur with earflaps, a fleece-lined Tibetan chuba or dress, and long leather boots. My father appeared busier than ever, tuning his radio and listening to All India Radio, with its banshee wail Lionel Fielden signature tune (which that station uses to this day), and rarely we heard something in Tibetan from Radio Chungking Radio. At night my father would be awakened by code messages that he had to decipher, and he would grumble like a doctor disturbed by a night call.

One day I heard that the Second World War had started. The news excited and interested me a great deal, and I asked my father to tell me how the war had started. I enjoyed showing off to an audience what I had heard. I used to make a very simple drawing on the Dekyi Lingkha ground and explain everything to the adults: Here was England and there Germany, and in between a country called Poland; Germany had attacked Poland, and England had come to her aid, and that's how the war had begun. France, with the largest tank force in the world, had sided with England. "Tank"—the very sound of the word had something hard and menacing about it. During one Christmas party, Dr. Morgan has asked me what present I had received, and I proudly showed him a tank: khaki-camouflaged, tracked, and a heavy gun emerging from its turret. France would certainly win, I was told, because she had so many tanks. Nobody spoke of Guderian's Panzers or about the blitzkrieg.

Reginald Fox's AC4YN radio station was now very busy, as he anxiously tuned into the BBC to listen to the latest news of the bombing of London, for Fox had his home in the East End, in a place that ended in "ham"—his wife Nyima once told us. Nyima was of Bhutanese extraction, and we had first met her in Yatung before we came to Lhasa. She was not yet twenty when she met Fox. I remember her visiting our house in Dekyi Lingkha, sitting near our iron stove and chatting with my mother. We knew that Fox was courting her at that time.

The radio station was worked by a generator that had to be hand cranked; as this task required some strength, a tall, large-boned Khampa was employed for this purpose. But Fox's right-hand man was another Khampa, and we used to call him Khampa Tashi—a toothy, walrus-mustached, wiry, middle-aged man with heavily veined muscular arms, an impulsive man with a quick speech. He said that the Germans were bombing London incessantly and the place was being blown to bits, fires everywhere, and the children being evacuated. He said that it appeared England was finished. He told us of a very sad song the Londoners were singing as their children were being sent away; perhaps it was Gracie Fields's "wish me luck!" ("Wish me luck/As you wave/Me goodbye . . . Not a tear but a cheer").[12]

Some very interesting people came to visit Dekyi Lingkha. There was a young Japanese priest, rather wild and eccentric. He was possibly the only Japanese in Lhasa then. Some said he was a spy. Once a Chinese pilgrim came to see us, and I remember him prostrating ceaselessly in our courtyard chanting, *"O-me-to-fo! Koying-fu-tsang!"* (a prayer to Amitabha, or in Tibetan *Hodpagmey*, the Buddha of Boundless Light, who dwells in the Western Paradise); a bump would rise on his forehead like a third eye, bruised from the prostrations on the stone-flagged surface. He was a latter-day Huien-tsang, the Chinese pilgrim who visited India many centuries before. I also remember the very tall, emaciated Indian whom we boys nicknamed "Om bhagwan" because this was the mantra that he intoned all the time, which means "O god." He would demand shelter, diplomatic immunity, milk, and *halua* (a sweet Indian dish). One day "Om bhagwan" died and was carried off by the Ragyabas. My mother's opinion was that the Ragyabas wouldn't carry him very far and that they would cut off his legs and keep the lengthy thigh bones and sell them to be made into kanglings (the thigh bone trumpets that were essential musical instruments in religious ceremonies).

A blind young man used to visit us regularly, and we knew he was coming when we heard him singing and beating two stones together to serve as percussion instruments. He sang well, but he was at the same time a Joan Rivers of gossip-gossip-gossip. He made a round of all the well-known aristocratic mansions in Lhasa and picked up all the gossip. In a city without a newspaper or telephone, he was a walking vendor of news, scandals, resignations, which officer had bribed which, and the likelihood of war. Sometimes what he reported was, of course, nonsense. Once he told us that Kazakhs from Russia were about to attack Lhasa and that the crack Drabchi regiment had been dispatched to face them. The leader of the Kazakhs was an Amazon with pendulous breasts, and, like all Russians, the Kazakhs relished human and horse flesh. Lhasa used to be rife with such rumors, which spread like wildfire. The young man also conveyed messages from household to household and delivered invitations. I can still see him, with his hollow, shriveled sockets and his sad, resigned face, beating two stones together and humming the latest Lhasa song.

A Geshe from the monastery of Sera (second largest in the world and with over six thousand monks) was very friendly with my father. Whenever he came, he brought us *shekaras* (lumps of hard crystalline sugar). A Geshe is a very high qualification for a monk, attained only through long, assiduous study of metaphysics, logic, rhetoric, dialectics, and philosophy and granted only after an extremely rigorous examination conducted by teachers famous throughout Tibet. There were many monks from Mongolia in the monasteries of Lhasa, who were usually the most brilliant students, and our Geshe Chödrak (Rook of religion) was from Mongolia. However, he was most unorthodox, or I suppose his learning and spiritual distinctions placed him on a pedestal far beyond all orthodoxy. He told us not to worship idols because it was nonsensical, but which Tibetan monastery did not have its thousands of idols worshiped by the entire populace? He said that if you slapped idols, they did not dance. Once we were playing outside, and one young boy knocked down a girl, climbed on top of her, and started to simulate sexual intercourse in public. "Good for you!" exhorted the Geshe, closely watching the fornicating pair. "You're only doing that which is perfectly healthy and natural."

My mother took us to Norbu Lingkha, the summer palace of the Dalai Lama, to receive his blessings. There were huge crowds controlled by monk guards wielding staves, and my mother told me that recently a woman who was wearing her coral headdress had been struck on the head, and all her corals had been scattered by the force of the blow. Inside the central hall, the crowds were silent, filing past quietly, offering their *khadas* and being blessed by His Holiness the fourteenth Dalai Lama, a little boy, with a tassel hanging from the end of a stick. The Dalai Lama never blessed the public with his hands touching them; the two-handed blessing was reserved for high officials, ecclesiastical and civil; the one-handed blessing was for all monks and junior officials. Women were never blessed by hand, except a one-handed blessing (the hand touching the head rather than a ribboned tassel) given to Samding Dorje Phamo, the only incarnate nun in the whole of Tibet.

At the monastery of Muru, I saw some religious dances that were very rarely performed, and somebody told me that I was lucky to be in Lhasa at that time. The realistic fearsome masks and costumes of the dancers depicting the Tibetan hell following death were so gruesome that some little monks had fainted while taking part. Entrails of animals were wrapped around their blood-smeared bodies, papier-mâché rocks were hurled on sinners chained and lassoed and led away by vindictive guards masked with the faces of animals. It was an unforgettable experience, and many in the populace must have reformed and radically changed their ways to the paths of virtue for fear of encountering the demons shown in Muru when their turn came to die. Almost all Tibetans, without exception, believed that hell existed and that it was exactly as depicted in the dances at Muru.

There was the hill of Bagmari, where there was a Gesar, or Chinese temple (Gesar the legendary hero from eastern Tibet is also a Chinese deity). In ancient times, we read that prisoners were executed at Bagmari by being skinned, but in the Tibet of my days there was no capital punishment. The temple was guarded by statues of giant idols—bearded, fierce, with protuberant bellies, and carrying swords and spears. Inside joss sticks would burn and one could have one's fortune told by kneeling and shaking a box containing tally sticks; when one of these fell out, the priest studied it and read out your fortune by consulting a religious text. In Bagmari, the monks kept a large number of cocks, I know not for what reason. In our school at Dekyi Lingkha, Mr. Tseten, our teacher, told one bright student to construct an English sentence with the word "cock" in it, and he was complimented when he shouted loudly, "There are many cocks at Bagmari." In London many years later, Sir Basil Gould showed a film he had taken in Lhasa of Bagmari temple, with its cocks, and I heard him make the only joke I ever heard from him: "You'll notice there are only cocks at Bagmari," he told the attentive British audience, "no hens. . . . It may be bad for the monks."

The temple of Ramoche, as old as the Jokhang, was built in the seventh century AD by Princess Wencheng Kungcho, the Chinese wife of King Songtsen Gampo. I remember visiting the temple on a hot, very sunny day. I was extremely thirsty, and our servant Trasi took off his Gurkha hat and, in the indented crown of the hat, brought me some of the temple water, very cold and delicious, and as I drank, I inhaled an aroma of felt from the hat. There were two colleges in Lhasa devoted entirely to the study of Tantric Buddhism, the Gyütö and Gyüme (*Gyü* meaning "Tantra" in Tibetan), and Ramoche was the chief temple of the Gyütö monastery. In the eighteenth century, an effort had been made by Christian missionaries (Capuchins, Lazarists, and Jesuits) to convert Tibetans to Christianity, but their work had been a total failure. Tibetans are the most difficult of peoples to convert to another religion, and in my entire life I do not think I have come across more than twenty Tibetan Christians.

One such missionary—and he must have been a fascinating man to meet—was the Jesuit Ippolito Desideri of Pistoia, who entered Ramoche in March 1717 and lived there until July of that year. He had studied the principal Tibetan religious texts and had even enrolled himself as a monk in the monastery of Sera, writing a criticism of the abstruse metaphysical treatise of the *Lamrim chenmo* of Tsongkhapa and debated on the subject with the learned monks of the monastery. However, on orders from Rome, he had to leave Tibet in 1721.

The small monastery of Nechung was situated four miles from Lhasa and lay close to Drepung. It had only about a hundred monks, but it was one of the most important monasteries in Tibet because here ruled and lived Tibet's most authoritative oracle, the Nechung Chökyong (Religious Protector of Nechung). In a land ruled by omens, superstition, clairvoyance, and prophecies, where every day of your life was dictated by the calculations and pronouncements of the astrologers, the Nechung Chökyong's predictions were received with awe and unquestioning belief. It was he who was consulted during times of national crises and disasters, during floods, threats of war, eclipses, appearances of comets, and the births and deaths of Dalai Lamas. His advice straitjacketed national policy and the roads that Tibet and Tibetans had to take when the future was uncertain and veiled.

At the time when I was in Lhasa, the Nechung Chökyong was a relative of Mr. Gyaltsen Yonten, a very good friend of my father, who later became the aristocrat Sumdow. Mr. Gyaltsen Yonten told my father to send me to Nechung to spend some days with his children. He was the complete opposite of the oracle, for he was happy-go-lucky and fond of singing and dancing and good food, as evidenced by his extremely Falstaffian corpulence. His servants told me that he and his wife slept stark naked in bed, which must have been quite a sight because his wife was just as fat and also just as merry.

Nechung was very pleasant, with a willow park where aristocrats amused themselves in archery of the Tibetan type called Beshu, in which the arrows have bulbous slotted tips that whistle as they are released and shot at rounded padded targets made of felt.

In Tibet, there were many oracles, the soothsayer being a medium who was possessed by a deity. He wore a helmet with plumes and feathers, a rich brocade jacket, a shining silver mirror on his chest, and an apron on which was painted or woven the face of a fierce demon with protuberant, glaring eyes and fanged teeth. Sometimes the medium held an unsheathed sword. To the chanting of prayers and the beating of cymbals and drums, to the sound of *gyalings* (trumpets) and the blare of giant horns, the air wreathed with the smoke of incense, the medium began to shake and to tremble and then broke forth into uncontrollable spasms, foaming at the mouth, his face plethoric, sweating and ruddy, and then suddenly he sprang up, leaped and gesticulated, and had to be held by several monks to keep from harming himself or others. When in the full throes of his trance, the deity having taken complete possession of the medium, he began to speak in spluttered whispers and creaking sounds, and a monk secretary wrote down his interpretations, to be studied with care after the ritual was over. The medium now became wild and frantic, spitting out his words, making threatening gestures with his sword. More monks would rush forward to control him, and then there was a final thrashing of arms and legs, tossing his head spasmodically so that the heavy feathered jeweled headdress almost fell off, and then he collapsed in utter exhaustion into the arms of attendant monks, who bore him away to his altar-room. Such was the Nechung Chökyong during his trance, but when we called on him one evening and I prostrated in front of him and sought his blessings, he was a quiet, subdued monk sitting cross-legged on his throne and did not say anything to us.

I slept in a tent in the garden at Nechung, snug under some blankets, and the older daughter of the family would stoop down and talk to me before she went to bed, and I precociously breathed in her closeness and femininity. Sonam, her younger sister, was my dancing partner, and we danced to the music of Indian film songs from the Bombay Talkies, produced by a hand-cranked His Master's Voice gramophone, encouraged by the clapping and cheering of an appreciative adult audience. I used to visit the Sumdow family often at their Lhasa mansion in the main part of the town, listening to *Ache Lhamo* songs or taking part in improvised scenes from these operas.

*"Kundün chibgyur nangyi du! Kundün chibgyur nangyi du!"* These excited words would be shouted: "The Honourable Presence is coming!" All of us would dash out to the road that led from the Norbu Lingkha to the Potala, for His Holiness the Dalai Lama was being carried in his palanquin to his winter palace. This could have been February 21, 1940, as recorded by Sir Basil Gould, and he says that the cavalcade was a mile long.[13] There was incense burning along the route, and hundreds of worshipers held incense sticks devoutly in their hands and stood there, hands folded in prayer, heads bowed, hardly daring to look at the five-year-old fourteenth Dalai Lama, who had now returned to his home after passing into the Fields of Bliss in 1933. Many were prostrating in the dust. Nobody stood on any of the rooftops of the nearby houses, as it was sacrilegious to look down on a Dalai Lama.

All the Lhasa nobility, who were officials in the government of Tibet, were there in the procession, dressed in their finery, and there were monks wearing metal hats and riding gaily decorated mules, hardly able to control their mounts in the noise and flurry. There were even the priest-cooks of the Dalai Lama wearing strange-looking hats. There was a fife-and-drums band of smartly marching soldiers from the *kusung* playing "Marching through Georgia," and the huge prancing tekyecha horses from the Dalai Lama's personal stable that caught our eyes. Then the golden palanquin of the Dalai Lama carried on the shoulders of rows of green-uniformed, red-hatted lay bearers and just a glimpse of a boyish face inside looking at us. The cavalcade would disappear into a swirl of dust, and we took a last look at the glint of marching feet and heard the fading sound of martial music in the distance.

Sir Basil Gould, British political officer for Tibet, Bhutan, and Sikkim, had arrived at the Dekyi Lingkha. We could make this out from the hive of unusual activity at the mission building and the many tents outside housing his Sikkimese servants, waking up sleepily (I was told they enticed pretty, coquettish Lhasa girls into their tents every night) to don their British-Sikkimese uniforms of red and black velvet jackets, striped kilt-like skirts, conical gnome-like bamboo hats adorned with peacock feathers and their British "Honi soit qui mal y pense" and "Dieu Et Mon Droit" badges, and Lepcha swords on their belts, unsheathed on one side; at the same time, Tibetan servants dressed exactly like those of Lhasa noblemen, with wide tasseled hats, embroidered long-sleeved jackets, and elaborate felt boots, also prepared for a busy day full of official calls and receptions, giving us that haughty, supercilious, condescending look of a Jeeves, for they were the personal attendants of *Burra Sahibs* who ran an empire on which the sun never set and whose outposts, colonies, protectorates, and dominions encircled the entire globe.

Sir Basil Gould had studied at Winchester and New College, Oxford, and entered the Indian Civil Service in 1907 and the Indian Political Service two years later. He had attended King George V's Delhi Durbar in 1911 and had served his country in the Northwest Frontier Province of India (of Khyber Pass fame), Persia, and Afghanistan. He had escorted the fleeing thirteenth Dalai Lama from Phari to Yatung in 1910 and since 1935 had been in charge of Tibetan affairs. In 1936, he had been invited by the Radreng regent to mediate in an old dispute that had arisen between the thirteenth Dalai Lama and the Tashi Lama, or Panchen Rinpoche, who was the head of the monastery of Tashi Lhunpo at Shigatse in the U-Tsang Province, the Panchen being the second most holy and powerful incarnate lama in Tibet after the Dalai Lama (in Tsang itself, some placed him even higher). Rivalry between Tibet's two greatest lamas went back several centuries, and the sixth Panchen after their dispute had fled to China in 1923 and had agreed to return to Tibet only with a Chinese escort. Gould was asked to persuade the Panchen to return without the Chinese but failed, and in 1937 the Panchen died without ever seeing Tibet again. Gould had left Gangtok, Sikkim, in January 1940 on his present mission to Lhasa, which was to attend the installation of the fourteenth Dalai Lama.

Gould's hobbies and interests were polo, shooting, pigsticking, hawking, sailing, gardening, skiing, and the study of languages. In 1913, for the first and last time in the history of Tibet, four boys in their teens had been sent to Rugby, England, to acquire some knowledge in electricity, mining, engineering, and military matters. In an official letter from the thirteenth Dalai Lama, it was desired that four first-class educations at Oxford College, London, should be imparted to these sons of aristocrats. It was Gould who was designated to take the boys to England and arrange for their education. The Tibetan official in charge was *Tsiba* Lungshar, the man who allegedly kept two fighting scorpions and suffered the fate of the biblical Samson. Not much came of this venture, although Ringang managed to get some useful training in electrical engineering and later worked for the Tibetan government. One boy even served in the Northumberland Fusiliers and the tenth battalion of the East Yorkshire Regiment during the First World War, special permission to do so having been obtained from Kitchener himself.

I saw Sir Basil Gould for the first time in my life standing near the tennis court at Dekyi Lingkha and staring into the distance toward the monastery of Drepung. I'm afraid Tibetans had irreverent nicknames for Sir Basil, such as "Lönchen porto" ("Great minister, the old man") and "Dah yangchi" ("Bald one," from a Chinese silver coin that had embossed on one side the profile of a bald dignitary). I would stare at his strange features and noticed that he had a tic of his neck.

Many cases were being unpacked in the courtyard of our house. One case contained air guns, and a Darjeeling Tibetan—mustached, arrogant, and looking somewhat like Errol Flynn—was being very un-Tibetan, as he was taking shots at sparrows in the rafters above. He was wearing a Gurkha hat, and he was a *Sirdar* (overseer) for Sir Basil (Tenzing Norgay was also once a *Sirdar* for Everest expeditions). I stared with boyish delight at some of the things that they were going to present to the four-year-old Dalai Lama: a tricycle, a car operated with foot pedals, a toy boat with a motor (my father telling our servant Rinchen to fetch a tub of water for him to try out the boat).

The fourteenth Dalai Lama, born on July 6, 1935, was now in Lhasa and would be formally installed in the Potala on February 22, 1940. Gould gives a list of presents made to the Dalai Lama by the British government in addition to those that I saw: a gold clock with a nightingale that came out and sang, a gold brick fresh from a Calcutta mint, ten sacks of silver, three rifles, six *polis* of broadcloth, a gold watch, a cane, a pair of binoculars, an English saddle, a picnic case, a musical box, and a garden hammock. A gift of two pairs of budgerigars was also made, my father being the emissary. Gould writes:

> Pemba Tsering, Rai Bahadur Norbu's Head Clerk, was dispatched to the Potala with the birds. It was well that he was sent, for yet other messengers were on the way, and on arrival at the Potala, a high dignitary of the Church was in readiness. Pemba, considerably overcome, handed over the birds and tried to make himself scarce, but he was sent for by the Dalai Lama who talking Tibetan, clearly and easily, discussed the birds' food and how to keep them safe. Pemba then noticed that the watch, nightingale clock, and musical box which we had presented, were all on the Dalai Lama's table and he was told that the Dalai Lama, when off "duty", would hardly let them out of his sight.[14]

Sir Basil Gould left Tibet in 1944. I met him at Brown's Hotel in London in 1950 and also at St. Thomas's Hospital, London (Somerset Maugham's old hospital, where he wrote *Liza of Lambeth*), where he was recovering from an operation for his duodenal ulcer, which had bled in 1944 at Gyantse and made him precariously ill. He was in a cheerful mood. While chatting to him about diverse topics, we discussed Gurkhas. He hadn't much regard for Indians; he thought twenty Gurkhas armed with *kukris* could cut their way from the Himalayas to Cape Comorin in the extreme southern tip of India—shades of General Dyer and his forty Gurkhas armed with *kukris* before the massacre of Jallianwala Bagh. After I had met Sir Basil, I wrote to my father at the British Mission in Lhasa (actually the Indian Mission then), and my father wrote back saying how vital Sir Basil had been in the shaping of his career. "He made me a man," wrote my father.[15]

The only German expedition ever to come to Tibet arrived in 1939, just before the start of the Second World War, and I remember them riding to meet the British at Dekyi Lingkha. The Germans probably belonged to a scientific expedition because I was told that they were collecting insects and fleas. On one occasion, they tried to film the Nechung oracle during one of his official trances, and the Tibetan crowd, resenting this attempt, stoned the Germans, who had to flee for their lives. After this incident, there were rumors in Lhasa that in retaliation the German government was sending planes to bomb Lhasa. At that time no airplane had ever flown over Lhasa. Of course, the rumors were quite unfounded. I only know two Germans or Austrians connected with Tibet: Heinrich Harrer, who wrote the famous book *Seven Years in Tibet* and whom I met for the first time in 1991 in Kalimpong, and Peter Aufschnaiter, his climbing partner as well as compatriot on his escape to Tibet, whom I knew in Gangtok, Sikkim, in 1955. Heinrich Harrer was a good friend of my father.

In the summer months, the occasions I looked forward to most were *Zamling Chisang* (incense offerings for the whole world) and attending the *Ache Lhamo* opera shows. During *Zamling Chisang*, all Lhasa went on holiday and government offices were shut for about ten days, beginning from the fifteenth day of the fifth Tibetan month. Families erected tents in the parks of Lhasa and picnicked. There was dicing, cards, *mah-jong*, feasting, singing, and dancing, and the famous Lhasa band from the parties held in Dekyi Lingkha would be kept busy every day. The air was full of carefree merriment, gaiety, and laughter, and Lhasa threw away the cobwebs acquired during the austere winter months.

The *Ache Lhamo* operas are unique to Tibet, and authorities are uncertain why they are so named and who originated them. *Ache* means "woman" or "sister," and *Lhamo* means "goddess," and these operas might in the beginning have been performed by a company of sisters. Others say that Thangtong Gyalpo, that fifteenth-century ascetic who engineered the iron suspension bridge at Chushül, was the one who started them. There were four or five famous troupes when I was in Lhasa, each excelling in a particular repertoire.

The opera season commenced with the first performance at Shide for the regent or after 1940 at the Norbu Lingkha palace for the Dalai Lama. They were held in the open air. Music was provided by drums and cymbals. Men, women, and children were the performers, but in front of the clergy the female parts were taken by men. The stories dealt with folklore, mythology, religion, and history, poetic license being liberally taken. There was singing, dancing, comedy, slapstick fun, drama, pathos, tragedy, and repartee. Traditional costumes were worn, but some of the rich silk dresses and costly jewelry were provided on occasion by the wealthy households and institutions that sponsored and patronized these shows. A running commentary on the incidents of the story was given by a person who spoke so quickly that the words were almost swallowed, who ushered in each new scene with the words *"Chala phesho!"* (Please enter!), very much like the Shakespearean "Enter," followed by a rapid beating of the drums and the clash of cymbals.

The famous operas included "Drowa Sangmo," the story of a king who is fond of the chase, who falls in love with Drowa Sangmo, the daughter of a mystic absorbed in meditation, and her suffering at the hands of the insanely jealous demoness wife of the king; "Norsang," another story of an ancient king of Tibet; and "Pema Hodbar" (Lotus Brilliant Light), a young boy undergoing the vicissitudes of life.

I especially enjoyed "Gyasa Beysa" (Chinese Consort, Nepalese Consort), an opera about the wives of Tibet's greatest king, Songtsen Gampo of the seventh century AD, during whose reign Buddhism began to flourish in Tibet. Songtsen Gampo sends his astute minister Gar to the Tang Chinese emperor's court to seek the hand of his daughter, and the emperor orders a series of tests to be undergone by the suitors and emissaries who have come from Persia, Mongolia, India, and Nepal. Gar is aided by an old maidservant of the Princess Wencheng Kungcho named Ache Genmo.

In one test, the princess stands in rows of statues of beautiful maidens, and she has to be identified. Gar, in a pretended act of prayer and supplication, scatters rice over each of the statues; the real princess blinks and gives herself away. In another test (which gave the actors a chance to improvise and indulge in much buffoonery and drunken fun), all the suitors are led into a maze, made completely befuddled with wine, and then have to find their way home. Ache Genmo tells Gar to mark his route secretly with a thread, and he succeeds, although he can hardly stand on his feet. A piece of jewelry impossible to thread is given to each contestant, and they are told to thread it; Gar wins again, following the advice of this old lady, who must have had a soft spot for the barbarian minister from Tibet—this time the stratagem is to tie a fine length of silk to the waist of ant, who then threads its way into the jewelry piece. Gar is the undisputed winner of all these tests, but the Tang emperor is unwilling to send his daughter into the wild wastes of Tibet. All pleas and remonstrations from Gar go unheeded.

Gar then pretends to be seriously ill and dying. The emperor's most skillful physician is summoned to treat him, but Gar refuses to be examined and only agrees after much persuasion to hold a thread in his hand for the physician to study this "long-distance" pulse. Gar now displays true Tibetan Rabelaisian ingenuity, tying the string to his penis. The Chinese physician is baffled and becomes terribly anxious, for never in his long practice and experience has he felt such a strange pulse, "akin to that of a dying chicken." The flabbergasted physician, certain now that Gar has an incurable condition, rushes to the emperor and beseeches him to send the princess and Gar immediately to Tibet, as it would be war between the two countries if the minister should die. The emperor has no choice. The princess brings with her as a dowry the statue of the Shakya-muni Buddha, which is in the Jokhang and is Tibet's holiest idol. She is also said to have hidden barley seeds in her vagina and introduced for the first time into Tibet the growing of barley, which subsequently became the country's staple diet. Tibetans arguing in a Lamarckian fashion say that is the reason why the barley seed looks like a vulva.

Once they leave, the Chinese appear to have undergone a change of mind and dispatch soldiers to retrieve the princess. They almost catch up with them at the very gates of Lhasa. Ache Genmo comes to the rescue once more. She waits at the Yuthog bridge (Turquoise-roof bridge), which is within shouting distance of Lhasa, carrying a basket full of worn shoes. The Chinese soldiers ask her how far Lhasa is; she points to her basket and says that the shoes were new when she left Lhasa. The Chinese soldiers hang their heads in dismay. They decide to return home, and Gyasa, the future wife of King Songtsen Gampo, is safe.

I have vivid happy memories of the *Ache Lhamo* shows; the warmth of summer; the clash of cymbals, the beating of drums, the singing and danc-ing and the *namthar* form of singing found only in these Tibetan operas; and the happy, merry, entranced crowds. I attended an *Ache Lhamo* show at the Norbu Lingkha in the summer of 1940, the Dalai Lama's first opera since his installation. It was very much like the description by Sir Charles Bell during his 1920–1921 visit.[16] In the evening, soldiers of the Dalai Lama's *kusung* marched in and presented arms; there was the flash of bayonets, and the band struck up a stirring British tune, or perhaps even "God Save the King" and "Auld Lang Syne."

One day my father received a telegram from Gangtok saying that his uncle Tashi Tsering's wife had died. My parents told me that thanks to her business acumen, the dead lady had left behind a great fortune, which Tashi Tsering was sure to squander, as he was extravagant and care-less about money. He was liable to give away things without a thought. Therefore, it was decided that my mother, taking with her my two sisters Norzin and Norden and my brother Norbu, should leave for Gangtok as soon as it could be arranged. I was to stay behind in Lhasa with my father.

We went to see them off at Shing Donkar (White-faced woods), four miles west of Lhasa, and said to be of strategic importance, as the place guarded the entrance to the city. There was a grove of poplar trees there. My mother, sisters, and brother said good-bye. I saw them leave and fade into the distance. I turned around and rode back to Dekyi Lingkha, holding on to my saddle while a servant riding close to me roped my mount to his. Tears were streaming down my face, and I have seldom been so sad. I couldn't say a word, and when I arrived home, I sought solace by visiting the wife of Dzasa Norbu; she consoled me and diverted my mind by making me sort out her British shoes, which were lying higgledy-piggledy in a large cupboard. Having done this, as it was getting dark and time for my evening lessons, for father was strict about such matters and that day was no exception, I went home.

I sat with a heavy heart next to our iron stove and did my mathematics (fractions and brackets), my Hindi (something about the Moghul rulers of India, with pictures of turbaned monarchs with drooping moustaches, bulging eyes, and wearing ropes of pearls around their necks), and my English (something to do with King George VI and Queen Elizabeth). I couldn't concentrate, but my father did not spare me, nor did he say a word of consolation or sympathy. I had to choke back my tears and persist with my lessons.

*Painting of author's mother by Indian artist Kanwal Krisha (Gangtok, Sikkim). Courtesy of Tsewang Norbu Pemba*

Then Krishna Kanwal came in. He was the head of the Art Department in the Modern School, New Delhi, and had come with Sir Basil Gould. Kanwal was a thin, hawk-nosed, dark-skinned Indian artist who did many watercolors and oil paintings in Tibet, particularly in Lhasa. He was a brilliant amateur conjuror, conjuring being called *migtrul* (eye-eluded) in Tibetan, and because of his conjuring skills he received many invitations into Tibetan homes and used these as opportunities to paint. Even the Radreng regent wanted a show. I resented his intrusion that evening and thought (perhaps unfairly) that now that the house was empty and my mother not there, he was taking advantage and coming to disturb my father, because my mother did not like too many visitors. Kanwal smiled at me and peered at my homework. I was too sad to be sociable.

After the installation of the fourteenth Dalai Lama (the present one) in February 1940, Krishna Kanwal did a famous painting of the five-year-old, seen in several books on Tibet. In the portrait he had colored the inside of the Dalai Lama's conical cap red; my father did not think this choice was right and persuaded him to change the color, which Kanwal did by painting in a flowery pattern, which is seen in the completed work. Years later, Kanwal did a watercolor portrait of my mother in all her finery in Gangtok, and this painting is at present in my brother Norbu's house in England.

## NOTES

1. Bell, *Tibet Past and Present*, 181.

2. Gould, *The Jewel in the Lotus*, 204.

3. Charles Bell, *Portrait of a Dalai Lama* (London: Wisdom Publication, 1987), 329–330.

4. Spencer-Chapman, *Lhasa*, 67.

5. Ibid., 165.

6. Bell, *Tibet Past and Present*, 128.

7. James Hilton, *Lost Horizon* (West Sussex: Summersdale Publishers, 1936), 1.

8. John Milton, *Paradise Lost, Samson Agonistes, Comus, and Arcades* (London: John Sharpe, 1823), 6.

9. Williamson and Snelling, *Memoirs of a Political Officer's Wife*, 109, 110.

10. Dr. Morgan, letter to the author, n.d.

11. Spencer-Chapman, *Lhasa*, 252.

12. Gracie Fields, "Wish Me Luck," Genius, accessed on January 13, 2022, https://genius.com/Gracie-fields-wish-me-luck-as-you-wave-me-goodbye-lyrics.

13. Gould, *The Jewel in the Lotus*, 221.

14. Ibid., 231–232.

15. Pemba Tsering, letter to the author, n.d.

16. Bell, *Portrait of a Dalai Lama*, 362–363.

# 7

~

# The Dalai Lamas and Reincarnation

Almost all Tibetans believe in reincarnation. Without indulging in the intricacies of Buddhist dialectics and metaphysics, I would state categorically that what Tibetans believe in is that at death, something concrete, something whole that constitutes a vital aspect of the dying person, travels for a maximum of forty-nine days in the *bardo*, the realm between death and rebirth, during which time the entity is judged by *Shinje*, the God of Judgment. This concrete whole is reborn again as an animal, god, or human being in any of the six regions that constitute *sripa* (the phenomenal world of existence), the form of rebirth depending entirely on the merit acquired in the previous lives.

There are some beings or deities who have reached Nirvana, or final salvation, who return to earth to be reborn again as a human being in order to help suffering humanity acquire more meritorious rebirths, and then finally obtain release into Nirvana. For the sake of clarity, one could term such deities Bodhisattvas, and *Chenresig*, or Avolokiteshvara (in Sanskrit), is such a one, the Bodhisattva of Compassion, often depicted as having eleven heads—hence called in Tibetan *chukchi shay* (eleven-faced) or *chatong-chentong* (a thousand hands and eyes), denoting all-feeling and all-seeing. As the deity of compassion, he is also addressed as *Thugi-chenpo* (Compassion-great). The Dalai Lama is believed by all Tibetans to be an incarnation of the Bodhisattva of Compassion, who is also the patron deity of Tibet. The mantra or divine vocal formula of this Bodhisattva is the well-known *"Om mani peme hum."* The exact meaning and significance of these six syllables would require volumes for their exposition, and I shall desist from trying to explain what this mantra means. Some have translated it as "Hail, the Jewel in the Lotus."

From the region of Amdo in northeastern Tibet, adjacent to the Chinese border (nowadays Amdo is incorporated in the Chinghai province of China), there came to Lhasa Tsongkhapa (which means "from the onion country"), whose ordained name was Lobsang Drakpa and who was born in 1358 AD. He founded a new tradition, which among other rules, advocated celibacy and abstinence from alcohol.

He built the third largest monastery in the world, which at one time had nearly four thousand monks—the monastery of Ganden, situated about thirty miles away from Lhasa. It became a tradition of this school to wear yellow hats, and they were originally called Gandenpas from their monastery's name but later came to be known as the Gelukpas (followers of the virtuous path). Tsongkhapa died in 1419, seventy years before Columbus landed in America, but his teachings still live on. He is famous for his monumental work, the *Lamrim Chenmo* (*Great Path to Salvation in Stages*). In Los Angeles in 1992, an answer-telephone in a religious center teaching Tibetan Buddhism informed me that a commentary on the *Lamrim Chenmo* would be given, and a clear female American voice called the course "Liberation in the Palm of Your Hand," a commentary on the Lamrim.

In 1391 was born Gedun Drubpa, who became one of Tsongkhapa's most devoted and famous disciples and wore his mantle after the death of his teacher. Gedun Drubpa's reincarnation was Gedun Gyatso, and after him Sonam Gyatso. The last converted the Mongols to Tibetan Buddhism. The Mongols were a powerful force in Central Asia at that time. Altan Khan, the chief of the Mongols, gave the title *Tale* to Sonam Gyatso, which means "ocean" in Mongolian. From *Tale* has come the name *Dalai*, with neither the spelling nor the pronunciation being the way the Tibetans pronounce the word. It is closer to *Tale*. Moreover, Tibetans seldom address their ruler by this name. He is addressed as *Kundün* (The Presence), *Kyabgön chenpo* (Great Protector), *Yishi Norbu* (Jewel of Wish Fulfillment), or *Gyalwa Rinpoche* (Victorious Precious One). Sonam Gyatso later gave the title retroactively to his two predecessors so that he became the third Dalai Lama. Strictly speaking, there are no first and second Dalai Lamas.

Sonam Gyatso also began the system of reincarnating Dalai Lamas, although such reincarnating lamas were in vogue in other schools. The fourth Dalai Lama was born into a ruling Mongol family and after him the fifth in an ordinary Tibetan household. The fifth, regarded as one of the greatest Dalai Lamas, Ngawang Lobsang Gyatso, ruled from 1641 until 1680. It was to him that Gushri Khan, another Mongol chief, offered in 1642 complete spiritual and secular power over the whole of Tibet, so that from 1642 until 1959 (when the present fourteenth Dalai Lama, Tenzin

Gyatso, fled from the Chinese Communists to seek asylum in India), the Dalai Lamas have always held complete spiritual and secular domination over the whole of Tibet.

The sixth Dalai Lama, Tsangyang Gyatso, has been mentioned before. He was the strangest in the sense that he spent much of his time composing exquisite romantic poetry and in the pursuit of beautiful women. He lamented that if he concentrated as much on his religious studies as on the thoughts of his beloved, he would surely attain Nirvana immediately. One of his verses sung throughout Tibet, and even in Bhutan, says:

> *Chade trung-trung karmo*
> *Shoktse yardang*
> *Thagring gyang ne midro*
> *Lithang korne leyong.*

> [White crane, lend me your wings
> I do not go far
> Only to Lithang and then back again.][1]

It was to Lithang, in far-away eastern Tibet, almost three months, walking distance from Lhasa, that one of his favorite maidens had been banished, and the Dalai Lama in his Potala palace must have pined for her and envied the cranes that migrated eastward, as they did even when I was in Lhasa. But his wishes must have been granted, or else he must have arranged his own rebirth, for the seventh Dalai Lama, Kelsang Gyatso, was born in Lithang. One of my Tibetan friends told me that the sixth Dalai Lama had the yogic ability to control his bodily functions so that during sexual intercourse he did not ejaculate. He is believed to have lost this control on one occasion, and there is a possibility that some of his descendants are still living.

His death, given historically as 1706, is controversial. He was being taken, a prisoner, to Peking with an escort of hostile Mongols. Some say that he became ill and died on the way; others claim that a mysterious desert sandstorm arose, and out of the swirling sand three goddesses appeared riding mules, manifestations of Palden Lhamo, patron deity of Lhasa (the goddess with the little mice running around her at the Jokhang temple in Lhasa), who rescued the priest-sovereign and bore him away to Mongolia, where he died of old age. There were several contemporary eyewitnesses who swore that they had seen the sixth Dalai Lama three times in the streets of Lhasa following his alleged death.

The eighth, ninth, tenth, eleventh, and twelfth Dalai Lamas all died young, and there is a strong possibility that they were poisoned by power-hungry ambitious regents. The thirteenth, Ngawang Lobsang

Thubten Gyatso, is now well known to my readers, for he ruled Tibet at the time of the Younghusband Expedition.

On the December 17, 1933, at the age of fifty-seven years, the thirteenth Dalai Lama passed away, and in 1934 the regent Radreng Rinpoche was appointed to rule Tibet. The regent; the heads of the three great monasteries of Drepung, Sera, and Ganden; the Cabinet; and prominent members of the Tsongdu (National Assembly of Tibet) began to ponder on the matter of a successor to the departed Dalai Lama. It was stated that after his death the Dalai Lama's body had faced toward the northeast spontaneously. The Nechung oracle was consulted, and he, too, in his trance utterances favored an easterly direction for a search, throwing *khadas* or ceremonial scarves in that direction.

In the summer of 1935, the Radreng regent, accompanied by some monks and civil officials, visited the sacred lake of Lhamoi Latso (Mountain-pass Lake of the Goddess) at Chokhorgyal, ninety miles southeast of Lhasa. After special prayers and meditation at the lake, the regent beheld in the depths of the lake a monastery with a Chinese-style roof, a villager's house, a hill shaped like an elephant, and the letters *Ah, Ka, Ma*, interpreted as meaning the province of Amdo. Tibetan officials were dispatched toward Amdo, inquiring after any household reporting miraculous occurrences during the birth of a boy, born after the death of the last Dalai Lama, although not necessarily simultaneous with his passing away into the Fields of Bliss.

In 1936, one such group came across a boy in the province of Amdo close to the monastery of Kubum (a hundred thousand images). It was reported that at the time of the birth of the boy, whose name was Lhamo Dhondup, a peach tree had blossomed in the winter and other miraculous events had occurred. The boy, three years old at the time, was tested by the officials, who disguised themselves, but the child saw through their disguise. A monk dressed as a civilian was addressed as "lama" by the boy, who also dragged out his rosary (which the man had hidden around his neck) and began to tell the beads. Some articles belonging to the last Dalai Lama jumbled together with identical copies were displayed to the boy, and he was asked to identify his "toys," which he did unhesitatingly and without a mistake except for a walking stick. One can infer from the above how literally Tibetans interpret the passing of the "entity or personality" of the last Dalai Lama into the body of a newborn.

The members of the search party were overjoyed, and some of them wept, for the boy was certainly the reincarnation of the "Great Thirteenth" and had returned once more to guide the destiny of Tibet. However, word of their discovery was kept secret, and the authorities in Lhasa were asked for further advice. The Tibetan government instructed the search party to bring the boy to Lhasa for further tests, but the Muslim warlord of the region, Ma Pu-fang, got wind of the whole affair and refused to allow the boy to leave unless a hundred thousand Chinese silver dollars were paid as compensation.

A very good Amdo friend of mine in Darjeeling, a Tibetan refugee, was living at that time in Ma Pu-fang's territory; he told me that Ma was fond of having stark naked girls dance in front of him and that he was an indiscriminate womanizer. At one time he had cast his eyes on a young girl and wanted her to live with him, but the girl was already in love with a young man. She requested Ma to allow her for the last time to go in a boat on a nearby lake with her lover and promised that afterward she would come to live with him. Ma agreed. The pair of lovers rowed out to the middle of the lake and then drowned themselves. Such a man was Ma—a tough, ruthless, lecherous man. The Tibetans paid the money, but Ma demanded three times the original sum, and after a great deal of negotiation, the money was loaned by some Muslim traders and the Tibetan officials began their long return journey to Lhasa with the young boy, his parents, and his relatives.

Ma Pu-fang had a powerful private army of his own, and even Chiang Kai-shek, the Nationalist Chinese generalissimo, now locked in battle with the Japanese, had no control over him. The Tibetans, fearing blackmail and escorting their precious discovery, kept a low profile until they entered "Outer Tibet." When Nagchukha, ten days away from Lhasa, had been reached on September 20, 1939, the Tibetan government formally recognized the four-year-old boy as the true incarnation of the thirteenth Dalai Lama. He was met by a prostrating cabinet minister with a letter from the Radreng regent declaring him the Bodhisattva Chenresig returned once more to work for the salvation of the people of Tibet.

On October 6, 1939, when World War II was a month old, and Poland had succumbed to Nazi Germany, the Dalai Lama was officially received at Rigya, two miles to the east of Lhasa. There the Radreng regent paid homage to the little boy, and there were representatives from the British Mission as well as Chinese, Ladakhi, and Nepalese delegates. I remember the occasion well, as all of us went to see the new incarnation: a pleasant sunny day, huge jostling crowds prostrating en masse, public prayers, the burning of incense, a surge of happiness, for Tibet now had the embodiment of the Bodhisattva Chenresig, the Deity of Compassion, and all would be well. There was a mass of tents with, at the center, the "peacock" tent erected specially for the Dalai Lama. My lasting memory of Rigya is this mass of tents and the immense, happy prostrating crowds, the intense display of worship, devotion, and religious fervor.

Two days later, Tibet's fourteenth Dalai Lama entered Lhasa and was escorted to the Norbu Lingkha palace, a dramatic social change that could only happen in Tibet through reincarnation—a farmer's son from far-away Amdo formerly living under the rule of a Chinese Muslim war-lord, now a god-king of Tibet with absolute spiritual and secular powers.

On November 24, 1939, the Radreng regent initiated the Dalai Lama into monkhood by cutting his hair and gave him the name of Tenzin Gyatso. On February 13, 1940, the British Mission, led by Sir Basil Gould, had a formal audience with the Dalai Lama in the Norbu Lingkha palace and presented him with some of the gifts I mentioned in the previous chapter, including the pedal car and the tricycle. Gould was dressed that day in British diplomatic dress, including a cocked hat, sword, and medals on his tunic. My father went with him, dressed in silk. All remarked on how delightful a boy the new Dalai Lama was, very well behaved for somebody not yet five, bright eyed, rosy cheeked, inquisitive, and sitting with patience and composure through long hours of official ceremony, cross-legged on his throne—how he performed all his duties naturally and with ease and without any awkwardness, as if he had been doing so for years!

On February 21, the Dalai Lama left the Norbu Lingkha for his winter palace in the Potala, and all of us ran to see the procession, for the road on which he was carried in his saffron palanquin was very close to Dekyi Lingkha. His brother and parents, in Amdo dress, riding ponies, were also part of the enormous cavalcade. On the next day, February 22, the Dalai Lama was formally installed as the new incarnation, to succeed the thirteenth. The regent would henceforth be known as the Sikyong Rinpoche and would handle the affairs of Tibet until the Dalai Lama reached his majority at the age of eighteen years.

On February 23, which was the fifteenth day of the first Tibetan month (and in the night was *Chö-nga Chöpa*, when butter structures were erected in the Lhasa streets, as described in another chapter), the British Mission was granted an audience at the Potala, and my father accompanied Sir Basil Gould again.

The future years of His Holiness Tenzin Gyatso, the fourteenth Dalai Lama in the history of Tibet, are not part of my narrative. Most readers know of the events that occurred in Tibet and how he fled to exile in 1959 from a Tibet under Chinese Communist domination. However, there are just a few points I wish to touch on that might interest my readers.

I met His Holiness on a few occasions in India. Once I had an audience with him alone for nearly two hours in Darjeeling, and we discussed many topics. I noticed he had large scar marks on his upper arm from smallpox vaccinations, for this disease was common in Tibet, and vaccination was carried out in the British Trade Agency hospitals. One frequently came across pockmarked Tibetans, and in the past several high incarnate lamas of Tibet had died of smallpox. His Holiness complained of itching in one wrist, and I told him that I thought it was due to contact dermatitis from

*Author and His Holiness the fourteenth Dalai Lama at Druk Thubten Sanga Choling Monastery (Darjeeling, 1993). Courtesy of the author*

his watchstrap. Otherwise, he looked very well and cheerful. When he gives a speech in Tibetan, he is very logical and eloquent and marshals his arguments skillfully. He wanted me to explain to him the physiology of bodily functions from a scientific point of view, for he has an inquiring mind. At one point we discussed reincarnation, and I asked him what it is that reincarnates after death. He mentioned something about a minute element in the personalities of all human beings that persists under all situations and even after death. He said that if you looked for it, you would never find it. I asked him how one could assert the existence of something that one could never find. He laughed.

We then discussed Marxism. He wanted to know what Karl Marx had meant when he said that religion was the *dug* ("poison" in Tibetan) of the masses and how religion could be called a poison. I suggested that *dug* is not the correct Tibetan translation of the word "opium," and that when Marx said, "Religion is the opium of the masses," what he was asserting was that religion made the masses forget their toils and tribulations in the same way that opium makes one forget one's cares and woes, and therefore the masses were lulled into complacency and did nothing to alleviate their sufferings.

The Dalai Lama is believed by all Tibetans to be an incarnation of the Bodhisattva Avolokitshvara, but even if he is not a deity, he would in any company stand out as a most vivacious, intelligent, and intriguing personality to meet.

A question often asked is whether the present Dalai Lama is the last in his line. Somebody has even quoted some source saying that there will be only seventeen, the present being the fourteenth. I think the Dalai Lama himself has answered the question. He has said that the task of a Dalai Lama is to return to earth after each death in order to teach human beings the path to Nirvana, and as long as this task remains unfulfilled, it is possible that a Dalai Lama will continue to reincarnate. Another topic is whether a Dalai Lama—or, for that matter, any other incarnate lama— reincarnates immediately after death into a conception occurring at that instant. That is not so, for the period can vary. The thirteenth Dalai Lama died on December 17, 1933, and the present was born on July 6, 1935.

In Los Angeles, in 1992, I saw a video in which a rich high-society lady living in the luxury of Beverly Hills professed to knowing the Dalai Lama very well and made the casual remark, "Of course he told me that he remembered every detail of his last thirteen incarnations." As far as I know, I have not heard him say so. I did, however, hear him once say that he didn't even remember details of his childhood of his present incarnation, let alone all his past incarnations.

The Dalai Lama is not the only incarnate lama in Tibet. In fact, there are hundreds of lamas believed to reincarnate, usually called *tulku-s* (magical body) and addressed as *Rinpoche* (Precious). When I was in Lhasa, a famous incarnate lama was the Radreng regent. He came from a family that was terribly poor. One day the parents went out, leaving behind some gruel cooking in an earthenware pot, and told the Radreng, who was then a little boy, to look after the pot carefully and not let the gruel boil over, as it was the only food they had for the day. The boy became engrossed in play and suddenly saw the pot boiling over; in desperation, he took off his cloth garter and miraculously tied the mouth of the pot as if it were a leather bag. When his parents came home and saw what the boy had done, they were astonished and felt sure that the boy was a devil. I was told that the pot tied with the garter was in the national treasure vaults in the Potala. One day the boy said that horses from his monastery were coming to take him home, and his parents, who were so poor that they did not even own a donkey, laughed at his fertile imagination. Gathering some wooden pegs, the boy drove these with his bare hands into a rock face and said that they were to tether the horses when they arrived. Sure enough, the next day, a cavalcade from the monastery of Radreng arrived searching for the new incarnation. Not a single Tibetan doubted the incidents that I have related above.

My brother, Norbu, was about the same age as the Dalai Lama. In Lhasa, early one morning, he told us that Geshe Chödrak of the monastery of Sera, the unorthodox eccentric Mongolian priest I have written about earlier, would come that day visiting us and would bring us *shekaras* (the rocklike lumps of sugar) to savor; we were all amazed to see in the afternoon Geshe Chödrak paying us an unexpected visit and he gave each of us a lump of *shekara*. Once a woman lost a piece of jewelry, and Norbu told her that she would find it near a stream where she had washed some clothes that day, and that, too, turned out to be true. At one time, we visited Dra Yerpa, some miles outside Lhasa, where the great Indian saint Atisha lived for many years in a cave in the eleventh century AD. We went to a chapel, probably built to incorporate the very cave where Atisha had lived, and there an old priest, on seeing Norbu, said excitedly, "This is my spiritual son! You must name him Jampa Lodrö." My mother was very upset and said that such attention from a priest was bad for a child and shortened his life. My father was keen to give his sons a modern education and not make them into Tibetan monks. Norbu's name was not changed, nor did my mother's apprehensions come true. He is still alive, a senior civil engineer and a British citizen who lives in England.

As I have said at the beginning of this chapter, almost all Tibetans believe in reincarnation, and in an absolute literary sense, as if a whole personality after death is transferred intact into another birth. Some may even comment on the smile and gestures of the new incarnation and say how exactly similar they are to his dead predecessor. An incarnate lama is reported as recognizing his old friends and favorite attendants, remembers exactly where he had placed his rosary or a book just before his death, or recalls vividly particular incidents from his past incarnations. What does one make of all this? Tashi Tsering, my granduncle, poured contempt on the gullibility and the childishness of us Tibetans in believing in reincarnation. His view was that children who displayed such almost miraculous powers were "infant prodigies" found everywhere in the world. They were just precocious beyond their years, like Mozart. It is possible that the plastic infant brain can display some forms of perception, not yet recognized or classified, which are gradually lost as the infant develops, to be replaced by other faculties of perception, more reliable, more concrete, more amenable to discipline, control, and training. The romantics call such forms of perception *clairvoyance*. Scientific physiology of the senses would dismiss them as vestigial remnants of evolution or something akin to the thymus gland that atrophies with age after having served its function in the development of immunity. These questions are open to debate and are not the subject matter of my present book.

## NOTE

1. The Sixth Dalai Lama, "O bird there—white crane—come," in *Songs of Love, Poems of Sadness*, trans. Paul Williams (London: I.B. Tauris, 2004), 117.

# 8

~

# Tibetans and Sex

So far in this book there has been very little mention of sex, and after this chapter I shall desist from doing so. For those who have no interest in this topic, which so obsesses modern society, especially in the West, this chapter can be skipped, and such an omission will in no way interfere with the thread of my narrative.

Until I had left Yatung and arrived in the Tibetan capital of Lhasa, I knew very little about sex. In Lhasa, however, it was quite different, and my best teachers were my own friends and our servants. Tibetans are very interested in sexual matters and are absolutely frank and open about it. There is almost no prudery, and there is no kinky sex. Child molestation, perverted sex, and sex murders are unknown. One never came across manifestations of sadomasochism, fetish, group sex, and so on. Tibetans as a race, I think, have the least neuroses about sexual matters. Lesbianism was unknown, and Tibetans burst into laughter and ladies cover their mouths in astonishment when one asserts that such a thing exists. Oral sex or the licking of genitalia in any form is considered repugnant, disgusting, and abnormal.

Among the monks, homosexuality certainly existed and was widely recognized and accepted, possibly sinful, but not enough to condemn one to hell. Some senior and elderly monks kept catamites openly, and everybody knew this. Chonyi Lhamo, a woman patient of mine living in Kalimpong, a refugee from Lhasa, was a very good *Ache Lhamo* opera singer. She told me that after an opera performance, a particularly beautiful youth who used to take the female parts would be pounced on by a horde of young aristocratic monks who had been waiting for him the whole day, and then he would be carried away like a child in the arms of a monk to their rooms even before the actor could change his costume. But homosexuality among the laity was something that young boys got up to as a prank; adults, other than monks, indulging in male homosexuality was very rare.

Masturbation by males or *dah dungya* (beating semen) was indulged in and considered a bit of a joke, or "no big deal," to use an American expression. Masturbation by women was probably very rare, although there was one form described to us. In this the woman lies down, gets a raw egg, makes a small hole at one end, and inserts the egg into her vagina, letting the contents trickle in slowly. It was said to be so pleasurable that even galloping horses would not make her stop. I think it sounds too good to be true.

Sexual intercourse was considered healthy, natural, to be indulged in, and then forgotten, not something to be obsessed by. Tibetans preferred romantic love rather than brute lust. There was no Tibetan *Kama Sutra* or a classical manual of sex that we knew of, although modern Tibetans say there are such works. I think that Tibetans did not have much imagination in this respect, preferring to use the missionary position or some modified version of it for sexual intercourse. It was believed that the rear entry or doggy position was that favored by European couples.

Tibetans never went in for abortions. They thought that the taking of a life was sinful. It was better for a child to be born out of wedlock than to abort the child. Bastards were not looked down on. For a young unmarried woman to have a lover and then to have a child by him was considered quite normal and socially acceptable to both families. Monogamy was the rule, despite what Bertrand Russell has to say about the mathematics of polyandry.[1] There was a vast monk population, but polyandry was practiced in some parts of Tibet, and also among the aristocracy of Lhasa, usually several brothers sharing one wife. Children born of such marriages were considered those of the oldest son, the other brothers being called "uncles." Occasionally a man might be polygamous. Many couples lived together without going through a marriage ceremony.

While I was in the United States in 1992, there was heated discussion about how much of the breasts could be revealed on the beaches, as well as the banning of swimming costumes that displayed the anal cleft. It made me smile and understand the relativity of all our social and sexual taboos. In Tibet, the breasts of women were considered lumps of meat with nothing "sexy" attached to them. Young women may show their breasts in front of their fathers or brothers and breastfeed in front of monks and religious dignitaries. The showing of uncovered breasts in public to all and sundry means nothing at all.

Young women in Lhasa lost their virginity on many occasions by being chased through parks by men, some of whom could be total strangers. Thus "rape" in the strict sense did not occur, as many women had their first sexual tryst by being "raped," and afterward the assailant might become their future husband. Perhaps the way she performed during such an encounter might decide whether it was worth courting her. "Performance" meant not only sexual passion, the making of sexy noises, and the smoothness of her thighs and the ease with which he penetrated her but also whether she was versed in *wangdah* ("pelvic thrusts," for which the women of Kham in eastern Tibet had fabulous reputations) or *tutsum* (contractions of the vagina on the inserted penis) utilizing those muscles of her perineum and pelvis with which Thai bar girls in Patpong, Bangkok, smoke cigarettes with their vaginas, blow out "Happy Birthday" cake candles, or burst balloons with unerring accuracy by shooting darts out of their vaginas.

Some Tibetan girls were lax about sexual matters, amoral rather than immoral, perhaps like the Tahitians and Polynesians of the sailing ship days. Tashi Tsering, my granduncle, no mean sexual athlete, used to tell me of the wood cutter girls who would pass by his house in the old days in Yatung and how he used to entice them to have sexual intercourse with him by giving them a few Indian rupees. He said a girl seldom refused. Of course, there were professional prostitutes in Lhasa and Phari and other major towns in Tibet, but business must have been rather slack for the poor girls, for they were floating a commodity that was easily obtainable. In Dekyi Lingkha, every evening a pretty young girl used to visit a servant of mine, and the two of them flirted and played amorously. In the morning the girl would be gone, but my servant would be standing up with a triumphant look of conquest on his face and would waggle a still erect penis at me. He must have been indefatigable, performing nonstop all night with the pretty wench, and then in the morning erect, unbowed, and raring to go.

For those champions of women's liberation, what I shall write now is not heartening. Women certainly played a full life in Tibet, working side by side with the menfolk in every way and doing a full day's work in the fields and carrying as heavy a load on their backs as any mother's son. There were no social restrictions at all for women except for certain shrines of protective deities in the monasteries where they forbidden to enter. However, in Tibet, women are called *kye-men* (low born) and are considered, as the name implies, as of inferior birth. In fact, when a person dies, the relatives, men and women, pray as follows: "*Kyepa pholü thobpar sho, dam pe chö dang jewar sho*" (May he be reborn as a man, and may he encounter the holy religion—the "holy religion" being Tibetan Buddhism). The only female incarnate nun is the Samding Dorje Phamo, and she receives only a one-handed blessing from the Dalai Lama. All other women of any rank receive the tassel blessing, the Dalai Lama not touching their heads. No woman held high government or monastic posts; in fact, I cannot think of any woman in my Lhasa days who was holding a government post. Once in a television program in Los Angeles, I saw the fourteenth Dalai Lama being interviewed by an American woman reporter. She sat with him side by side on the same sofa. In Tibetan eyes, this would be absolute sacrilege, like sitting with the pope in a pub and standing him to a drink.

Tibetans do not kiss in public; kissing being regarded as somewhat obscene and crude. Couples are seldom demonstrative in the company of others, such behavior being regarded as embarrassing for the others and slightly distasteful. Tibetan women did not inquire why women have periods. It was believed that a fetus was formed by the mixing of semen with menstrual blood. Tibetans love telling ribald jokes to each other accompanied by explicit gestures, and even the highest born aristocratic lady might relate such a tale. Men and women tease each other, and they believe in calling a spade a spade. One young aristocrat confessed to me that he had seduced several young aristocratic nuns at parties by regaling them with lascivious tales, which presumably turned them on. Once a celibate nun or monk loses her or his virginity, they have to become lay (pardon the double entendre), and there is no stigma attached to such folk.

Known and perhaps even revered throughout Tibet is a folk hero named Akhu Tönpa (Uncle Tönpa). He is supposed to have come from a place called Phenpo. At parties and in households, his stories are told with great hilarity. Telling Akhu Tönpa stories is quite a pastime in Tibet. My mother used to tell some to us, which shows how broadminded she was—nothing unusual in Tibetan families. I will now relate two stories that are typical of the genre and well known.

One day, Akhu Tönpa was passing through a field where a farmer was planting potatoes, and Akhu, being a friendly, sociable person with an amiable disposition, went up to the farmer and asked him what he was planting. The farmer was an ill-tempered, uncouth man, and he replied gruffly, "Penises." "Penises?" questioned Akhu Tönpa, rather amused. "Yes, penises," said the farmer. "Now be off with you! I've got no time for inquisitive folk." "All right," said Akhu Tönpa, "then let it be penises."

After some months, Akhu Tönpa returned to the same field, and a distraught farmer came running after him. "Heh, aren't you the same fellow who came here when I was planting potatoes? You must have cursed my field . . . look . . . everywhere there are only penises growing! Unthinkable: I'm the laughingstock here. And everybody thinks it's an ill omen. They've never seen penises growing in a field. Surely there will be war or famine this year . . . or perhaps even a terrible earthquake. . . . What can I do? What can I do?" The farmer wrung his hands in despair. Akhu looked at the field, with penises growing in profusion everywhere of every variety, stiffness, and size. "That'll teach you to be more civil the next time," said Akhu. "Do you remember how I asked you what you were planting and how you replied?" The farmer nodded. "You've got to help me," he pleaded. "I'm ruined. Nothing to eat or sell this year. How can I pay back all the debts I owe?"

"All right," said Akhu, feeling sorry for the farmer. "My dear fellow, don't be so upset. You may be sitting on a gold mine." The farmer couldn't understand Akhu's words. "Listen to me," said Akhu. "Do you see that nunnery up there? Go up there and sell the penises to the nuns. You'll be rich." The farmer's face lit up, but he wasn't exactly sure how the sales would go. After all, a lot of static penises were no good for any nun. Akhu drew the man aside and said some things to him, and the farmer listened with rapt attention.

The next morning, the farmer cut all the penises down, packed them in sacks, loaded them on his donkeys, and drove the team to the nunnery. There he unloaded his goods, spread them out in front of him according to size and shape and texture, and nonchalantly sat there as if he were selling turnips. Some nuns went past, giggled, and ran away in alarm as well as embarrassment. There were no customers. Some dogs came by and sniffed at the exotic goods, and the farmer beat them with a stick and drove them away. His heart sank, and he despaired of ever paying his debts that year.

Then a demure teenaged nun came along (possibly sent out on the errand by a senior), covering her mouth as if she was viewing something repulsive and abhorrent. She kicked at a magnum-sized penis and whispered, "How much?" The farmer put on a poker face and named his price. "God, that much?" protested the pretty nun. "Yes," replied the farmer. "No reduction and no bargaining. No sales and no discount." (The very words that Akhu Tönpa had taught him.) "Does it work?" asked the nun. "You bet it does," said the farmer. The nun wanted to know how the penis worked. "Just leave it outside your cunt," instructed the farmer. "Say *tsk tsk*, and when you are completely satisfied and exhausted, just give a deep sigh and say *hushhh*, and the penis will come out on its own. Simple. Works like magic." (Now it must be explained to the readers that when Tibetans make a clucking sound and say "*tsk-tsk!*" it is an exclamation expressing wonder, astonishment, and surprise; "*Hushhh!*" whispered with an exhalation of breath indicates utter exhaustion.) The nun bargained, but the farmer was adamant, Akhu Tönpa having advised him not to reduce the price on any account, for it was not every day that penises were on sale in the market. The nun went away, but after a while she returned and surreptitiously handed the farmer the full price asked for and took the penis away. Soon there was a fairly brisk sale, but the next day it was an avalanche, for no sooner had the farmer laid out his goods than every item was sold, every nun in the nunnery wanting to buy one, including grey-haired abbesses and little girl nuns. The farmer made so much money that he contemplated giving up planting potatoes and going into business.

Peace as well as disappointment descended on the nunnery after the farmer declared that he had sold every penis that grew on his field and there wasn't even a shriveled one left. After some weeks, the head of the nunnery, a dignified, solemn old lady, famous throughout the valley for her piety, wisdom, and learning, was invited to the house of a rich man to chant prayers and carry out rites to propitiate some devils that had seized his son and made him very ill. The abbess went, accompanied by her entourage of nuns. Toward the evening, just before sunset, the abbess showed distinct signs of becoming restless and anxious. The rich man had insisted that she stay at his house for the night, as the nunnery was some distance away and it was getting dark, but the old nun wouldn't listen and was determined to return to her nunnery. Her patron inquired why she was so anxious, and she replied that she had left a treasure behind in her room and feared that somebody might steal it. The man then reassured her, saying that he would forth with dispatch his most trusted servant, riding the fastest of his horses, and he would go and fetch the treasure and that she need not have anxiety about the whole matter. The abbess had no choice but to agree, but she did explain in great detail where her treasure was kept—in the special altar wrapped in the richest brocade—and that on no account must the package be opened because the contents would miraculously fly away and disappear. The rich man again reassured her and told her that the last thing his trusted servant would do would be to disobey the abbess's orders and instructions. The servant rode away at a gallop and collected the treasure.

While returning, the servant, a young man with a very inquisitive mind, was seized with curiosity. What was this treasure that the abbess was so anxious about? What did the brocaded package contain that could fly away into the skies? He dismounted, tethered his horse, and very carefully opened the package. On seeing what it contained, he burst out in laughter and, expressing great astonishment, made the clucking sounds—"*tsk-tsk!*"—and up flew the penis into his arse. The servant, panic-stricken, ran away, uphill and down dale, but the penis wouldn't come out; instead, it worked away at him with unflagging zeal. At last, the man could run no farther; he collapsed in exhaustion, almost dying, and exhaled, "*Hushhh!*" The magic incantation (a Tibetan "open sesame!") having been uttered, the penis flopped out. The servant was so seized with rage and exasperation that he picked up a stone and beat the penis into a pulpy mess, wrapped it up in the brocade again, and set off for his master's house, arriving there late at night, and handed the package to a very anxious abbess. The abbess said she was tired and wanted to retire for the night. She opened the package and laid it between her thighs and uttered the familiar sounds, but there was no response from the patient. "Oh thou, a thing of joy and beauty," she whispered coaxingly (this was long before Keats), "come to your lovely nest . . . do come," but nothing happened. And the story ends, abruptly, as most Akhu Tönpa stories do.

The second story is of Akhu Tönpa enrolling himself in a nunnery disguised as a nun. After some time, several nuns became pregnant. The abbess was perplexed. There wasn't a single man to be seen for miles around, and yet these pregnancies . . . She felt sure that there was a man or men in their midst pretending to be a woman.

One day, she ordered all the nuns to strip naked and get their genitalia inspected. Akhu Tönpa tied a cord to the tip of his penis and, attaching a large cowrie shell to the other end of the string, tucked it into his anus, thus creating a semblance of a female pudenda. He came unscathed through the inspection. The pregnancies, however, continued. Then the abbess summoned all the nuns again, made them strip naked in front of her and forced them to perform a Tibetan-style long jump, like the long jumps we used to do at Dekyi Lingkha. Akhu Tönpa gave some prodigious jumps and was declared the champion long jumper among all the nuns, but, like the one fatal mistake that all men are destined to make sometime in their lives, Akhu turned into a showoff, encouraged by all the delicious naked teenaged nuns dancing around him, pleading for just one more jump that would be the greatest ever performed in the history of the nunnery. Akhu Tönpa duly obliged, took a fabulous run, and leaped up into the skies, and he surely would have earned a gold medal for Tibet in any Olympics. He cleared the pitch, the abbess beamed, and all the girl nuns danced with delight, but out came Akhu's cowrie shell. Now all the nuns belabored him, torturing him by tying a string round his penis and a stone as large as those used for milling Tibetan barley attached to the other end and forcing Akhu to crawl around the nunnery carrying the terrible millstone around his genital neck. (A stone attached to the penis, *lig-do* or testicle-stone, and punishment as described for our poor Akhu Tönpa, was used playfully in the villages of Tibet by girls during games with the young men in the summer, when they "captured" such an unfortunate victim.)

"You've done enough to me," pleaded Akhu Tönpa, "and now probably you have exhausted all forms of torture known to man. Let me suggest some to you because I'm truly repentant. What a wicked, wicked man I am," Akhu pretended to cry through remorse. "What suggestions?"

asked a husky, suspicious nun, the one who had tormented Agu the most. "Tie me with leather thongs," he said, "and throw me into the river. That way I shall die a slow agonizing death." This sounded good. The nuns did as Akhu had suggested, forgetting that leather loosens in water; Akhu released himself in the river, swam across to the other shore, waved farewell to the flabbergasted gaping nuns, and disappeared into the distance, undoubtedly for more hilarious adventures, to be continued. . . .

And now for another folk story, not starring Akhu Tönpa. To the north of Lhasa is the wild and desolate Chang-thang, or the "Northern plains," and even farther north one finds the Goloks. These Golok tribesmen ride bareback and are robbers, bandits, and herdsmen. But they are robbers with a strict code. They never attack women, and they never attack a man from behind. They domesticate some of the fiercest mastiffs in the world. But life among these herdsmen is hard and harsh, and there is very little diversion.

Once upon a time, there was a herdsman and a herdswoman living in a yak-hair tent in the wilds of the Chang-thang. Every night after a hard day's work, when the yaks had been pastured, the horses tethered, the mastiffs secured, and the huge butter loads piled away, they would indulge in passionate sexual intercourse. One night the wife said to her husband, "I'm getting a bit bored with our usual form of intercourse, let's do something different. Let's get your penis as well as the two balls inside me. That's what I really want." The husband acquiesced, for he was an understanding and sympathetic husband and Golok women have ferocious tempers.

Preparations were made for this unusual sexual feat, which even the learned Kinsey does not tabulate. Unknown to the herdsman and his kinky wife, that very night three robbers were hiding outside the tent who had planned to steal the butter loads. The husband penetrated his wife, and just then one robber entered the tent. "That's the first one," whispered the wife in delight but loud enough for the robber to hear, who stood there rooted to the spot. Then the second robber came in and the husband-wife team, working literally hand-in-hand, managed to get one testicle inside. "That's the second," shouted the wife, louder this time, for she was now getting uncontrollable with ecstasy.

The third robber waited for some time, wondering what had happened to his two colleagues, for everything appeared unnaturally quiet inside the tent. The herdsman and his wife tried repeatedly to get the second testicle to go in, but it was not easy, for she had a tight vagina. However, with a final stupendous effort from both of them, it, too, slid in, but with a simultaneity that would have defied and baffled Einstein, who denied that there was such a thing in the space-time universe, the third robber entered the tent. "There's the third one!" screamed the demented woman.

"My god, what pleasure! So tight inside my tent and all of them inside! I'll never let them go . . . never! I won't let them escape. . . . I want to eat them!" The robbers were like humans turned into statues of stone. Surely they were in the tent of an ogress, and a cannibalistic one at that. Prayers froze in their breath.

"My loved one," whispered the herdswoman to her husband, "lift me up and carry me around." The husband obeyed and began circumambulating the tent. The robbers were now certain that the tent was occupied by a demoness because the apparition advancing toward them had two heads and numerous arms and legs. Stark fear forced their rigid limbs to move. They ran helter-skelter in every direction. Seeing so many people in the tent, when all the time they had been thinking they were alone at their amorous pranks, the herdsman, too, ran carrying his wife in the Kama Sutra position of the "Lotus serpent" recommended to sexual athletes. He bumped into a robber, who, thinking it was a colleague dashing off with a butter load, whispered in astonishment, "My god, fancy knocking off a butter load in a crisis like this!" At this, the herdsman dropped his wife, and everybody scattered.

## NOTE

1. Bertrand Russell, *Introduction to Mathematical Philosophy* (New York: Dover, 1993), 15.

# 9

### ~

# Lhasa to India

## *A Journey to School*

On certain full-moon nights, I used to listen to the sound of the *gyalings* (trumpets) played from the roofs of the Potala, the moon full above the shadowed branches of the willow and poplar trees of the Dekyi Ling-kha, the clear starry Tibetan night sky above, an air clearer and purer than any in the world, and one held one's breath at this first sight into serenity and tasted the mystic.

One day, my father told me that we were leaving soon for Gangtok, Sikkim, because he wanted to send me to school. Mr. Tseten Wangdi, my teacher, again told me that I must go to an *Enji* (English school) in India. He said that I would be like an idiot for the first few months and wouldn't be able to talk to the English boys, but after that I would be able to converse like the *Sahibs*. This excited me, for I have always been fond of the English language, and I wanted to speak it well.

On the return journey from Lhasa, we took the same route as before, and I shall not describe it in detail. It was sometime in the month of February 1941, in the Iron-Snake year, that we left Lhasa, and it was bitterly cold. My lasting memory is of the freezing cold crawling over my hands and knees, parts that I could not hide, and my father standing there laughing, trying to turn me into a Spartan. I feel no shame because Spencer-Chapman, who crossed the 15,400-foot Gampa La pass from Chushül at night (and he was a man who in 1937 was the first to climb the 24,000-foot Mount Jomolhari, which lies close to Phar; lived behind Japanese lines during the Second World War; trained commandos; wrote a book on jungle tactics; and went by sled across Greenland), has written the following: "Tuesday December 15, 1936: Hell of a day! A day that will be remembered among many grim days."[1] I, too, like him, crossed the Gampa La in winter.

I remember galloping across a wide plain and the horse steaming with sweat. We stopped for a day at Gyantse, the town where I was born, and met Mr. Dawa, who was the head clerk at the British Trade Agency there. He was bespectacled, rather Chinese looking, wearing a long silk Tibetan dress lined with fleece. He was a great comedian, and in Lhasa, in the theatricals held at the Dekyi Lingkha, he used to take the part of a clown with a pillow stuffed under his shirt to suggest corpulence. It was sunny and windy in Gyantse, and I enjoyed the comforts of the rest-house, with its English armchairs and mattresses and chimneys and again the familiar magazines—*Blackwood's, Illustrated London News*, and *Punch*. I don't recall looking at a single magazine during my time in Lhasa.

In Yatung, I was very happy to see my grandmother again after spending over three years in Lhasa. I told her about the goat in the Jokhang temple and about all the other places I had visited in the city, and she told me that I was a lucky boy.

When we approached Gangtok, I came across mist for the first time in my life. In Tibet, I had never seen mist, and for some time I thought that I was walking through clouds. Soon my father pointed to a car waiting for us about four miles from Gangtok. It was the first car I had ever seen in my life. How exciting it was to see my sisters Norzin and Norden and my brother Norbu again, and they all looked so different. And they were all talking in Nepalese, as people in Sikkim do. I did not know a word of the language. The only language I could speak was Tibetan, that too proudly in the Lhasa dialect (which had such expressive phrases as "keeping your mouth shut like a walnut"; "you can go in as a needle and I'll follow you like a thread"; "mouth like a crevice in a wall"; and when we took an oath and swore, it was in the name of the Jowo or Shakyamuni Buddha in the Jokhang temple, "*Jowo-shel!*" like saying "By Jove!"). I knew a little Hindi and English, although my English had not gone very far beyond "the fat cat sat on the mat" and "there are many cocks in Bagmari" (Bagmari now felt so far, nearly twenty riding days away). In mathematics, I knew more than the average boy of my age, thanks to my father's private tuition reinforced by threats with the camera tripod. The car drove toward Gangtok, and my brother and sisters chatted away excitedly, and I couldn't understand a word of what they were saying until they switched over to Tibetan. And then we arrived in Gangtok, the capital of the state of Sikkim.

My first impressions were of afternoon sunshine and the smell of orange peels. No oranges grew in Tibet, but here in Gangtok they were present in profusion. One could eat as many as you liked. And then there were bananas everywhere, the first I had tasted since my Yatung days. I used to call them the fruit that looks like a horn. Ever since those days, the smell of an orange peel instantly reminds me of Gangtok. It was warm and pleasant after the intense cold of Tibet. It seemed like afternoon all the time, like the sailors arriving in the land of the Lotus-eaters. Our hard and very difficult journey from Lhasa in the middle of the Tibetan winter had ended, and I had arrived at a land where it was always afternoon.

> A cold coming, we had of it,
> Just the worst time of the year
> For a journey, and such a long journey:
> The ways deep and the weather sharp,
> The very dead of winter.
>
> A hard time we had of it.
> At the end we preferred to travel all night,
> Sleeping in snatches,
> With the voices singing in our ears, saying
> That this was all folly.[2]

Like in this T. S. Eliot poem "Journey of the Magi," I had made the long journey from Lhasa at "just the worst time of the year," looking forward with eagerness to going to an English school. I had not acquired the wisdom and the years to realize that "this was all folly."[3]

Thus began my first days in Gangtok, a place I would be familiar with for the rest of my life. I met my grand-uncle Tashi Tsering again, spending his time in enforced retirement and the pursuit of English literature. In those days, Gangtok, although the capital of Sikkim, was a tiny town, with the bazaar just two rows of single-storied houses with corrugated roofs, Tashi Tsering's house being the biggest and the most imposing in the bazaar.

In the bazaar, there were lots of boys and girls to play with. I specially remember an "English" song sung in the fading evening light by hordes of laughing children holding hands and marching backward and forward:

> Oranges and laymons
> Sole for a paynay
> Alldus guldus are so many
> The grass is green, and the rose is red
> Eiven vensur I choo you.

My father, contrary to the advice of Mr. Tseten Wangdi, my teacher in Lhasa, had decided against sending me to an English school. He wanted me to go to an Indian one in Kalimpong where all Tibetans from Sikkim and Yatung went in those days, where Mr. Tseten himself and Mr. Gyatso, the football player in the yellow sweater, had gone. Sending a boy to a *Sahib* school was rather ambitious and might turn me into a misfit. It was also expensive. So he applied to the Scottish Universities Mission school in Kalimpong. Back came the reply. There were no vacancies that year, and school had already started. Perhaps next year. My father was perplexed.

It had never been difficult to get a place in Kalimpong. Then a friend of his told him that he had sent his son to Victoria School, in Kurseong, nineteen miles away from Darjeeling and about a hundred miles from Gangtok if one went the long way. The school was English but gave special concessions and priority to the children of parents working for the British government, and since the British Trade Agencies in Tibet came under this category, the fees were not beyond the reach of a head clerk. My father had no choice but to follow the advice of his friend. Some days later, a letter arrived together with a brochure and a school prospectus. Victoria School would accept me.

In those days in Gangtok, riding in a car was something rare and as exciting as a roller-coaster ride at Seven Flags, Great America, near Chicago. Once the mail van was parked in the bazaar and a gang of urchins (including myself) hid in the luggage compartment to enjoy a free ride, but we were discovered by the enraged driver, who hauled us out one by one like rats in a sewer and began to box our ears. He was a formidable man. When he caught me, my mother came running to intercede and told him that I was her son, and I was spared. My mother scolded me. "Fancy trying to hide yourself in that car," she said, "in a few days you'll get fed up riding in cars. You've got a lifetime of riding cars in front of you." Prophetic words, dear Amala.

One day we left for Kurseong, where Victoria School, the *Enji lapdra* or "English school," was situated. We reserved a car and set off—my parents, my sisters Norzin and Norden, my brother Norbu, and our servant Rinchen, pigtailed and in Tibetan clothes and wearing a large earring in his left ear. The driver was Nepalese. The journey was a nightmare for me. My mother was right when she had told me that I would be fed up with car journeys, because I was continuously car sick. My father tried to reassure me, saying that once we got close to Kurseong the road surface would be as smooth as the tennis court in Dekyi Lingkha and that I would stop being carsick. However, this was not so. Kurseong is certainly no metropolis, but it was the first city I had seen in India, and my first impression of the town as it drew into sight was very akin to seeing San Francisco for the first time, or so it seemed. In Kurseong, we stayed with my father's relatives.

One morning we left for Victoria School, which is about 1,200 feet above the town. Our car entered through the school main gate, above which was monogrammed on the steel arch the letters V. S. We got out,

*Left to right: Kaila (driver), Tsewang (author's younger brother), author, author's mother, Norzin (author's younger sister), and Rinchen (attendant) at Coronation Bridge (Siliguri, West Bengal, India, 1941). Courtesy of the author*

all of us dressed in all our finery in silk clothes, as if we were celebrating Losar. Rumors spread that "the King of Tibet" was visiting the school. We walked across the upper playground, and all the boys stared at us. They were the strangest lot of boys I had ever seen: blue eyed, yellow haired, pink faced like little monkeys and with shrill voices. They were the first English children I had seen since my Yatung days, and I had never played with any. Boys ran about trailing wind-blown nets, chasing butterflies across the field. In the air was the incessant chirruping of cicadas. The school was surrounded with cryptomeria trees. Everything looked foreign and outlandish to me.

The headmaster was Mr. E. C. G. J. Hessing, a Cambridge man who specialized in history. He invited all of us to his study, lined with photographs of the past. There were cups, shields, and sporting trophies standing on the shelves and inside cupboards. Hessing wore a gown; he was thin and had a sharp face, a type of face you associate with an officer of the Nazi Wehrmacht, although Hessing was the least Nazi of men. My father introduced me to him, and he shook hands with me warmly and smiled. He said he would like to show us around the school. He took us to the spotlessly clean school dormitories with their rows of neatly arranged beds with bedsheets and counterpanes, and we were welcomed by the English and Anglo-Indian matrons who supervised these dormitories.

My mother expressed delight at the rows and rows of washbasins and the cleanliness of the latrines (I had never yet used a cistern flush toilet). Then off to the school dining room—napkins, knives, and forks—and then a look at the day's food laid out in the storeroom, Victoria School having the reputation of serving the best food among the schools of its type. All this pleased my parents, and they told me again and again how lucky I was in getting into such a school; how assiduously I must study and not let my father's hard-earned money go to waste; how well behaved I must be and do the best in school in every way and not let the family down. My mother reminded me that I, being the oldest, must set an example to the rest of the family and that they would follow the path I had pioneered. In all this, she was being a typical Tibetan mother. My father told the headmaster that he would bring me to school on the Friday of the next week (I have a suspicion my mother consulted the Tibetan calendar to find out the most auspicious day) but to allow me to go out that weekend. Then we left. My parents and Rinchen did not cease praising the school.

The next few days were spent on completing my school outfit and in visiting neighboring Darjeeling, nineteen miles away, where my father wanted to meet a cousin of his and where he himself had gone to school; we passed through Jorebungalow, where my father was born, and he related something of his own schooldays and how hard life had been for him, an orphan at the age of eight, and Tashi Tsering, his uncle, squandering all the family wealth. He told me that I must study hard and later go to a college and obtain a university degree without fail. Darjeeling in those days was a very British town, with English girls with long blonde hair and hats playing with hoops and chaperoned by their Nepalese *ayaas* (nannies) and British army bands playing every Sunday in the parks where British tea planters congregated after chapel.

It was in Darjeeling that an uncle of mine taught me how to put on a tie, for he said that in English schools, unlike Indian schools, all boys wore ties. My school outfit, the prospectus list followed closely by my father with a pencil ticking off the items, included a sola topee (pith helmet, like those used by Ronald Coleman and others in *Gunga Din on the Khyber Pass*); long rubber boots called gumboots for the torrential monsoon rains; a hockey stick; toothpaste and toothbrushes (I never used these in Tibet); and also a nailbrush. All the clothes had to be marked with my name. A "hold-all" was de riguer, which truly lived up to its name, for it was a bedding roll that, in addition to blankets and pillow, could hold any and everything. A tin attaché case for toilet and personal articles was also essential.

One day, I had to discard my Tibetan clothes and put on the brand-new English clothes. The only possession I had in my steel trunk from my Dekyi Lingkha days was a brown suit specially ordered for me from

Calcutta by Rai Bahadur Norbu as a gift for taking part in the theatrical show in Lhasa, when I had acted as a prince murdered by my Sadhu father. Those happy carefree Dekyi Lingkha days were rapidly fading away.

We drove up to Victoria School again. My father reminded me often that the day was a Friday and that on the next day he would send Rinchen to get me for the weekend. We met Mrs. Grace Clark, the art mistress, who went into raptures over the gorgeous silk clothes worn by my parents, brother, and sisters. She said that she must do a painting of them one day. Then I entered my class, which was Standard Two, with thirty-two boys. The class mistress was Mrs. Hill. I sat down at a desk given to me while all around me the boys stared. In that class there was one Indian boy and two Nepalese; the rest were all British or Anglo-Indians. My parents stood at the door for a while and then left. I was alone on my own.

The class was reading a poem titled "The Snow-drops" from an English poetry book. They recited in unison with hissing voices, with perfect English enunciation and pronunciation, and my heart sank. Where was my "the fat cat sat on my mat"? Would I ever catch up with these boys whose mother tongue was English? I despaired of ever doing so. Mrs. Hill was kind. She was a slim, beautiful English lady, who had long white-pink fingers with glossy lacquered manicured nails like the models in the catalogs of Hall and Anderson, Army and Navy Stores that I had seen in Yatung and Lhasa. She was smooth legged and high heeled and had a scented alluring presence as she leaned over me to point out something on the page. I was solemn, embarrassed, shy, but I tried hard, remembering what my mother had said. I must never let my parents down, and I was so lucky to be in an *Enji* school. And I thought of what Mr. Tseten Wangdi had said in Dekyi Lingkha about being a complete *kukpa* (idiot) for the first few months (Tseten Wangdi, under the willow trees of Lhasa, used to play for us on his harmonica, "Marching through Georgia").

The next day, I was delighted to see Rinchen, who came with a letter from my father to Mr. Hessing, asking him to issue an "Exeat" for me to go out for the weekend. But Rinchen returned sadly and said that the British headmaster had inexplicably refused to let me go home. I was heartbroken. Rinchen descended the 1,200 feet to the Kurseong town and returned with another letter from my father to Mr. Hessing. Then he gave the "Exeat." What had happened was that a boy had been diagnosed with a case of chicken pox on the Friday evening and had been admitted into the school hospital. The school had been put into quarantine, and Hessing, true to inflexible British principles of sticking to rules and regulations, had refused to issue the "Exeat." My father had written back saying that he was returning to Tibet and that he would not be seeing me for many months, as it took three weeks from Lhasa to India. I took the coveted "Exeat" joyfully to my dormitory mistress Mrs. Heywood, whose husband was then away in the British Royal Navy. She issued me a brown jersey and khaki shorts and told me not to forget to take my attaché case and my pajamas (we never wore these in Tibet), as well as my toothpaste and toothbrush and the soap in the soap dish. Having complied with these explicit instructions, I descended toward Kurseong town, with a smiling Rinchen carrying my attaché case.

I had a very pleasant weekend, but in the morning on Monday I broke down. I cried and cried, not because I did not want to go to school, as I realized all the advantages of an English education, but because I would not be seeing my parents, brother, and sisters for a long time. My parents were very upset. Father kept quiet. He confessed later to me that he had felt so sorry for me that if somebody had advised him to take me out of that school that morning, he would have done so. My mother once more poured in her advice and told me how lucky I was to be able to go to such a good school as Victoria. I decided to wash my face and get ready to go to school.

The classes began, but there was an interval of twenty minutes before the second morning session started. My parents had waited for me under the cryptomeria trees, and when the interval came, I went to see them. My mother gave me some oranges. I put them in my pocket. Suddenly the bell rang; the twenty minutes interval was over. "Pale dang Amala shuah," I shouted as I ran off to my classroom, tears running down my face—"Father and mother, good-bye!" I ran, anxious that I would be late. I suddenly remembered that I would be punished if I carried foodstuff in my pockets and took out the two oranges and threw them on the playing field. My legs carried me mechanically across the sandy ground, bright in the warm sunlight of a spring day, surrounded by the swaying cryptomeria trees and the chirruping of the cicadas. I did not turn around. I was running toward a new life and away from the old one forever.

## NOTES

1. Spencer-Chapman, *Lhasa*, 282–283.
2. T. S. Eliot, *Collected Poems 1909–1962* (New York: Harcourt, Brace and World, 1963), 99.
3. Ibid.

# 10

~

# A Tibetan Schoolboy during the British Raj

## *Metamorphosis*

The town of Kurseong, lying at an altitude of 4,864 feet, was about 640 kilometers from Calcutta and 19 miles from Darjeeling. It had an average rainfall of over four meters in a year—over ten times the rainfall of Lhasa, as it bears the full brunt of the monsoon rains. Victoria School was at an altitude of 6,100 feet, almost 4,000 feet lower than Yatung.

The school had been founded around 1879, moved to its present premises in 1898, and named to honor the Golden Jubilee of the reign of Queen Victoria. Originally only children of European descent were admitted to the school, but later a quota of 15 percent had been allotted to Indians. Its first headmaster was a Mr. Pegler, born in Cromhall, Gloucestershire, in 1852, who trained in Cheltenham, served in India from 1875 until 1907, and had died a few years later in Cheltenham. A typical devoted servant of the British Empire, when he first came to Victoria, the boys traveled in bullock carts. I saw a photograph of Pegler with his butterfly collars, gown, and mortarboard, somebody who could have stepped right out of Tom Brown's *School Days*.[1]

The school was based on the model of an English public school, and many of its teachers had Oxford and Cambridge degrees. A boy finished school when he passed the Senior Cambridge School Leaving Certificate, which he sat for in the Ninth Standard—the examination papers being set in Cambridge. In 1941, there were nearly two hundred boys in the school. There were three houses in the school: Kellas (named after Dr. A. M. Kellas of the British Reconnaissance team to Mount Everest, who died in the Chumbi valley in 1921), Irvine, and Mallory (named after Andrew C. Irvine and George Leigh Mallory, who died under mysterious circumstances on June 8, 1924, on Everest). The blazer of arms of the school read, "Azure, a fess dancette argent; over all a torch, flamed in pale proper, in base Ashok Chakra or; Crest on a wreath of the Colours, a yak's head, erased gules." Its motto: "Quo lux ducit." (Even James Joyce would have nodded in approval.)

The opening verse of the original school song was:

> We have no high historic roll,
> No list of glorious names,
> Like Harrow on her steepled hill
> Or Eton by her Thames.[2]

Some extracts from the headmaster's diary dating back many years give a taste of the milieu of the school:

26 June 1905: The King's Birthday. A holiday was given. The boys sang "God Save the King" and gave three cheers for His Majesty. [In my early years at the school, after every important function, we sang the British national anthem, but it was for King George VI, Rex Imperator, Fidelis defender, emperor of India.]

4 August 1915: . . . anniversary of the war . . . cadets turned out in uniform. I made a speech upon the war and its objects; there was a march past, the flag was saluted, and three cheers were given for the King Emperor. [During my schooldays, the cadets belonged to the North Bengal Mounted Rifles, although by then there were no mounts. They drilled smartly in forage caps, with bandoliers across their chests and 303 Lee Enfield rifles with fixed bayonets.]

29 March 1917: I have just received news that James Wilson, an old boy, has been awarded the Victoria Cross for conspicuous gallantry in the western front.

>Staff for 1935:
>Mr. E.C.G.J. Hessing (Cambridge) Headmaster.
>Mr. E.V. Staynor (London University) Second Master.
>Mr. T.W. Clark (Nottingham University). English and Latin.
>Mr. V.C. Prins (Cambridge) History and Latin.

(Undated): Three houses were created in 1928 and named after those who had lost their lives in an attempt to reach the summit of Everest. In 1933, I obtained from Mrs. Mallory, as a momento of Mallory himself, the gift of a compass used by Mallory on his last expedition.

(Undated): The school Amateur Dramatic Society in the presence of His Excellency the Governor of Bengal presented the play *The Late Christopher*

*Bean* at the Gymkhana Club, Darjeeling. His Excellency, Sir John Anderson in thanking the school stated that he thoroughly enjoyed the play, the entire proceeds will be given to His Majesty's Jubilee Fund through the Darjeeling Committee. [If I'm not mistaken, Sir John Anderson is the same person who was a minister under Churchill during the London Blitz and supervised the construction of the bomb shelters that bear his name.]

3 September 1939: England declared war on Germany at 11 o'clock GMT.

3 March 1940: R. Smart appointed Head Boy.
The Editor of the school magazine, *The Vic*: N.St. Romaine
Sub-editors: C. Dodsworth and R. Moulding
Photographic Club: President Reverend G.B. Elliot
Secretary: R. K. Stuart
[Readers will note from the above that all the boys were WASPs. Smart later immigrated to Australia and was at one time a state soccer player. Moulding I saw in later years attending the Old Boys' Dinner in British army uniform and carrying a revolver in a camouflaged khaki holster with a lanyard as used at El Alamein. R. K. Stuart created a pole-vault record that still stands, and I was there in 1941 when he did it. I, too, won a prize on that day in the nippers' race running the hundred yards.]

7 October 1940: Frederick Berry, DFM, RAF lost his life at Boulogne in the defence of Britain. A large number of our boys are serving with His Majesty's services, and two of them have so far obtained decorations; A. deGruyther, Squadron Leader, RAF, DFC and F. Berry, Sergeant; RAF, DFM. [Victoria's boys were also taking part in the Battle of Britain. The sons of the empire had returned home to defend their motherland. To most of the boys in Victoria, "home" always meant Great Britain, even to those whose grandparents had been born in India. India was never regarded as "home."]

28 October 1940: I received definite information that Squadron Leader Albert deGruyther, DFC, has been killed in action.[3]

"I say, what's your name?" a boy would ask me. "My name is Tsewang Yishey," I would blurt out, remembering how my father had taught me to answer the question. "What?" with a surprised supercilious look. "Tsewang Yishey," I would repeat. "What a funny name!" commented the boy. Soon a chain of boys came asking the same question and choking with laughter at my reply.

In the dining room, there was food I had never tasted or seen and which I loathed: rissoles (salads with raw bleeding beetroot, stews, and cutlets). I hated treacle too, which surprised many of the boys, and they wanted me to give them my share. "Don't open your gob when you eat," a boy told me, making a face in disgust. "It's bad manners."

And then I received my first letter from my father. It was addressed to "Master T. Yishey," and at first I was reluctant to open it, not knowing what "Master" meant and whether it was for my teacher, because in "Baa baa black sheep" there occurred the line "one for my master." And there were the three British words: *skit*, *swot*, and *sneak*. One must never be a "skit" because that was girlish. One could be a "swot," because hadn't my mother told me to study hard and not waste my father's hard-earned salary? But one mustn't be caught "swotting," as that was bad form. Finally, one must never be a "sneak." That was as bad as hitting a chap when he was down or kicking him from behind. One didn't do those things. Once during a torrential monsoon downpour, with the rain cascading on the corrugated roofs so that the noise drowned even conversation and the drains overflowed and one raced little wooden boats, a boy named Wise pushed a friend of mine into a drain. I was so incensed by the attack, which was a form of bullying (Wise being quite a big boy), that I went straight to Mr. Hessing and reported what had happened. Subsequently I was labeled a "sneak," and some of the boys said I should be sent to "Coventry," wherever that was.

The Second World War was very much in the air at Victoria. Sometimes, on special solemn occasions, the boys intoned in the assembly hall, "They shall not grow old as we that are left grow old; age shall not weary them, nor the years condemn; and at the going down of the sun and in the morning, we will remember them."

The school belonged to the Church of England denomination, but there was a small church for Catholics. There were also a few Jewish boys. No religious services were held for Buddhists and Hindus. Before and after each meal, grace was said by a prefect: "For what we are about to receive may the Lord make us truly thankful for Christ's sake . . . amen!" And we all chanted "Amen!" in unison. Church attendance was not compulsory for the non-Christians, but in the evenings I would listen to the Christian boys at their paternosters: "Our Father who art in heaven . . ."

In Victoria, we played cricket, football, and hockey. It was while watching a game of cricket that I suddenly understood what Dr. Morgan was trying to do when he threw stones with a whirling action of his right arm against the willow and poplar trees of Dekyi Lingkha. There was an Edinburgh Challenge Shield for cricket for the schools of the Darjeeling district and the tea planters, and at one time, I think it was 1912, it had been won by the third battalion County of Middlesex Regiment. For the Scouts, there was a Jackson Shield, presented by His Excellency, Colonel the Right Honorable Sir Francis Stanley Jackson, P.C., G.C.I.E., governor of Bengal. Whenever the school won any of the shields, the trophy was paraded in by the team in the dining hall, like a Roman emperor returning in triumph to Rome, and the boys shouted hoarsely and threw their napkins in the air, and the day would be declared a holiday.

In class, I learned about Romulus and Remus, Horatius defending the bridge, King Alfred and the burned cake, King Canute trying to hold back the waves, and the Spartans at Thermopylae under Leonidas. We read Stevenson and Keats: "Then felt I like some watcher of the sky, when a new planet swims into his ken."[4] It was a far cry from "the fat cat sat on the mat" and "there are many cocks at Bagmari." In geography, we learned about Eskimo igloos, the pygmies of the Congo, the fisheries of Lowestoft, Boston market and the Tuaregs of the Sahara. Nature study taught us about tadpoles and how they metamorphosed into frogs. Later there was Latin with *"Vir bonus non miser est"* ("The bony man is not a miser," joked the Latin teacher in an effort to rouse our interest in this strange subject; "dead as a dodo," complained some boys). But there was a flowing beauty and grace in such sentences as *"Quam bella est ora ma ritima."* I entered a fascinating, captivating world in the stories of Hans Christian Andersen and the Grimm Brothers and in the thick encyclopedias, full of pictures, during leisure study. "The Snow Queen" made my imagination soar, and I thought of her as a blonde, blue-eyed maiden in the snowy vastness of Tibet.

But it was not all fun and games. There were dark sides to Victoria, and I was very miserable for months. Punishment was severe. The least painful, but taxing to the patience and an absolute guarantee if you wished to acquire writer's cramps, was the writing of lines, the number of lines inflicted being a case of the punishment to fit the crime, with "I shall not be late" or "I shall keep my desk tidy" having to be written out again and again. We were beaten with hockey sticks, had to kneel with bared knees on iron bedrails, had to keep our hands out holding books and being beaten if the hands dropped (oddly reminiscent of punishment then being meted out in Japanese prisoner-of-war camps). And all the time, there was the exhortation to be fast—fast—learning in Victoria the tyranny of time, the price modern man has to pay for his glitter and creature comforts. In Tibet, time was something we all had. There was always leisure, always enough time to do anything. Not so in Victoria. Hessing would come into the dormitories in the evenings—scholarly, slightly stooped, gowned. "Hurry! Hurry!" he would say all the time. Hurry to undress, hurry to dress, hurry to your classroom, hurry to the dining room, hurry to the games. Why? When did one ever stop?

And the prefects, many of them cruel and vindictive (and now, when I look back, possibly sadistic), shouting, "The Jhug chap to undress gets three licks with the hockey stick!" ("Jhug" was the Victoria slang for "last.") No matter how quickly you undressed, there was always

inevitably a Jhug chap, and one took the three licks like a man, unflinch-
ingly. Even a Speedy Gonzales was liable to come Jhug when it wasn't
his day.

Then there was being gated in for hours on a Saturday or Sunday, mass
punishment for something done by somebody who wouldn't own up—
sitting mute, unmoving in the assembly hall, not even allowed to read
or to write. And especially no reading of comics when you were gated:
*The Beano, The Dandy, The Legend of Lord Snooty and His Pals, Desperate
Dan, Pansy Potter the Strongman's Daughter, Rockfist Rogan—RAF, Batman
and Robin, Roy Rogers and Trigger*, and of course *Captain Marvel*. Instead,
one glued one's eyes to the names carved on the desktops, like those
that I saw at Rugby School, the names of boys who had been in school
long ago, just like us, and had bequeathed their autographs to posterity,
seeking an egoistic immortality. But it was entertaining. Outside, the
teachers walked briskly in the corridors, laughed, and joked. They were
free. Theirs was another world. When would I ever be free! I despaired.
Sunshine outside, the chirruping of cicadas (did they never stop?). One
looked around at the walls and read what was written on the boards—
the names of boys who had passed the coveted Senior Cambridge School
Leaving Certificate. (Lucky chaps! When would I ever get my Senior
Cambridge? The goal looked, oh, so distant.) And there was the "Roll of
Honour": F. Berry, DFM, 1940, Boulogne; T. Grosvenor, F/Sgt.1941, England; L. Manser, F/Lt., V.C. 1942—in the "thousand bomber raid" over
Cologne; N. Beadle, Sgt. RAF, 1942, Libya; G. Harris, Chief officer, 1942, at
sea; A.de Gruyther, DFC, RAF, 1940, England. The whole history of Great
Britain and the British Empire in the Second World War was condensed
on that board, and Victoria School could be as proud of her record as any
school in the whole world.

Mrs. Heywood, our dormitory mistress, was looking for new recruits
for her singing class. We filed upstairs to her room adjacent to the dormitory, passing on the way the little room stacked with well-ironed
clothes delivered by the tall sinewy Indian *dhobis* (washermen) who carried the laundry on their heads (like the pictures of the Indian women I
had seen in Dekyi Lingkha at the British Mission in Lhasa), the clothes
impregnated with that peculiar musty smell that clothes washed by the
Indian *dhobis* possess, and past the Indian *darzi* (tailor) mending our torn
pockets and stitching on shirt buttons, and then there would be Mrs.
Heywood waiting for us: spectacled, rouged cheeks, rather stern and
forbidding. Her husband was a captain in the King's Navy. First, she
wanted to know who could whistle for the song "Whistle While You
Work" (the last thing any of us would have dared to do; otherwise there
would be several "licks" with the hockey stick).[5] Then she sat down at
her piano; one by one we advanced to her side, and she played a note

and we had to sing that note. "Do-Re-Mi-Fa-Sol-La-Ti-Do," you sang with your hands folded in front of you, chin up, eyes looking straight ahead, and singing out the notes from your diaphragm and not just from your throat—certainly a yogic feat.

Padre Gilbert B. Elliot was the school padre, living under spartan conditions just above the armory where the cadets kept their 303 Lee-Enfield rifles chained neatly together. Despite his cramped quarters, he had allowed the rooms in the verandah to be used as a recreation center, especially welcome during the heavy monsoon rains, which kept us indoors for days. There would be the *Statesman* newspaper to read, an assortment of magazines, and a carrom board. In his spotlessly clean dining room cared for by his uniformed turbaned old Nepalese bearer, there was a decanter of boiled water covered with a square of neatly starched cloth, weighted at the edges with glass beads. On the dining table he would spread out stamps on a newspaper and distribute turn by turn a stamp for each of us, picking up each stamp with meticulous care with a pair of tweezers. I still have some of the stamps he gave us.

Padre Elliot was always neatly dressed and his clerical collar immaculate. He was tall, thin, with a smooth shiny bald dome, bespectacled with clear merry eyes, twinkling with laughter, a man of God at peace with God, his vocation in life discovered, his mission fulfilled. Years later, when I saw the British actor Wilfrid Hyde-White acting as a missionary and running through exotic South Sea streets, twirling his umbrella against the tropical noonday showers, I was instantly reminded of Padre Elliot. But Hyde-White had a somewhat frivolous, sinister, and mischievous air about him; our padre was never frivolous, sinister, or mischievous.

At weekends, if the weather was good, Padre Elliot would take us for long walks, wearing a short-sleeved cricket pullover and carrying a walking stick. Some evenings he visited us in our dormitories and, perching himself on a cupboard to get close to the wall light, would read to us delightful tales: Rudyard Kipling's *Just So Stories* and *The Jungle Book* and a host of other authors. In case there was a power outage, Padre carried a long torch. And when the stories were ended, he would come to each bed and had a cheerful word for us all.

We had two baths a week at Victoria School, the little boys being scrubbed by Indian bearers with Lifebuoy soap, the bearers having such nicknames as "Cock-eye," "Handsome," and so on. In the mornings, the same bearers shined our shoes with Cobra, Cherry Blossom, and Kiwi shoe polish and made our beds, arranging the counterpanes neatly.

In our school, we had all shades of skin color, from coal black to Nordic white. The majority of the boys were Anglo-Indians, though one wouldn't think so by looking at some of them, who had blue eyes and blonde hair.

*Author on horse, en route from Tibet to India (1941).*
*Courtesy of the author*

Anglo-Indians, almost without exception, identified themselves with the British and thought of Britain as "home." The history of the British in India and European colonialism were written in their names: Clark, Howe, Macdonald, O'Leary, Riordan, D'Cruz, Beaupert, Dubois. I, too, owed my presence in Victoria School to the British and especially to Sir Francis Younghusband.

The Anglo-Indian teacher thought of himself as British. He poured scorn on the Indians with their *Babu* English, saying "Proceeding to my residence" instead of "Going home" and so forth. He flicked pieces of chalk at any boy whose attention was diverted elsewhere. One day he caught me looking, during class, at a photograph I had. He came up to me and took the photograph from my hand, peered at it, read the caption at the back written in stilted English ("Myself at Tibet, 1941"), and then, with a supercilious look, handed the photograph gingerly back to me, holding it in his fingertips as if it was a repulsive worm. I was particularly fond of that picture, for it brought back memories of Tibet. It was taken by my father. I was riding a horse, wet with sweat, and I was wearing heavy, fleece-lined Tibetan clothes and a *maksha* (soldier's hat) with fur-lined earflaps. The horse carried huge saddlebags, and I wore thick, dark, snow-blindness-preventing goggles. I remembered that wild gallop across the plains with the main cavalcade far away traveling at a leisurely pace with my father in their midst. Now I was at an *Enji* school at the mercy of this teacher who could inflict any number of lines he fancied, and, robot-like, I had to jump to every command.

The magic enchanting world of the cinema compensated for much. When I first came to the school, there was no cinema. We had to go dawn to the town of Kurseong, almost 1,600 feet below us, to the only cinema hall there, the "Plaza"; walking back to school after a show was exhausting, but this did not deter us from seeing every film to which we were allowed: Sir Richard Attenborough's debut performance at the age of nineteen as a cockney sailor in Noel Coward's *In Which We Serve*; *Drums Along the Mohawk*, with Henry Fonda and Claudette Colbert; Mickey Rooney and Spencer Tracy in *Boys' Town*; Nelson Eddy and Jeanette Macdonald in *I Married an Angel*; and Charles Laughton and Clark Gable in *Mutiny on the Bounty*. Each show was preceded by Pathe News and British Gaumont News ("Presenting the world to the world"), as well as Donald Duck and Mickey Mouse. At the end of the show, all of us stood up as they played "God Save the King" with a smiling King George VI waving at us from Windsor Castle.

If you did not feel well, you climbed up the stairs leading to a dormitory, and then an English nurse would be there on the landing, in charge of her improvised dispensary. She stood behind an array of mixtures, a Juno-esque figure, with a starched uniform, sleeves rolled up displaying her sturdy forearms, her skin as white as snow. She asked you what the matter was, and if you had any "tummy" complaints, she dispensed a good "opening" dose of Mag sulph. If you complained of a fever, out would come a thermometer, and she inserted it in your mouth, and it instantly brought back memories of my father with his clinical thermometer in Yatung and his anxious face as he peered at the reading. If you were really ill, you were packed off to the school infirmary, which was about a mile or less away, and a report was dispatched to your parents.

A school year lasted for nine months, and then one went home for the winter vacation, most of the boys traveling to Calcutta in specially booked trains with the school monogram strapped to the front of the engine.

No more Latin, no more French
No more sitting on the hard old bench
Two more weeks and where shall we be?
Out of the gates of misery.

Before the year ended, there was the school concert (scenes from Shakespeare's *Julius Caesar* were favorites), the school fete, and then Speech Day. At the fete, I enjoyed buying magazines, especially *Lilliput* and *Victory*, which were for the Allied armed forces in India. I still remember one verse in *Lilliput* interspersed with luscious pictures of the pinup girls, Betty Grable, Rita Hayworth, Lana Turner, and Esther Williams:

Jack and Bill went up the hill
Carrying a two-inch mortar
Jack got the Japs
But Bill got the bhisti's [water carrier's] daughter.

On Speech Day the guest of honor was the governor of Bengal, the Muslim Fazul Huq—rare in those British and Anglo-Indian days to have an Indian dignitary giving away the prizes in an English school. I got the class Application Prize: Rudyard Kipling's *Jungle Book*. Padre Elliot borrowed it for a night. The final examinations took place and I passed, coming third in a class of thirty-two boys. It was with a light heart that I returned home to Yatung.

## NOTES

1. Thomas Hughes, *Tom Brown's School Days* (London: Macmillan and Co., 1868), 94.

2. *The Spectator: A Weekly Review of Politics, Literature, Theology and Art*, Vol. 100 (London: John Baker, 1908), 669.

3. Headmaster of Victoria Boys School Diary, 1905–1940.

4. John Keats, *Poems* (London: Blackie and Son, 1903), 131.

5. Disney, "Whistle While You Work," University of Pittsburgh, accessed on January 15, 2022, https://voices.pitt.edu/TeachersGuide/Unit7/WhistleWhileYouWork.htm.

# 11

~

# Back Home to Tibet

In Gangtok, I found that my sister Norzin was waiting for me. She was at a local school. The two of us traveled to Yatung together. She was wearing in her hair some ribbons I had bought for her from Kurseong

*Left to right: Gendun (author's friend), holding a kite; author; Sangay (friend); Tsewang Norbu (author's younger brother); Chimie la (daughter of Rai Sahib Dr. Bo); Norden and Norzin (author's sisters). Taken during kite flying season in spring (Lhasa, Tibet, 1940). Courtesy of the author*

from my pocket money. It was a very pleasant journey, and we sang most of the way. I sang for her "The British Grenadiers" ("Sing tow-row-row-row-row/For the British Grenadiers").[1]

In Yatung, my father was living at our old house close to the British Residency. My mother and my grandmother were also there, and I was very happy to see them again. My father was very pleased to hear me speak English so fluently, and in just nine months. I had bought for him a tin of Gold Flakes cigarettes as a present, for in Tibet it is customary to give each other presents when meeting again after a long separation. Then he asked me to sing for him an English song while my mother and grandmother became the attentive audience. I sang "Hearts of Oak" ("Come cheer up my lads, 'tis to glory we steer . . . for who are so free as the sons of the waves?").[2] Even Mrs. Heywood and Padre Elliot would have beamed with pleasure and appreciation. I did not know then how "the sons of the waves" were waging a grim life-and-death struggle against U-boats in the icy North Atlantic depths and Churchill giving his "We shall fight on the beaches" speech.[3]

One evening my father took me to the residency to meet a British gentleman and his wife. We sat close to the fireplace and chatted away, and my father appeared pleased with my social ease and good manners (British) learned at Victoria (the hard way with many "licks" with the hockey stick). I didn't tell him about the harsh discipline and the sadistic monitors supervising us as we knelt bare-kneed on iron bedsteads, our eyes heavy with sleep. That would be sneaking. Each year I heard the discipline became less harsh, and eventually, in Standard Nine, we, too, would be prefects, and then nobody would boss us.

The English lady, young, smiling, and charming, appeared amused when I told her that dictation was my favorite subject. I never came to know who the British couple were. Later they sent me a Frog model airplane, a Battle of Britain Spitfire that I took with me back to school.

One event that went unheralded and unnoticed that winter in Yatung was the Japanese attack on Pearl Harbor on December 7, 1941. The United States of America was now in the war on the side of the British, and this news pleased us Tibetans. My mother and several ladies whose husbands were on the staff of the British Trade Agency in Yatung were knitting long groin-length stockings with thick Tibetan wool. I was told that this was voluntary work and that the stockings were going to be donated to the Royal Air Force to be used by pilots. I don't know whether they ever received them.

That winter in Yatung, I began to take a precocious interest in the Tibetan religion, joining my grandmother at her prayers, holding her rosary, and telling the beads. A Tibetan rosary has 108 beads, and one tells them in a clockwise direction. The whole aim of the Tibetan religion as practiced then was to acquire merit in order to obtain a higher rebirth, which was done through prayers, pilgrimages, giving of alms, good deeds, telling of beads, spinning the *mani* (prayer wheel), lighting oil lamps, prostrations, and not committing sins, the worst sin being the deliberate killing of anything living. Tibetans talked all the time of *tshe ngönma, tse di, tse chima* (past, present, and future lives). *Dikpa* (sin) was to be avoided at all costs, or else when one came to be judged by *Shinje*, the God of Judgment, there would be too many black pebbles that would outweigh the white pebbles of good.

1 saw my mother and grandmother practice the Tibetan religion, and it probably was in no way different from the way the religion was practiced in other homes throughout the whole of Tibet. Superstition, the mechanical saying of prayers, belief in omens, avoidance of sin, and every moment spent acquiring merit for a higher rebirth were the hallmarks of this religion. Many Tibetologists and scholars of Tibetan religion, especially Europeans, dismiss this as "folk religion," but that was the way it was actually practiced. Thousands of monks reading the vast Tibetan religious texts—the 108 volumes of the *Kangyur* (translated commandments of the Buddha) and the 220 volumes of the *Tengyur* (commentaries and texts on dialectics, logic, medicine, metaphysics, etc.)—did not comprehend what they were reading. The mere reading of these volumes, usually done in a rapid cursory way, was an act of merit, and that sufficed. It was not necessary to understand what one was reading. Very few did. There were monks who could read but not write; so much of their lives were spent in memorizing texts.

At present, Tibetan Buddhism has had a resurgence in the world outside Tibet, with Buddhist centers scattered all over the world in San Francisco, Los Angeles, Hawaii, Taiwan, Singapore, and many parts of Europe, but the Buddhism taught and practiced in these centers, with their emphasis on meditation, ontology, mysticism, and metaphysics, is only one tiny aspect of the living Tibetan Buddhism practiced by the people of Tibet. The Tibetan Buddhism preached in the United States, Europe, and the Far East at slick modern centers with answer telephones, word processors, glossy brochures, programs, and courses is an esoteric arcane form of the religion comprehended and practiced by very few of the clergy in Tibet.

Grandmother led me through the prayers, though with some disapproval. She said it was good to be religious, but young boys should not take it seriously. That was for later life. Boys should be their age and go out to play and have fun, get up to pranks and roam the surrounding mountainside. She mumbled something about "*tsela barchay yong*" (some harm will befall you).

One night I could not go to sleep because of a splitting headache. There was a skylight above my bed, and I could see outside a flurry of snow. I stared at our altar with the incense sticks and the seven silver bowls empty and piled in a neat row (in the morning mother would fill them with water as an offering for the day, but in the evening it was the custom to empty them); the light from the oil lamps flickered on the faces of the idols in their glass-fronted chambers: Ugyen Rinpoche, or Padmasambhava, the patron saint of the Nyingmapa (Old School), who had consecrated Tibet's first monastery at Samye in the eighth century AD; Jetsun Dolma, or the goddess Tara, the most revered of female deities and guardian of travelers; Jampelyang, or Manjushri, the Bodhisattva of Wisdom; Tsepagme, the Buddha of Boundless Life (my own guardian Buddha, as Gendün my friend in Lhasa had told me and taught me the special prayer to him). All were asleep in the room, but I was restless and tossed and turned.

In the morning, I watched my mother make the water offerings, light the incense sticks, and prostrate many times in front of our family altar while she chanted prayers to the goddess Dolma, for this was her favorite prayer, which she never failed to say several times in a day. I told her about my headache. I also had a severe pain in my right elbow. My father was upset, took my temperature, laid his palm across my forehead, and then asked what my main complaints were. In the whole of Yatung, there was only one ill-qualified Indian doctor. My father didn't want to consult him yet. I told my father about my headache and also a stomachache that had started in the morning. He brought some Maclean's stomach powder and said I would be instantly cured with that. I drank the prescribed dose but brought it all up.

Each day I became worse. My grandmother now revealed to my mother my obsessive and precocious interest in religious matters lately, which meant that I was going to die. They blamed my father for sending me to an English school, saying that such schools were not meant for Tibetans, as we came into contact with *Chö chiba* (outer non-Buddhist religions). My father dismissed all this talk as so much superstitious nonsense.

An astrologer was consulted, and he said that my illness was due to the Tsan demon that dwelled behind our house, the demon I was told about long ago when I had come across the *tsa-tsas* images near the *chödten*. This demon must be appropriately propitiated, and a monk was summoned to carry out the rites. He constructed a dough image of the Tsan—fierce, vindictive, red faced, fanged—and placed in front of it a bamboo framework and on it wound strips of wool of different colors in a symmetrical geometrical pattern to catch the spirit of the Tsan. Dough balls were rubbed on my body. I had to spit on them, pull out some hair from my scalp, and embed them in the dough balls, and the monk, shouting incantations and screaming magic formulae, hurled them into the night together with the Tsan image at the junction of three paths.

Seeing that I was still not improving, the monks from the Dungkar monastery, where my cousin Thubten was a monk, were called. The head of the monastery, Geshe Rinpoche, had given me my name when I had arrived in Yatung in 1931. He had died a few years previously, and his new incarnation had not yet been discovered. The books of the *Kangyur* were brought, all 108 volumes, and monks intoned from them the whole day. They also said prayers meant especially for sick children called "*Chi-wai bumchung*," as well as "Tsela" (for a long life). The house resounded to the beating of drums, the blowing of the *gyaling* trumpets, the deep sonorous blare of the giant *dongyer* horns, the clash of cymbals, the staccato beat of little handheld drums, the melancholy moaning of the conches, and the eerie blare of human thigh-bone trumpets. The chanting of the monks was unceasing the whole day, and I could hardly sleep.

My mother was told to buy a sheep, as I was born in the Iron-sheep year, and then donate it to the monastery, where the animal would be kept as pet. Such animals, called *tsethar* (life granted), had parts of their fleece dyed red and were forbidden to be slaughtered—hence their name. A boy from a very poor family of the same birth-year as myself was found. A complete set of my clothes was given to him as well as some money, and he was sent away from the house after undergoing a rite by which my disease was transferred to him as a scapegoat.

Despite all these elaborate rituals, I continued to deteriorate. My father, in agonized despair, quarreled with my mother and told her to send away all the monks, for they were no good. He said that there was no God or gods, and that religion was a sham, for no deity could be condoned for making a boy suffer so much. The presence of evil gave the lie to the existence of any omnipotent benign deity. In Tibet, there is a saying, surprising in a race imbued with religion: "When man despairs, he resorts to the gods. When the gods despair, they resort to lies." My grandmother, more serene, more sage-like in her wisdom, comforted and consoled my father and told him not to say such things. The workings of the universe were due to the irresistible spontaneous force of *le gyudre* (action-link-fruit, or *karma*, or the law of cause and effect), and nothing could oppose its inexorable course except the religious life, the acquiring of merit and the avoidance of sin. Even if I died, it could not he helped, for death was something that came to us sooner or later; some died in their mother's wombs and others when they were over a hundred. Who could tell how long each of us would live? And even if I died, there were three other children, for some families were childless.

My father was inconsolable. He looked up medical textbooks and family health volumes full of glossy photographs of the human anatomy. He tried every British remedy that he possessed in his medicine cupboard. Finally, he sent for the Indian doctor. He was a short, round-faced, spectacled man. He was kindly, felt my abdomen, drummed it with his fingertips, put a stethoscope on my chest, and appeared perplexed. He said there was too much gas in my abdomen. "Why is the boy passing so little urine and his face swelling up?" asked my father. He examined me again, went back to the hospital to fetch a rubber urethral catheter, and catheterized me. I screamed with pain, but there was no urine, for empty bladders do not produce urine.

My father began to worry about the lack of urine. I was now getting a little confused and delirious at times, and I found myself muttering nonsense. I was also hiccupping. One night I was very ill. My mother sat next to my bed the whole night, holding my hand. I asked her to tell me a story, and she did. It was about three ants who tried to climb up the Gampa La (the pass now familiar to my readers), near Chushül on the way to Lhasa. The ants were laughed at because it was such an ambitious, difficult task, but they tried and tried, and eventually they succeeded—a Tibetan Robert Bruce and the spider story. Later she told me that she had a foreboding that this was to be my last night and that I would die the next day. I asked my mother to say the English word "Bible," and she did so. I don't know why I did that. I wasn't a Christian, and at school I did not attend church. It just seemed to come out of me; perhaps I was trying to get the Christian God on our side as well. Soon I fell into a dreamless sleep, and when I woke up, my mother was still at my side.

The next day I was very ill. My father decided that there was only one recourse, and that was to take me to Gangtok, four days away, with the 14,140-foot Nathö La pass to cross in the winter. In Gangtok, there was a hospital, diagnostic and treatment facilities, and many doctors. Since I was too ill to ride, a box was made for me to be carried in and porters hired for the next day. I could see my mother busy in the house preparing to travel to Gangtok. I had not passed urine for nearly three days.

Grandmother came to see me, and I made a dramatic speech about this life ending for me and that we would all meet again in *tse shume* (the next life). She dismissed my words and told me not to talk of such things. I would be all right in Gangtok. Toward the evening, Ah Migmar (Brother Tuesday), the compounder of the local hospital whose boss was the catheterizing doctor, came with a bottle containing some pills. They were "De Witts" pills, and he said that they helped the kidneys to function, and he had got them from Babu Injung, the shopkeeper whose shop was our favorite during Losar, the shop with the posters of the circus. My father told me to swallow some at bedtime. That night I had a very peaceful sleep. I felt calm, serene, euphoric. Everything was quiet, and time seemed to stand still. I wondered whether I was approaching death, for Tibetans say that just before dying there is a period of great peace, calm, and serenity and a vision of a silent all-encompassing light.

The next morning, the porters arrived, the box in which I was to be carried was made ready, and we prepared to set off for Chumbithang, the first stage on the road to Gangtok. Suddenly I had an urge to urinate, and Ah Mingma came running. He brought a urinal and then carried it away in triumph to show to my parents. I asked for the urinal again. I just couldn't stop. This was diuresis, or the excess secretion of urine by the kidneys. My parents were overjoyed, for they felt that once my kidneys started to function, I would recover. The urine was a beautiful blue in color. I think "De Witts" pills contained methylene blue, which is a mild diuretic. The porters were given gifts and dismissed, and Ah Mingma was congratulated.

From that day I began to recover, and each day I became stronger, although it was weeks before I could walk again. My father gave me a Laurel and Hardy comic book to read. An *Ache Lhamo* show was put on at the British Residency, and I was carried on somebody's back to see the show. All my father's friends remarked on the miraculous cure of his son. I had been snatched from the jaws of death and was a *shilog*, one who has returned from the dead.

Despite my illness and my grandmother's objections, my father decided to send me back to Victoria School. He came to see me off at Chumbithang, and I can remember spending the night at the dak bungalow there very clearly. Long ago, in 1933, my father had gone hunting in Chumbithang with Captain Rerrie of the Marathas and Dr. Tennant of the Indian Medical Service.

The next morning, I rode away up toward the Nathö La pass, my father touchingly holding my saddle and walking at my side until it was time for parting. He said that I must not come to Yatung on my next holiday in case of another illness. He had been through a terrible nightmare. It would be preferable for me to stay in Gangtok with my grand-uncle Tashi Tsering during the next winter vacation. The day was sunny, but there was a great deal of melting snow on the slushy road.

## NOTES

1. "The British Grenadiers," Genius, accessed on January 15, 2022, https://genius.com/Traditional-the-british-grenadiers-annotated.

2. William Boyce, "Hearts of Oak," Exouth Shanty Men, accessed January 15, 2022, https://www.exmouthshantymen.com/songbook.php?id=169.

3. Winston Churchill, *The Speeches of Winston Churchill*, ed. David Cannadine (London: Penguin, 1990), 165.

# 12

~

# Further Metamorphosis and Another Winter in Yatung

From Gangtok, I traveled with my servant Trasi, who had once been on the estate of a nobleman in Lhasa but had now worked for my parents for some years. In Lhasa, he used to be sent *trenma tsamba* (roasted milled pea flour) from his village, and I used to exchange my barley flour with his *trenma tsamba*, as I preferred it. A friend of his used to let me smoke from a long-stemmed Tibetan pipe with a tiny metal bowl, and the Tibetan tobacco had a delicious aroma. That wasn't the first time I had smoked in my life. Long ago, when I spent some days at the Dung-kar monastery in Yatung, I was forced to smoke a cigarette to relieve a severe toothache.

Trasi was a tough, gnarled man with pigtails and earrings, with jaws like a tiger's from constantly chewing stony-hard *chura* (dry Tibetan cheese). Tibetans chew *chura* as addictively as Americans do their chewing gum. We traveled by the Gangtok mail bus to Geille Khola, near the Tista River below Kalimpong. A small narrow-gauge train, which does not exist anymore, took us to Siliguri in the Indian plains. It was quite a rush to buy tickets at Geille Khola as the train was about to depart. I bought Trasi a third-class ticket and for myself second class. The second-class compartments were full of British troops returning to Siliguri after their leave in Kalimpong. In those days, the cool, pleasant hill stations of Kalimpong, Kurseong, and Darjeeling were like the "rest and recreation" stations in Thailand for the American troops during the Vietnam War. The British soldiers and officers told me that I couldn't get into their compartments, as they were packed, and some, they declared, were part of the "hospital train." But I had to catch that train. I forced my way in, placed my "hold all" on the carriage floor and sat on it with my attaché case close at my side. The train gave a shrill whistle and left.

I watched the sun set over the Kalimpong mountains and felt very homesick. I was alone once more, with Trasi in another compartment. He would have found himself a place even if he had to sit on another passenger. In my attaché case, packed with toothbrushes and toothpaste tubes to last a year, was also a tin full to the brim with Indian four annas coins (less than one U.S. cent at present exchange rates), but in those days each coin would buy me my tuck for the day from the Indian *roti-wallahs* (breadmen), who sold confectionery from their steel trunks, which they carried perched on their turbaned heads (patties, cream rolls, and queen cakes). I also carried dried *chura* bits; they were popular among the British boys, who called them "yak's milk"—a few lumps could be exchanged for a tin of Tasmanian jam, a bottle of tomato sauce, or a tin of Argentinian corned beef. Despite the consolation offered by the hidden wealth inside my attaché case with my name painted on it, I was very sad. I thought of home and of my brother and two sisters.

Siliguri was hot, dusty, crowded, noisy, and full of British soldiers and airmen, for in those days there was the war on the Burma front, and the Japanese were at the very gates of India. China was entirely cut off except for American airplanes lifting supplies from Assam to Kunming, in the Yunnan province of China, over the formidable Himalayan Hump. The battles of Imphal and Kohima were about to be fought, and Siliguri was an important railway junction for trains that traveled toward Assam, Imphal, and Kohima.

Hundreds of coolies—brown, lithe, sweating, and carrying enormous loads on their heads—jostled with British soldiers and civilians, and there was absolute pandemonium. I hurried with Trasi to the second-class waiting room, deposited my luggage there, reserved a corner for ourselves, and told Trasi to wait while I went off to buy tickets for the next day's train journey that would take us to Kurseong.

Outside the heat, noise, and crowds overwhelmed me. I had come down that day from Gangtok, which was 6,000 feet high, and a week before that I had been in Yatung, almost 10,000 feet in altitude, cold, peaceful, and with snows on the surrounding mountainsides. I went past the drink stalls selling lemonade bottles with marble stoppers, past the A.H. Wheeler and Co. railway book stalls, with their erotic magazines and novels, *Lilliput* and *Victory* army magazines, inside which I knew I would find pictures of Rita Hayworth and Betty Grable in skimpy titillating costumes. These bookstalls used to sell Jean-Paul Sartre's novels, advertising them as "hot" novels. At the ticket window, the Bengali railway clerk was amused when I asked him for one second-class ticket for myself and "a third-class for my servant."

Having bought the tickets, I leisurely made my way back to the second-class waiting room. In those days, one never entered a first-class waiting room, for that was only meant for the British *Sahibs* and their *Memsahibs*. One also kept clear of the dining room for first-class passengers. I did, however, manage to peep in. The year 1947 wasn't very far away, and then the two-hundred-year British Raj would vanish, but just then the Raj held full sway. The Second World War was being waged on many fronts, and now the United States of America had also become a belligerent. I used to follow the war with great interest, especially the Russian front, and place names like Orel, Kharkov, and Rostov were quite familiar to me. My father used to relate how the Germans had come so close to Moscow that they could actually see the domes of the Kremlin with their binoculars, and then they had been driven back by camouflaged quilted Russian troops, and the Germans had frozen to death because Hitler had not supplied them with winter uniforms. The first-class dining room customers, *Sahibs* and *Memsahibs*, sat under the spinning *punkhas* (fans), as if they didn't have a care in the world, as if they weren't aware of the Japanese threatening India and trainloads of troops, just outside, moving to the fronts. They sipped their drinks nonchalantly served by Indian Jeeves, wearing gold-bordered turbans, cummerbunds, and immaculate white gloves, and ate their soup delicately, with the soup spoons turned away from them (as we were taught in school by the Anglo-Indian dining room matron), conversing and laughing, the women distantly alluring and beautiful. The pre-war British Raj of gracious living and unhurried elegant conversations still lingered in that dining room amid the bustle of war.

There were the RAF airmen in their smart uniforms having their shoes brushed and their brass buttons polished—pilots, navigators, and observers (half a wing with the letter "O")—as well as Scots soldiers with patterned caps or berets with a pompom, but one seldom saw any sailors. I remember on one occasion traveling with a British officer from Kurseong to Siliguri by train, and we had a long chat about various topics, and he asked me where I had learned to speak English. He had been on leave in Darjeeling and was traveling to Calcutta to join his unit. He was young and pleasant, and I hope he survived the war, for the fiercest battles were then yet to come.

The next day, Trasi and I reached Kurseong and, after spending the night, walked up the 1,400-foot slope to my school. A Tibetan woman coolie carried my luggage, the steel trunk, the "hold all" on top and my attaché case in her hand. She looked older and tougher than Trasi. There is a legend about a Darjeeling Tibetan woman who carried a grand piano two thousand feet up a mountain. She stopped now and then, heaving a sigh, and smoked a cigarette, which she rolled herself, refreshing herself and regaining strength, as I suppose Andean natives do when they chew coca leaves.

When we reached Victoria School, many of my friends ran to greet me. "I say, is he your dad?" somebody asked, pointing at Trasi. "Go and grab a desk," said another. "Put on your hasp and latch. . . . Don't forget to sit next to me in the dining room," said a chum of mine. "I say, you do look thin!" And so life in Victoria School began again for me. Trasi told me to study hard, to behave well, to pass my examinations, and to look after my health, as I had been so ill in the winter in Yatung. He took out some *chura* pieces from his pocket and gave them to me. He began to walk down to the Kurseong railway station and turned around to look at me as he left. He was grinning at me, showing me his perfect teeth. His jaws, I knew, could crush the hardest walnuts in Lhasa when I wanted to eat some.

We learned about the boy who stood on the burning deck; the wreck of the schooner *Hesperus* ("Blue were her eyes as the fairy flax. . . . That ope in the month of May"); and young Lochinvar, who had come out of the west.[1] There were the Tudors and a play to read about Abraham Lincoln ("This is the wonder, always everywhere/Not that vast mutability, which is event,/The pits and pinnacles of change,/But man's desire and valiance that range/All circumstances, and come to port unspent") and about Dame Barbara Frietchie ("Shoot, if you must, this old grey head,/But spare your country's flag," she said).[2]

In the night, while the jackals howled weirdly in the background, boys in close-knit gangs walked about the top playground, singing and whistling, "Roll out the barrels," "Pack up your troubles in the old kit-bag and smile, smile, smile," "Coming in on a wing and a prayer," "This is the Army Mr. Jones . . . she had you worried but this is war, and she won't worry you any more,"[3] and some wicked George Formby songs. Little boys darted here and there, playing pranks on each other: there was the play of light and shade on the field, the Indian servants clearing up the crockery and cutlery in the dining hall, and the beginning of an exciting school weekend while outside, far away, there were battles being fought in Russia, China, Africa, the Pacific, and the jungles of Burma, and in the Indian plains Nehru, Gandhi, Patel, and Jinnah plotted and planned the dissolution of the British Raj.

I enjoyed boxing, but in those days we followed the Marquess of Queensberry's rules, the straight left and the right cross. No uppercuts or hooks were allowed. My first opponent was Boardman, a Scots boy, overgrown and slow on his feet. When he had been punished in the Victoria School style with the hockey stick (and in those days, India was the world champion in this game), he commented with amusement in his quaint accent, "I never 'ad a lick on my boom before." I was wiry and underweight. After my Yatung illness, I didn't grow for two years. I fancied myself closer to the "hank of steel," as George Bernard Shaw described Montgomery after he had won the battle of El Alamein and was sitting for a portrait by Augustus John.[4] It was a massacre at Glencoe, but on this occasion the perpetrator was a member of the race of Genghis Khan. "This isn't boxing," lamented Mr. Moore the referee, giving me the bout. After this Twiddy (no relation of Mrs. Marion Bloom), and it was a fixed match of pulled punches and feigned knockdowns, for Twiddy was a good friend of mine who cared little for pugilism. In the finals, I squared up to Brian Dozev, schoolboy exponent of the "floats like a butterfly and stings like a bee" Mohammad Ali style, and he certainly stung me to bits. He was declared "the most scientific boxer of the evening," and I felt quite humiliated, for Dozey had made me look like Desperate Dan battling wearing oversize boxing gloves.

The attractions of the Plaza cinema continued to beguile us: Eugene O'Neill's 1940 *The Long Voyage Home*, directed by John Ford, which had won an Oscar; *Major Barbara*, with Rex Harrison and the twenty-year-old Deborah Kerr; *So Ends Our Night*, based on Erich Maria Remarque's novel *Flotsam* about three people fleeing Nazi Germany in 1937. Jeanette Macdonald and Nelson Eddy were unforgettable, and it was a thrilling moment for me in 1992 at Mann's Chinese Theatre in Los Angeles to see her hand- and footprints on the cement. Although we were an English school and most of my school years were spent during the British Raj, the United States of America also influenced our outlook and culture. We saw a number of American servicemen in the streets of Darjeeling, with their friendly ways and openheartedness. Once a U.S. soldier visited our school and showed us his torn earlobe, which he said was from a bullet he had received in North Africa. We knew everything about the U.S. Marines, whom we admired greatly, and Merrill's Marauders, who captured Myitkyina in Burma. We were familiar with the bloody fierce battles of Tarawa, Iwo Jima, and MacArthur's "I shall return" promise.[5]

I remember the American "C" and "K" rations of the soldiers, which even provided some sheets of toilet paper. And there was *Yank* magazine, full of war pictures and the cartoons of Ernie Pyle. There was Wrigley's chewing gum, Butterfinger, Babe Ruth, and Hershey chocolates. Surreptitiously, we smoked Camel, Chesterfield, and Lucky Strike cigarettes. On occasion we saw some American Volunteer Group (AVG) pilots wearing leather jackets, on the back of which were printed American and Chinese Kuomintang flags and a notice in Chinese. They could have very well have belonged to Chennault's "Flying Tigers" group. Hollywood and its films influenced us immensely without our becoming aware of it. Clark Gable, James Cagney, George Raft, John Wayne, and Humphrey Bogart were our heroes. We sang the songs of Bing Crosby, Frank Sinatra, and

Perry Como. In the glossy film magazines, which we read from cover to cover, were the photographs of all our film heroes and heroines.

We read Zane Grey and followed the exploits of Perry Mason. It was fashionable to use American slang and expressions such as "hit the hay." And there was jitterbug dancing and American songs: "Lay That Pistol Down, Babe," "You Are My Sunshine," "Drinking Rum and Coca-Cola," "Johnny Zero" ("The Yanks they call him Johnny Zero, Johnny's got a Zero today!"), and the lilting "Going to Take a Sentimental Journey."

In 1943 came the Bengal famine, in which more than a million people died, and the intensification of the war everywhere. The number of bread slices that we received at each meal was cut down. We were told to be careful of food and paper and not to be wasteful. "Paper boats make battleships," wrote Mrs. Grace Clark, the art mistress, and she pinned this statement on the notice board. Mr. T. D. Nugent, the headmaster who took over from Hessing, red faced and forbidding, waggling a finger, addressed the school in the dining room: "Any boys caught spreading rumors will be severely punished."

We had boys who were refugees from Burma, who had harrowing tales to tell of arduous treks through the malaria-infested Hukawng valley, escaping from the Japanese. British troops holidaying in Kurseong were entertained to tea by volunteer groups organized among the school staff. Trains left from Kurseong railway station packed with fresh Gurkha recruits waving white scarves to us and shouting *"Basa-hail! Basa-hail!"* (Good-bye!). The school cadets of the North Bengal Mounted Rifles practiced bayonet drill and carried out intricate, realistic battle maneuvers, and many joined the armed forces as soon as they finished school.

Our drill instructor was a Scots serjeant, Jock Davis (odd name for a Scotsman) of the Black Watch, which, he reminded us, was the 42 Royal Highland Regiment. He taught us how to stand at attention, chin in, chest out, with the tips of the turned-down thumbs in line with the creases of our shorts. He had difficulty pronouncing my name at rollcall. We felt proud of ourselves, for we belonged to the same tradition that had inspired the charge of the Scots Greys at Waterloo and the Light Brigade at Balaclava. Davis devised some kind of an Eton Wall Game in which boys piled on top of each other and then, oblivious to the back-breaking strain, had to sway from side to side in conga fashion chanting in unison something that sounded like "Horky-dock, horky-dock, one two three." Serjeant Jock Davis's oft-repeated command to all boys was "Hands out of your pockets!"

During the winter of 1944, I met Sir Basil Gould in Gangtok, I think it was during Christmas. We were all invited to the British Residency and had dinner with him. Sir Basil, I noticed, kept on teasing a young Sikkimese Gurkha soldier. Later I learned that he was Ganju Lama, and in

*British Trade Agency Residence (Yatung, 1933). Photo by author's father, Rai Sahib Pemba Tsering*

years to come I became good friends with him, and he was a patient of mine. At Victoria School, listening to the BBC news every evening, I heard that a Victoria Cross had been won by a Gurkha from Sikkim. Ganju (the name is a British version of a Sikkimese name) Lama was a true Sikkimese, who are ethnically closely related to the Tibetans. He had been recruited in Jalapahar, Darjeeling, by Lieutenant-Colonel A. V. M. Mercer (who, as a retired British Gurkha officer and a patient of mine, gave me this account), who told me that at first,he had been reluctant to recruit Ganju into the Gurkhas, as the Sikkimese did not fall into the martial races sought by the British.

He became Rifleman Ganju Lama, No.78763 of the "B" company, 1/7 Gurkha Rifles, who on June 12, 1944, using a PIAT anti-tank gun on the eastern front close to Burma, knocked out several Japanese tanks and had been severely wounded. For his exploits, he was awarded the Victoria Cross. Ganju Lama told me of "Ten Kaal ayo bhaney marcha" (If your time has come, you'll die) and that in his days the motto of his Gurkhas was "Maarchu kyi marchu" (Kill or be killed). During the Second World War, a cousin of mine, Lama Thubten's brother, was in the first battalion of the Tenth Gurkha Rifles, and a granduncle, an officer, served in the same battalion. He was Lhakpa Tsering Lama, and I saw a photograph of him taken with Field-Marshal Claude Auchinleck of the British Army. The caption read, "A typical Gurkha officer." He had served in the First World War in what was then Mesopotamia (Iraq nowadays) and in the Second World War saw active service in Burma against the Japanese. He told me how once he had been thrown sky high by an exploding shell but had landed unharmed.

It was in the winter of 1944–1945 that we visited Yatung again. My sister Norzin was going to an "English" school in Kalimpong, St. Joseph's Convent, run by the Sisters of Saint Joseph of Cluny, mostly British and Irish nuns. Her school motto was *"Cor unum et anima una"* (One Heart and One Soul), and the school badge read, *"Cum beato Joseph in cordibus Jesu et Marie."* There were now many Tibetan children, boys and girls, mostly the sons and daughters of Lhasa aristocrats, who were going to schools in Darjeeling, Kurseong, and Kalimpong, which were *Enji* schools like Victoria School. My brother came with me to join Standard Two in 1945, and Norden also went to St. Joseph's Convent in 1948. There was now no novelty in going to an *Enji* school.

As soon as we had crossed the 14,140-foot Nathö La pass, we shouted *"Lha gyalo!"* (Victory to the Gods!), as is the custom whenever Tibetans cross a high mountain pass, and heaped stones on the cairns festooned with prayer flags. But now Norzin and I found it easier to talk to each other in English, and we sang the same songs that Bing Crosby and Frank Sinatra were singing, and she also thought Errol Flynn and Clark Gable were wonderful. The alien cultures and philosophies that the two of us were exposed to in the *Enji* schools were now overlapping, and we had much in common.

In Yatung, my father was now the British trade agent, but he did not live at the residency, for he had instead bought a house in the middle of the town. The house was like a Swiss chalet, and there was a large room on the first floor with glass windows that received the sun for most of the day and was very pleasant to stay in and read, especially when the afternoon dust storms occurred, shaking the rafters and the prayer flags on the rooftops and threatening to knock down the stones that secured the shingles. Wallpaper for the house was provided by old English newspapers gathered over many years, a feast for anybody having nothing to do: photographs of Ginger Rogers and a boyish Fred Astaire; a visit of a pre–World War II Balkan monarch to Britain; Hitler's stormtroopers goose-stepping.

In the storeroom, there was yak meat hanging, and outside the ground floor was neatly piled chopped wood for the winter fires. There was a toilet with a shaft down which one threw toilet paper and straw after use. There was the same altar with the same images that I recalled clearly from that night when I had been so ill in the house of the head clerk (*Burra Babu*). My father was no more a *Babu* but a *Burra Sahib*.

We visited the British Residency, and many hours were spent there looking inside every room. There was now a small library there, and I remember picking up a novel in English about Tibet; it was about a European being chased by giant mastiffs belonging to a monastery followed by all the monks. It made me laugh, because obviously it was all made up and bore no resemblance to anything Tibetan that I had experienced or heard about. And we regaled all our Yatung friends with stories from the movies and Errol Flynn's exploits and the sinister Peter Lorre and Sidney Greenstreet duo, which held them all spellbound, and soon the demands for "Ellol-finn" stories were unceasing. We put on our school clothes (blazers emblazoned with badges) and our school caps and showed off to our friends in their Tibetan homespun. All the Yatung boys and girls, with their ruddy faces and wind-blown hair, said how lucky we were to be able to go to English schools, dress in such glamorous clothes, speak English with such fluency, and see so many "Ellol-finn" movies.

I used to wait eagerly for the mule trains carrying mail to arrive, so that I could read all the magazines that my father received. Tibet was still the same: no electricity, no sanitation or plumbing, no cars, a few telephones that had to be hand cranked and blown into incessantly to make conversation audible (and this also only for official use). The mule trains made the four-day journey from Gangtok to Yatung in two days—big, handsome mules with bells around their necks—and the muleteers, tough Tibetan employees of the British Raj, carrying their six-celled torches and driving their mules through snow and storms wearing balaclava caps or Tibetan fur hats and thick snow goggles.

One day, we put on a concert to entertain my grandmother. We sang many of our school songs and did some jitterbug dancing. She preferred the "Song of the Volga Boatman" to "Pistol Packin' Mama." Perhaps the former stirred some ancient memories in her Tartar blood.

Mr. Mingma, my old teacher, visited us, and he said that he was pleased to see his old students doing so well. He said that our English put him to shame. Seeing his smiling face as he sipped his tea, I could not help thinking of those early days in Yatung, when I had learned the Hindi alphabet by forming the letters with pebbles, and how he used to make the iron filings "march" with a magnet.

Sometimes we sat outside in the sun, with the snow melting on the roofs, and our grandmother told us once more those stories of Kham that we so enjoyed hearing. But we smiled when she talked of the tortoise holding the universe on its back and of *Shinje*, the God of Judgment, weighing the black and white pebbles and deciding your fate when you died. The Christian version of death and the afterlife was so different, and the Muslims taught one thing and the Hindus another, so who was right? Or were they all wrong? Or perhaps each only glimpsed a part of the whole.

Some events had taken place in Tibet while we had been away at school. In 1942, Lieutenant-Colonel Ilia Tolstoy and Captain Brooke Dolan, U.S. Army officers of the Office of Strategic Services, had come to Tibet and had become the first and second Americans ever to have met a

Dalai Lama in Lhasa. They brought gifts and an autographed photograph from President Franklin Roosevelt. Because of Japanese encirclement, China, under Generalissimo Chiang Kai-shek of the Kuomintang party, was completely cut off from the rest of the world except by air over the "Hump" from India. How long this state of affairs would last, nobody could foretell, but the country's condition was critical, and a total collapse could not be ruled out. The U.S. government believed that a land route from India through Tibet to China was feasible, and it was to explore this possibility that the two men from the OSS had come to Tibet. Nothing concrete came out of the venture, and Tibet continued to maintain her policy of isolation and neutrality. In fact, the first time in history that a U.S. president met a Dalai Lama was many years later, in 1991, when President George Bush received the fourteenth Dalai Lama in the United States.

The "Hump," the name given by American fliers to the section of the eastern Himalayas over which they had to cross on their extremely hazardous journeys to China, was also responsible for the first airplane ever to fly over Lhasa. In November 1943, a U.S. four-engine cargo plane, with a crew of five, piloted by Lieutenant Robert E. Crozier of Texas, while returning from Kunming in China to Jorhat in northeastern India, developed engine trouble, had to encircle Lhasa, and then crashed at Samye, fifty miles to the southeast of Lhasa, the crew managing to bail out. Samye has the first monastery ever built in Tibet, by the Indian saint mystic-magician Ugyen Rinpoche, or Padmasambhava, in the eighth century AD. From Samye, the crew were taken to the Dekyi Lingkha in Lhasa and were cared for by the British Mission. I hear Chinese Nationalists in the city also helped them. From Lhasa, they traveled to India, leaving that city on December 19, 1943. I have a photograph of the American fliers taken with my parents at that time outside the Yatung British Residency. Later Crozier wrote a book about the whole incident called *Jump to the Land of God*.

Soon it was time to return to school. We had bought permanent marking ink in Gangtok (because at that time I don't think you could have bought a single bottle of permanent marking ink in the whole of "Outer Tibet"), and Norzin and I got down to the task of marking all our clothes with this indelible ink. There was only one man in Yatung who could tailor in the Western style, and he wasn't exactly from Saville Row! My mother had a suit made for me of excellent Tibetan cloth of a natty checked pattern, but when I donned the suit that I had nurtured with secret hopes of making it my "Sunday Best" at Victoria School, I looked like a circus clown!

## NOTES

1. Felicia Dorothea Hemans, "Casabianca," in *Best Remembered Poems*, eds. Martin Gardner (New York: Dover, 1992), 45; Henry Wadsworth Longfellow, *Favorite Poems* (London: George Routledge and Sons, 1878), 44; Walter Scott, "Lochinvar," in *The Book of Scottish Ballads*, eds. Alexander Whitelaw (London: Blackie and Son, 1857), 66.

2. John Drinkwater, "Abraham Lincoln," in *The Collected Plays of John Drinkwater*, Vol. 2 (London: Sidgwick and Jackson, 1925), 55; John Greenleaf Whittier, "Barbara Frietchie," in *Poems of American Patriotism*, eds. J. Brander Matthews (New York: C. Scribner's Sons, 1882), 207.

3. Will Glahe, "Roll Out the Barrel," Songfacts, accessed on January 20, 2022, https://www.songfacts.com/facts/will-glahe/beer-barrel-polka-roll-out-the-barrel; Felix Powell, "Pack Up Your Troubles," University of Missouri–Kansas City, accessed January 20, 2022, https://dl.mospace.umsystem.edu/umkc/islandora/object/umkc%3A23228#page/1/mode/2up; Jimmy Mc Hugh, "Comin' in on a Wing and a Prayer," University of Missouri–Kansas City, accessed January 20, 2022, https://dl.mospace.umsystem.edu/umkc/islandora/object/umkc%3A21093#page/1/mode/2up; Irving Berlin, "This Is the Army Mr. Jones," Antiwar Songs, 2010, https://www.antiwarsongs.org/canzone.php?id=24313&lang=en.

4. Colin F. Baxter, comp., *Field Marshall Bernard Law Montgomery, 1887–1976* (London: Greenwood Press, 1999), 67.

5. Karen Harris, "'I Shall Return': General MacArthur's Promise," History Daily, accessed January 20, 2022, https://historydaily.org/i-shall-return-general-macarthurs-promise.

# 13

~

# Farewell, Tibet

Extracts from the diary of the headmaster of Victoria School:

24 August 1944: The school got a holiday to celebrate the liberation of Paris. [I remember our boys singing "La Marseillaise" in French.]

19 November 1945: I, Vernon Prins, took over charge from Mr. T. D. Nugent . . . quoting Arnold, I told the boys what I looked for here was "religious life, gentlemanly conduct and intellectual ability."

1945–1946 winter vacation: "Quis custodiet custodes?" I think it is very necessary to revive the system of inspection by the Headmaster . . . not in the spirit of carping criticism but that of guide, philosopher and friend.

3 March 1948: The partitioning of Bengal and the exodus from India of European and Anglo-Indian families have affected our numbers very adversely. Only 120 at the moment.[1]

Vernon Prins was a Cambridge man who taught us Latin and history. At the time of the victorious Allied advance in Europe during World War II, he drew a large map of the battle areas and marked each capture of a strategic town with the appropriate Allied flag, looking at the map studiously, smoking a pipe. I remember him telling us that Aix-la-Chapelle was the modern Aachen, and many years later, when I passed through that town, I remembered his words. He called stupid students "blitherers," and he would berate us with "You blocks, you stones, you worse than senseless things." Once, when I wrote a good essay in history that

179

*Robert Ford (left) and author's father (1948). Photo by
author's father, Rai Sahib Pemba Tsering*

pleased him, he praised me to the skies and wrote in my exercise book, "*O
si sic omnia!*" (Oh, would that all had been done/said thus!).

To reinforce our understanding of the Napoleonic wars, he made us
sing,

> Boney was a warrior,
> Way hey ya
> A Warrior, a terrier,
> John Francois.[2]

Victoria School was situated in the heart of the Himalayas, and on clear
sunny days we could see, not at any great distance, a range of some of
the highest mountains in the world, including *Gang-chen Zö-nga* (Five
Treasures of the Great Snows), popularly called "Kanchenjunga," the

third-highest peak in the world. The story of the attempt at the summit of Mount Everest by the British mountaineers Andrew Irvine and George Leigh Mallory in 1924 fascinated us with its drama and mystery. They had been seen climbing steadily at a height about a thousand feet below the summit by a man named Odell looking through a telescope. Then a mist had hidden them from view, and when Odell looked again, they were nowhere to be seen. Did they reach the summit? Did they get lost during the descent? All this is a matter of conjecture, because, as of 1992, their bodies had never been found. Mallory and Irvine were now names of houses at Victoria School. It is interesting to note that Mallory had been a "fag" for Sir Basil Gould when the latter was at school in Winchester. Many years later, I met Mallory's son in London. That was before Edmund Hillary and Tenzing Norgay climbed Everest in 1953 (both of whom I have met, the former when I treated his wife in Darjeeling for an injured ankle and the latter as a friend as well as a patient of mine in Darjeeling).

In the night, along the dark passages that led to the school lavatories, past the gymnasium, I could hear some of the senior boys singing,

> Oh merry, oh merry, oh merry are we,
> We are the boys of the Artillery.
> Sing high, sing low, wherever we go,
> Artillery gunners they never say no.[3]

And the boys who belonged to the "Glee Club" founded by Mr. T. W. Clark, the headmaster, would sing:

> Drake is sailing West, lad,
> And here's to Drake and his merry, merry men,
> Who'll never return to Devon again
> Till they've laid the enemy low.[4]

These boys, with the blood of Drake and others in their veins, would soon see a total disruption of Anglo-Indian families as they at last sailed "home" to Blighty. They would very soon be in the land where "the boar's head . . . bedecked with bays and rosemary" was "the bravest dish in all the land."[5]

The Jewish boy was at his prayers, wearing his black skullcap, a black band wound round his arm, a striped shawl wrapped around his shoulders, reading from a book. He was my rival in mathematics. He was awkward, acutely intelligent, gentle, no good in boxing, and sometimes bullied; he never refused a fight, nor did he win any. Far away at Dachau, Auschwitz, and such places, Jews were being bullied, tortured, and exterminated, but we knew nothing of all this!

Other events took place during the final years of my life at Victoria School, and some of them can be best summed up by quotations from a diary my father kept for the year 1945. He was at that time traveling in western Tibet as the British trade agent, a legacy of the Younghusband treaty concluded in Lhasa in 1904 in which one clause read, "The Tibetan government undertakes to open forthwith trade marts to which all British and Tibetan subjects shall have free right of access at Gyantse and Gartok, as well as at Yatung."[6] That clause was the reason why I was born in Gyantse and spent so many years in Yatung and why my father was then traveling to Gartok. In those days, the easiest route to western Tibet was through northwest India, passing through the Indian town of Almora on the way.

Friday, 15 June: Halt at Almora—Altitude 5200 ft. Jawaharlal Nehru released from Almora jail. [Nehru had been imprisoned there by the British for subversive action against the Raj. Two years after his release, almost to the date, on August 15, 1947, he would become the first prime minister of an independent India.]

Saturday, 4 August: Arrived Gyanyima. [Heinrich Harrer, in his book *Seven Years in Tibet*, has this to say about Gyanyima: "The biggest market in this region is that of Gyanyima. Here hundreds of tents form a huge camp given over to buying and selling."][7]

Wednesday, 8 August: Halt at Gyanyima. 40 degrees. Atomic bomb. [It is strange that at such a remote place as Gyanyima in western Tibet my father should learn on his radio about the ushering in of the atomic age. In school, we also heard about this cataclysmic event. Our science teacher gave us a talk explaining nuclear fission. When I met my mother during the winter vacation of 1945, she, too, discussed the atom bomb and said that the flash from the explosion had been brighter than the noon-day sun.]

Thursday, 9 August: Russia declares war on Japan. Second atomic bomb.

Wednesday, 15 August: Halt at Gyanyima. Japan surrenders.[8]

When we went down to the town of Kurseong, we had to be careful. It was early 1947, and the Indians, on seeing us wearing school ties, blazers, and caps, would jeer at us and challenge us to fights, shouting, *"Bhotay Baba! Bhotay Baba!"* (*Bhotay* meaning "Tibetans" and *Baba* was what European children were called). "Quit India!" notices meant for the supporters of the British Raj were plastered all over the town and on the cinema posters of the Plaza theater. *"Inquilab zindabad!"* (Long live freedom!), *"Bande mataram!"* (Hail the Motherland!), *"Jai Hind"* (Victory to India!), shouted the massed voices of the agitating crowds. My friends at school told me that they and their parents would be leaving the next year for Australia, New Zealand, and "home." None of them wanted to stay on in India, not with the "wogs" and the "Babus." Australia was especially attractive to them, for most of the boys were mad about cricket—it was the era of Don Bradman, Lindsey Hassett, and Ray Lindwall.

The Hindi master was tormented. Hindi, the national language of independent India, was a subject that one took for the sake of the Senior Cambridge examination, just a means to an end. After that, it would be absolutely useless for all those emigrating from India. The Hindi teacher was a Muslim: bearded, gentle, pathologically tolerant, who dressed in a long black coat, a Maulana Azad (cabinet minister) of a figure, elegant and buttoned to the chin. "Boys, open your books and read '*Toto ka Sandesh*,'" he would say in his "Babu" accent, later imitated inimitably by Peter Sellers. "*Toto ka sandesh*" (The parrot's message) happened to be a particularly difficult passage. "Not bloody '*Toto ka Sandesh*' again! Can't we revise something else?"—a howl of protest from British and Anglo-Indian voices. The Hindi master would not budge. All over India, in those days, Indians were refusing to budge when confronted by their British rulers. The boys, seeing that the Hindi teacher was adamant and would not give way, filed out of the class in protest; only the two of us were left, the Jewish boy and myself. He later immigrated to Australia. The rebellious boys then ran past the window of the classroom and, imitating screaming Apaches attacking encircled cowboys, bombarded and pelted the Hindi master, who, when he stood up, did not realize that his immaculate black coat had imprinted on it in powdered chalk "Kick me," which the boys had written in reverse before he had sat down absentmindedly at the beginning of class. My Jewish friend and I kept mum. No good reporting to the British headmaster, and in any case one didn't sneak.

August 15, 1947: Indian Independence Day, the end of the British Raj. On the lower field a parade of cadets, Boy Scouts from Victoria School, and Girl Guides from Dow Hill School, the neighboring sister school of Victoria—the whole school assembled, and all the school servants joined the assembly, including the bearers, *dhobi-s* (washermen), *darji-s* (tailors), and the bearded Muslim *roti wallah-s* (who sold confectionery from tin boxes balanced on their heads), as well as the *pani wallah-s* (plumbers and watercarriers). There was silence. The headmaster spoke in three languages: English, Nepali and Bengali. The Union Jack was slowly lowered, and the Indian tricolor with the wheel of Asoka in the center flew from the flagpole.

In 1948, I would finish school. My father wanted to know what I wished to do after leaving school. He said that if I wished, I could join the British Trade Agencies in Tibet, now called Indian Trade Agencies after Indian independence. But he didn't think there was much future there. I could go to a college in India and then join the Indian Administrative Service, the successor of the Indian Civil Service during the Raj. Or perhaps I might join the Indian army, as I was athletic and fond of games. My mother, however, wanted me to study medicine. She said that the medical profession was a noble one; a doctor was respected everywhere and could always earn a living. The life of a doctor was full of merit that would ensure a higher rebirth. I wasn't particularly interested in medicine but agreed to give the matter some thought.

My father wrote and told me that a Major Guthrie, a British doctor working in an agency hospital in Tibet, would be passing through Darjeeling and that I should go and see him. Guthrie was a Scotsman. In 1935, he had been a captain in the Indian Medical Service and had been at one time the agency surgeon at Gyantse. I went to see him at a hotel in Darjeeling. He gave me news of my parents in Lhasa and asked me whether I wanted to be a doctor. His wife warned me that a medical course was very difficult and required a great deal of hard work. Major Guthrie agreed to see whether there was any possibility of my studying in Edinburgh, then considered as having the finest medical school in the world. Going to Edinburgh to study medicine was far more ambitious than applying for a place in an English school when I had first arrived in Gangtok from Lhasa. The Guthries promised to keep in touch with me and see what could be done. We left it at that.

Thomas Welbourne Clark, the headmaster, born in Derbyshire and educated at University College, Nottingham, gathered us in his study to give us extra "prep" in English. During the Second World War, he had been a lieutenant-colonel in the Indian Intelligence Corps, and he had been made an OBE (Officer of the Order of the British Empire). We went through the elegant essays of Addison and then revised some Shakespeare:

> Two truths are told,
> As happy prologues to the swelling act
> Of the imperial theme.[9]
>
> The evil that men do lives after them
> The good is oft interred with their bones.[10]
>
> Blow, blow, thou winter wind,
> Thou art not so unkind
> As man's ingratitude.[11]

His wife, Grace Clark, was born in Ambala, India (a favorite town of Rudyard Kipling). She was a kind vivacious English lady who used to teach us art. I can still remember her lecture to us in perspectives when she taught, "The ellipse that you cannot see is bigger than the ellipse that you can see." She was the one who had wanted to paint our family when we had first come to Victoria wearing our Tibetan silks. She had been to the Slade School of Art at University College, London, the university where I was destined to study medicine in the future. She went into raptures when she discussed the work of Jamini Roy, the Bengali artist.

Tashi Tsering, my grand-uncle, born in 1886, was living in retirement in Gangtok ever since April Fool's Day 1930, when Lieutanant-Colonel J. Weir, the British political officer in Sikkim, had terminated his post. Since then, he spent his time attempting to solve the crossword puzzles of the *Illustrated Weekly of India* magazine, which in those days gave rich cash prizes; playing carrom with a Muslim shoe shop owner in the bazaar, who was reputed to be the Gangtok champion; and reading English literature and drinking.

He took a constitutional in the evenings, walking backward and forward like a caged animal outside his house, always wearing his long Sikkimese-Tibetan dress, disdaining the Western clothes worn by many Sikkimese and Tibetans in Gangtok. Lately he had been delving into politics, becoming the leader of the Sikkim State Congress, which was affiliated with the Indian National Congress Party of Jawaharlal Nehru, then prime minister of India. Tashi Tsering wanted Sikkim to accede to India, as many princely Indian native states were doing voluntarily (or otherwise) after Indian independence. He was opposed to the ruling royal family of Sikkim. He often visited New Delhi and had meetings with Nehru and other national leaders, with a hip flask full of gin inside his chuba dress.

Tashi Tsering liked his gin and whiskey, quoting Omar Khayyam to justify himself:

> I often wonder what the Vintners buy
> One half so precious as the Goods they sell.[12]

> The Grape that can with Logic absolute
> The Two-and-Seventy jarring Sects confute:
> The subtle Alchemist that in a Trice
> Life's leaden Metal into Gold transmute.[13]

He was full of such quotations—wise, witty, ribald, or just smutty. He lumped the whole of Tibetan religion, of which he had considerable knowledge and experience, as "just a lot of mumbo-jumbo," and incarnate lamas were "only child prodigies like Mozart." He once turned around at me and asked whether I had read Rider Haggard's *She*, and when I professed ignorance, he asked me what sort of an English school Victoria was! When some British troops on holiday in Gangtok came to look at his shop, full of silks, ceramics, and jade cups, and inquired where he had learned to speak such good English, he replied, "Oh I just picked up the lingo here and there." He would laugh and quote Topsy in Harriet Beecher Stowe's *Uncle Tom's Cabin*: "I just growed."[14] I have a great love for English literature, and I think I owe a great deal of this interest to my father and to Tashi Tsering, who encouraged me to read the English classics.

Once he was quite drunk and rather pathetic and maudlin, perhaps lamenting over the career he had brought to a halt at its most promising stage by some misdemeanor that couldn't be helped and had to do with an affair with the wife of a senior Tibetan officer in a British agency and at seeing the promotion of his rivals and the grand titles and privileges they enjoyed, rivals who were intellectually his inferiors but who had stuck to their jobs, and he would quote,

> that which we are, we are;
> One equal temper of heroic hearts,
> Made weak by time and fate, but strong in will
> To strive, to seek, to find, and not to yield.[15]

And then with a wry smile he would go on: "Seven cities claimed the Homer dead; through which the living Homer begged his bread."[16] Once when I was whistling "Highland Laddie," he gave me his version:

> When the donkey wants to shit
> Hold its tail up, hold its tail up.
> And when the donkey wants to pee
> Shove a nail up, shove a nail up.

During the Second World War, some girls from Gangtok went to Calcutta to become prostitutes. Tibetan and Sikkimese girls, being pretty, attractive, and uninhibited in sexual matters, probably drew an appreciative clientele, especially in Calcutta, which was full of Allied soldiers at that time. Some of the girls used to come up to Gangtok, presumably to recuperate but also to flaunt their wealth. Tashi Tsering, who was a bit of a satyr, once invited to his house in broad daylight a particularly alluring prostitute to titillate him with intimate details of her sexual performances and clients' preferences. This incident created quite a bit of eyebrow raising, and my mother, who never liked Tashi Tsering and thought him a bad influence on me, objected strongly, in no uncertain terms, that she would leave the house if he did anything that scandalous again. "I used to know your mother ever since she was a little girl in Pipithang," he would say to me. "She's done very well in life considering the fact that she hasn't spent a day in school. She's the type who won't let the grass grow under her feet."

There was a very amusing incident one winter in Gangtok. Late one night, I didn't feel very well and wanted to go to the toilet. We had no flush toilets at our house, only "thunder boxes," which were at the basement. I had to open the shop door, go out into the street, and then descend some steps. I left the shop door open. Just then, Rai Sahib Dr. Tonyot Tsering, who was then living in Gangtok, happened to be returning from a party, and he was somewhat tipsy. He saw the door of the shop open and thought he would come in and see what Tashi Tsering was up to at that hour of the morning. He was fast asleep. Dr. Tonyot woke my grand-uncle up and hauled him out of bed. Tashi Tsering couldn't believe his eyes and how an apparition like Dr. Tonyot had managed to enter the house at that ungodly hour. They began to talk nineteen to the dozen, and it went on for some time. At one stage, a serious (yet at the same time hilarious) metaphysical argument broke out between the two of them about the existence of God. "Where is God? Where is God?" asked Dr. Tonyot, shaking Tashi Tsering by the shoulders and repeating his question with great vehemence. My grand-uncle was a confirmed atheist. "God is asleep," was his retort.

I wish to give two more of Tashi Tsering's quotations and report them verbatim with apologies to the authors of the originals:

> For it's Tommy this and Tommy that, an' "Chuck him out, the brute!"
> But it's "Saviour of 'is country" when the guns begin to shoot.[17]

> I'm full a'nu and I'm absolutely full and I dinna know the country
> I was born in; for my name is Jock McGregor and I dinna care a straw
> for I've something in the bottle for the morning.

During some of my winter holidays, my father was stationed in Lhasa, and he could not get leave to come to see us, and the journey to Lhasa for us in the middle of winter would have been just as hazardous and exhausting as ever before, for communications in Tibet then were exactly as they had been in the past. Tibet had not changed. The atomic age had arrived with the destruction of Hiroshima and Nagasaki, and the Second World War was over; the British Raj had vanished, but Tibet was the same in every way.

Since we would not be meeting my father, we would go to the radio station at the Gangtok Residency and talk to him on the radio telephone, and my sister Norden might even be persuaded to sing a Hindi film song for my father. The radio operator at one time was a young Englishman named Robert Ford. He was a very pleasant person, and we got to know him well. Later he joined the Tibetan government and was stationed at Chamdo in eastern Tibet, where he was captured by the Chinese

Communists when they attacked Tibet in 1950. His terrible experiences at the hands of his captors have been told in his book, *Captured in Tibet*.

I also met Reginald Fox one winter in Gangtok, I think it was the winter of 1947–1948. He, too, was now working as a radio operator for the Tibetan government in Lhasa. He was badly crippled with rheumatoid arthritis and could hardly walk. His tap-dancing days were over. He gave me a present of Lancelot Hogben's *Science for the Citizen* and for my brother, Norbu, *Mathematics for the Millions*.

I sat for my school finals, the Senior Cambridge School Leaving Certificate, still set from Cambridge and the papers corrected there, at the end of 1948. I was a school prefect that year, but by then licks with the hockey stick had been abolished. The boys who passed that examination with me that year were Beveridge Q. Junior, Bull, Dunbar, Frost, and Twiddy (my boxing opponent). I think our lot was the smallest that had passed the examination for many years. All of them left India in the following years with the exodus of the British after Indian Independence in 1947, and I do not know where they are. I heard one of them was in Dundee, and when I passed through that city in 1951, I had half a mind to look him up but didn't.

During the winter of 1948–1949, my father managed to come down from Lhasa to see us in Gangtok. He was still working for the British (now named "Indian") Mission in Lhasa. He had not lost his interest in photography, dating from his magnesium flare days in Yatung in the early 1930s. But now he had acquired a Leica camera. Later in Lhasa, he sold the camera to Heinrich Harrer. Harrer told me how glad my father had been to have been able to sell it to him because my mother had continuously nagged my father for being so extravagant in buying such an expensive camera. For Harrer, it was a profitable investment because he used it to take some of the photographs that appear in his book *Seven Years in Tibet*.

One day, we received news that my grandmother was very ill in Yatung, and my mother hastened to go to her bedside. I accompanied my mother. At Karponang, on our first halt after leaving Gangtok, I met Mr. Frank Ludlow. He was the British schoolteacher who had unsuccessfully run a school in Gyantse in 1923. He was now a well-known ornithologist and a botanist and later was employed by the Natural History Museum in London.

Ludlow was tall, gaunt, and hatted, and he stood there in breeches, puttees, and heavy boots, wearing a sweater and a tweed jacket—the very incarnation of a British explorer. There was melting snow all around us, and the day was sunny. I stood there, conversing with him casually and at ease, and I thought my mother looked pleased and proud as she stood behind us smiling, for she spoke very little English. Her son was talking to Ludlow *Sahib* and seemed to hold his own.

Ludlow told me that he had a Muslim bearer named Daoud who was an expert at making cakes. In Lhasa, when Ludlow gave parties, all tasted Daoud's cakes. Soon Daoud was being invited to the houses of well-known aristocrats "on loan" to make their confectionery when they gave parties of their own. When Ludlow left Lhasa, Daoud had declined to accompany him, instead remaining behind to start his own confectionery shop. "He's now minting rupees . . . simply minting rupees," Ludlow told me, rubbing his thumb and index finger together to emphasize his words. Several compounders from the agency hospitals had also absconded, starting their own clinics in Lhasa and giving penicillin injections indiscriminately for syphilis and gonorrhea and for any kind of illness as a panacea, charging fantastic sums of money in the process. "It was not quite right and proper," lamented Ludlow, "but then what could anyone do?" As we rode toward the 14,140-foot Nathö La pass that forms the boundary between Sikkim and Tibet, as laid down in the Anglo-Chinese Convention of 1890, I told my mother that I wanted to walk to the top of the pass and not ride. I wanted to prove my toughness.

I had developed a dread for pulmonary tuberculosis, which was very common in Sikkim and Darjeeling. The disease was called *Phthisis* by many people in the hills. *Phthisis*—the word with the silent *ph* had such a sinister ring. I walked briskly, breathing in the pure, clean, germ-free air. If there was any *phthisis* in my lungs, I was determined to wash it all out. I remembered what the Monster in Aldous Huxley's *Antic Hay* said: "The young girls of Sparta, they say, used to wrestle naked with naked Spartan boys . . . their breasts were hard, their bellies flat. They were pure with the chastity of beautiful animals. Their thoughts were clear, their minds cool and untroubled. I spit blood into my handkerchief and sometimes I feel in my mouth something slimy, soft, and disgusting like a slug—and I have coughed up a shred of my lung."[18] I shuddered as I recalled these lines. And there was that haunting portrayal of Chopin by Cornel Wilde in the film *A Song to Remember*—Chopin plays the piano, and suddenly the immaculate keyboard is spattered with drops of blood. I, too, longed to possess a flat belly, my thoughts clear and my mind cool and untroubled. I felt reassured when I crossed the Nathö La pass without much fatigue.

I waited in Tibetan territory some distance below the pass. This time I did not pile stones on the cairns or shout "*Lha-gyalo!*" Such behavior appeared redundant and did not befit a young man with a Victoria School education. It was superstition and, in the words of Tashi Tsering, just so much mumbo-jumbo. Instead, I reflected on how kind my mother was, how concerned for all of us and for my grandmother. How much must she have suffered in the past while taking us on our journeys in Tibet: four little children, first to Lhasa from Yatung in 1937 and then in 1940 from Lhasa to Gangtok with my sisters and brother when Tashi Tsering's wife had died. From Lhasa to Gangtok was three hundred miles, a short distance in these days of freeways and autobahns, but it took almost three weeks riding in the Tibet of that time. I remembered saying good-bye to her at Shingdonkar and how I had wept. And I could see her at each halting station at night saying her prayers, smoking a cigarette, the children all asleep, and preparing for the next day's journey and the tasks to be performed before they woke up. And that toy pistol that she carried in the leather holster for place like Dzara.

On the way to Yatung, the descent was easy, and my mother and I talked of many things. She wanted me to become a doctor. That was the best profession, she said. Certainly, it was hard, and you needed guts. If I agreed to study medicine, she was willing to send me to England, even if that meant selling all her jewelry to pay for the expenses. And we talked of the Radreng revolt that occurred in Lhasa in 1947. The regent, Radreng Rinpoche, had continued in office for a few years after I had left Lhasa but had then handed over his powers to the Takdrak Rinpoche, the senior tutor (or Yongzin) of the Dalai Lama. The events of 1947 had been triggered by some of Radreng's coterie trying to seize power again. Sera monastery, where Radreng had studied, had fought against the government, and howitzers had to be fired by Jigme Taring to quell the rebellion. At one time even Reginald Fox had been drawn into the troubles when he had to carry out some mechanical repairs to the guns.

The monastery of Radreng, built in 1057 AD (almost contemporaneous with William the Conqueror's invasion of England), had been taken and looted, and the Radreng Rinpoche was brought to Lhasa and imprisoned in the Potala, where he died on May 8, 1947, some even suspecting murder by his testicles being squashed, although medically I'm not sure whether anybody could be killed in this way. So, the incarnate lama, I argued with my mother, the child-deity who had miraculously tethered horses to pegs driven into hard rock with his bare hands and tied a boiling earthenware pot with his garters, had suffered the ignominy of being put to death by having his testicles crushed! Somehow it was not plausible. Why didn't Radreng perform some miracle? Why didn't he just fly up in the air? The proof of the pudding was in the eating. "*Chönga chöpa shebo yöna nyime gungla dönsho!*" (Butter offerings of the fifteenth, if you've got any guts, come out in the midday sun!), I quoted to my mother. My mother laughed. "One must not make fun of religion," she said.

Radreng monastery had been looted by the soldiers. They took whatever they could lay their hands on from the altars and temples. They crushed golden oil lamps with their boots and put the gold into their pockets. Later, my mother related, because they had committed such *dikpa* (sins), all the soldiers had died agonizing violent deaths, vomiting blood, becoming delirious, and many committing suicide. The spirit of the dead Radreng was taking revenge. My mother told me that one does not practice religion in order to obtain some benefit or to witness miracles. Religion must be practiced for its own sake, not because one wants to get something out of it. It was in this sense different from all other worldly pursuits, in which we do something in order to get something. In the end, she explained, when everything else has faded and turned stale, when everything has become like a painful dream, and human beings, disillusioned with their striving, taste the bitterness and impermanence of their deeds, there remains only religion.

As we approached Yatung, I asked my mother whether I could gallop ahead. She warned me not to. She told me the story of a young monk who had been sent to a distant land to fetch a fragile jade idol for his master. After many hazardous adventures, the young monk had returned triumphantly with the idol, but just before reaching his destination, he had become impatient and impulsive, spurred his horse to a gallop, and was thrown, and the precious jade idol had been smashed. She cautioned that the most dangerous stage of every endeavor was at the very end.

We reached our house and dismounted, and we climbed the wooden staircase that led to the large room used as a kitchen and a bedroom for my grandmother, for she said that the kitchen was the warmest part of our house. She was lying propped up in her bed and appeared quite breathless. She was being looked after by Nyima Wangmo, our old maidservant.

Nyima Wangmo drew back the bedclothes to show us grandmother's grossly swollen legs, the skin smooth, tight, and pale. My mother sat down at the foot of the bed and rubbed the swollen legs. I stood there and watched in sympathy. I was wearing a U.S. Army jacket and U.S. Army paratrooper boots laced to the knees—all war surplus goods sold by Gangtok Indian Marwari traders making enormous profits. I fancied myself a paratrooper who had jumped at Arnhem during Operation Market Garden or fought with the "Screaming Eagles" at Bastogne, where General McAuliffe had given his famous "Nuts!" rebuff to German demands to surrender.

The next day, my mother sent off Nyima Wangmo to inform the monks of Dungkar Monastery to come to the house to carry out some rites and say prayers for my grandmother's recovery and told me to go and fetch the Indian doctor from the Yatung Indian Trade Agency hospital.

I came out of the house and went through the town of Yatung, the streets full of barking dogs, horses, and mule trains. I met some people who knew me, and I told them that I had finished school, and they wanted to know what career I intended to pursue. I couldn't give any definite answers, as I wasn't sure myself. I went past my old school, where I had learned my first words of English; walked across the playing field where my father used to play hockey, where Mr. Gyatso Topden took part in archery and sometimes the British officers played polo; and then came to the hospital, a cluster of new buildings. The military escort to the Indian trade agent was still there, and I could see the army barracks where long ago they had staged theatricals and where Nyima Wangmo took me in the evenings when we sold milk to the soldiers, and they gave us their *chappatis* and *dal*. In the evenings then, when the sun set, a bugler would sound the "Last Post" and lower the Union Jack. The Union Jack was now no more. The British had left India.

I met Dr. Makhija, a pleasant young Indian army doctor who was in charge of the hospital. I explained to him my grandmother's condition and asked him to pay her a visit in the evening after his surgery. Having done that, I had an inclination to see the residency, which was quite close.

The gate to the residency was still there, perhaps the very gate I had come to when I had first learned to walk. I remember (but the memory is blurred and indistinct, and possibly the first thing I remember of anything at all in my entire life) negotiating a stile there, and everybody had clapped and jumped with joy and admiration because I was able to walk up and then down the stile without aid. The residency itself was empty then, and I didn't go inside the rooms. But the arbors, pergolas, and flowerbeds were all the same.

I went to the agency offices and met the young clerks. My father had been such a clerk at one time. They still stood close to the fireplaces, warming themselves. The servants stood up when I came, and I felt rather flattered at this show of respect. They had changed the badges that they wore—no more "Honi soit qui mal y pense" but the Asoka pillar and lions of independent India, or Bharat. I borrowed some magazines to read. They had *Life* and *The Illustrated Weekly of India*; nobody knew anything about *The Illustrated London News*, *Blackwood's*, or *Punch*.

The Indian army doctor examined my grandmother carefully, and he was very professional about the whole thing and told me that she had heart failure and that he intended to prescribe digitalis. He told me that she must restrict her salt intake and not eat any of Khampa roast meat. He explained that digitalis slowed the pulse and that I must take her pulse regularly and note down the readings accurately. We served him tea when he had finished, and we sat in the room that was full of glass windows and caught the sun the whole day. He wanted to know why I was so interested in medicine, and I told him that I might take up medicine. He wanted to know my grandmother's age, and when my mother told him that she was eighty-one, he wondered whether there was any point in trying to keep her alive. My mother told him that we all loved her and wanted her to live as long as possible.

The monks arrived from Dungkar monastery. An astrologer had carried out a *mo* (divination) using the beads from a rosary and calculations based on my grandmother's birth-year. Tibetans then used (and still use) the lunar calendar, each year being male or female and named after twelve animals (rat, bull, tiger, hare, dragon, snake, horse, sheep, monkey, bird, dog, pig) and an element (earth, iron, water, wood, fire). I was born in the Iron Sheep year, and 1992 was the Male Water Monkey year.

There was once more the chanting of prayers and the sounds of drums, trumpets, cymbals, conches, horns, and thigh-bone trumpets. I stood for hours watching and listening, trying to understand the rites and rituals and the reality behind the symbols. I talked to the monks and asked what each ritual meant. While they were chanting and reciting texts, I stood behind them, peering at the books, and asked them to explain the meanings of the things that they read. What did *nang-tong* (inner emptiness) and *chi-tong* (outer emptiness) mean? What good was the reading of all these voluminous texts if you didn't understand what it all meant? The monks laughed and teased me. They said that all this was "the commands of the Buddha"—intrinsically pure, unalterable, unchangeable through all eons, forever true—and that they were beyond the comprehension of most human beings.

Certainly, some of the learned sage-like lamas understood every word, but that wasn't the point. The important thing was to recite these texts with devotion and fervor, which became a meritorious deed. If one tried to understand what one was reciting, you wouldn't get through a single page in a day. But some things they could explain, such as the significance of the very common ritual objects they held in their hands, like the *dorje* (supreme-stone, or scepter) and the *drilbu* (bell). These objects signified "wisdom" and "method"—the two essential ingredients required on the path to enlightenment. That was interesting. Many of the texts dealt with extremely abstruse metaphysical and philosophical doctrines concerning ontology. I found Tibetan religion a strange, intoxicating, intriguing mixture of the abstruse and the superstitious, the primitive and the intellectual, and there was so much symbolism. It was true that the vast majority of Tibetans worshiped the symbols and accepted them literally.

The Shakyamuni Buddha had preached a simple doctrine of suffering, the cause of suffering and the way to escape from this suffering. It was a purified cleansed religion shorn of the complications of Hindu Brahmanism. But in Tibet, it had grown into this immensely rich, vast, complex amalgam of rites, rituals, ceremonies, incantations, astrology, divination, and the worship of a multitudinous pantheon of all forms of gods, goddesses, and demons. Abstruse metaphysical doctrines of great intellectual purity had become inextricably mixed with demonology, superstition, and the magic of the shaman. Buddhism does not believe in a personal god, but Tibetans who use the term *Könchogsum*, which literally means the "Three Rare and Precious Ones" (the Buddha, the scriptures, and the congregation of monks) take it to mean a supreme deity, and in daily use it is almost synonymous with the personal God of the Christians; *Kyabsu chi*, meaning "I seek refuge," is similarly used to express adoration, awe, or worship.

However, the Tibetan religion also had its secret esoteric aspect, understood and practiced by very few, but impressive in its profundity and magnificence of thought and not incompatible with any of the philosophies of modern science. There were expressions such as *yingrig yerme*, which meant that there was no difference between the unfathomable depths of space and the intellect of man. I was determined to learn something about our Tibetan religion, to understand the meanings behind the symbolism, to look beyond the rites and rituals. There was a possibility that within its inner secret core, in our Tibetan religion, "there is another kind . . . across a whole Thibet of broken stones/That lie, fang up, a lifetime's march."[19]

One evening, an array of intricate butter and dough images sculpted by specially trained monks, representing valleys, gods and goddesses, demons and witches, were laid out on the floor of a room. To the chanting of the lamas and the blowing of conches, interspersed with the eerie wailing of human thigh-bone trumpets, the evil demons that had been discovered from the astrological calculations to be the cause of my grandmother's illness (not the failing of an old heart with hardened arteries) were propitiated by Nyima Wangmo symbolically crossing twelve mountain ranges and valleys. Like a little girl playing hopscotch, she had to skip over each range as a monk standing next to her officiated and indicated when she should jump; at each jump, the din of ritual music ceased, there was absolute silence, and Nyima Wangmo had to shout, *"Tharo!"* (Be delivered!), and all the monks shouted in unison, *"Tharo!"*

I do not know whether Dr. Makhija's digitalis, my obsessive taking of grandmother's pulse, or the magic rituals of the monks of the Dungkar monastery contributed to her recovery, but Grandmother was "delivered" of her illness and was soon well enough to get around the house. He was very worried about her, and at one stage my grandmother had even invoked the name of Dr. Tonyot Tsering, like the dying Balzac asking for the physician Bianchot, and had said that only the Sikkimese doctor would be able to save her. But Dr. Tonyot was in Gangtok, possibly making surprise calls on Tashi Tsering in the middle of the night and arguing about the existence of God over a hot tot of rum or a glass of Scotch.

I had plenty of time in Yatung and decided to improve my Tibetan. I had paid scant attention to this subject, as my father said that a knowledge of Tibetan would be of no use in my future career and I should not to waste my time over it. Instead, it would be more profitable to read up biology in my spare time. He said that I could easily pick up Tibetan sometime in the future if I was still interested. But talking to some of the monks, peering into their scriptures, and occasionally experiencing flashes of illumination from their explanations made me anxious to study my own language. My knowledge of English was so much better, and I even thought in English. That couldn't be helped after being in an English school for eight years.

At home, all of us, my brother and sisters, talked in English to each other, and all our books, magazines, and interests were English-oriented. I would sit at night by the light of a hurricane lantern (still cleaned by Nyima Nangmo and still exactly the same in appearance) and study Tibetan. Tibet, too, was like that hurricane lantern—changeless. There was no electricity or sanitation or plumbing in Yatung. In the whole of "Outer Tibet," there were no cars, railways, electricity, or anything modern. The American cargo plane that had crashed at Samye in November 1943 was possibly the only one that had flown over Tibet and certainly the only one to crash in Tibet. Tibet, it seemed, would never change. We thought it then the height of backwardness, almost entirely due to the iron rigidity of the monks. The romantic, however, might yearn for such times and the disappearance of their Shangri-La.

During the day, wherever my mother went, I would tag along with her, with a notebook and pen in hand, and whenever a nice turn of Tibetan speech or a catchy phrase caught my ears during her conversations with her friends over cups of Tibetan butter tea and delicious Yatung cakes, I would immediately produce my notebook, a young Tibetan Henry Higgins, writing down everything. Later I would reproduce these words and phrases in my own conversations with my mother to put them into practice, and my mother would give me a quizzical "déjà vu" look.

Nathö La had somewhat erased my obsessive fear of the dreaded *phthisis*, but I still had to turn myself into a Spartan with a flat belly. I would grind nuts, raisins, and raw eggs into a glass of hot milk and drink the concoction at breakfast to give me super strength. Later I exercised, holding stones collected for me by Nyima Wangmo from the Yatung riverbed to substitute for dumbbells. I searched for my father's Eugen Sandow (My System) dumbbells but couldn't find them. My mother showed me his Pelman books, his fretsaw works, the tables, and the bookshelves he had made in Yatung long ago. I went through the Funk and Wagnall dictionaries (which were still so heavy that I had to hold them with both hands) and the little volumes of "the world's greatest literature." I flipped through the pages of *The Vicar of Wakefield*, which my father had studied so diligently, underlining certain phrases, and making a note of the words whose meanings he did not know. To me, the meanings of the words were clear, and the phrases had nothing very special about them. It was easy going after *The Pickwick Papers* and "It was the best of times, it was the worst of times" of *A Tale of Two Cities*.[20] Mr. T. W. Clark of Victoria School had done his job well during our English "preps" in the winter evenings in his study with the sun setting over the snows of the Himalayas. I would never be returning as a schoolboy to Victoria again. Unbelievable.

It began to snow. Snow falling in Yatung is an unforgettable experience: the peace and serenity outside, soft heavy flurries of snow, thickly falling, falling the whole day until you couldn't make out the roads or houses. And in this snow, undeterred, you heard the ringing of the neck bells of the mule trains bringing mail from Gangtok. It was pleasant to lie in the snug warmth of our Tibetan *tsugtrug* blankets, with their fleece-like insides, and hear my mother at her prayers, making her prostrations and filling the silver bowls with water offerings. She possessed an inner indestructible spirit and tranquility and serenity rare in this modern world. Grandmother also joined her in her prayers as every household in Yatung became isolated from each other, for the snow fell ceaselessly into the night and Grandmother said that even the most tenacious of mule trains could not venture out on such a night.

It was time to return to Gangtok: Grandmother had improved so much that she said there was no need for my mother to stay any longer in Yatung. Instead, she ought to return to Gangtok to get the other children ready to go back to school. Grandmother and I sat down together one night, and she asked me what I wanted to do and whether I would be working for the Indian Trade Agency in Yatung. That would be nice, she said, because then I could stay with her and go to the office every day. I told her that I might become a doctor. That, too, was good, she said. There was nothing like being a doctor and helping those in pain. One earned much merit and ensured a better rebirth. She told me that if I became a doctor, I must devote myself to my profession and be kind and compassionate to all those who suffered. Above all, she told me, be compassionate, because compassion for every living creature was the essence of religion.

The horses were saddled and ready. I said goodbye to Grandmother. She didn't say a word but held my hands and nodded. I went out of the house, down the wooden stairs, turned at the stacks of wood, neatly piled for the winter, and then looked up at the window of the kitchen. Grandmother had her bed in the corner there. She was looking down at me as I waved to her. I never saw her again.

My mother and I rode down the valley, and when we came near Pipithang, on the other side of the river, I saw a group of Lhasa Tibetan soldiers, in Tibetan uniforms, with fur hats and earrings. They were arrogant, like most Lhasa soldiers, and were laughing. One of them turned toward my mother and started to urinate, the wind breaking up his stream of urine.

There was a great deal of snow on the Nathö La pass. We came across mule trains with tough Khampa muleteers hurling stones at their struggling mules, whistling at them, and shouting curses. One of them stood on a rock, jigsaw patterned with unmelted snow, arms akimbo, his face caked with dirt, his breath vaporous in the icy air, with a long sword across his waist, putteed legs, army booted, a Gurkha slouch hat on his head held down by pigtails intertwined with red ribbon. They were Khampas, warriors of Tibet and of the same blood as my grandmother.

We arrived at Tsho-go after crossing the Nathö La and halted for the night at the dak bungalow near the lake. The *chowkidar* (caretaker) called us and gave us eggs, roasted meat, Indian Cream Cracker biscuits, and Tibetan pancakes. There was a roaring fire, and I sat in a comfortable chair next to the fire and read a novel by Aldous Huxley. My mother and the Tibetan *chowkidar* were talking about Indian independence, which had been gained eighteen months previously. The Tibetan was complaining about his personal affairs since and said he had been better off under the British Raj. He admired their pomp and *terso* (style). The British *Sahibs* were so elegant and honest. They were *Pukkah Sahibs*. No *Sahib* cheated you. Did you hear anything bad said about a single *Sahib* who had worked in Tibet in all these years ever since the Younghusband Expedition of the Wood Dragon year? He was in his teens when the British had come in that *Shing-Druk* (Wood Dragon) year of 1904, and he had worked for the British Trade Agencies ever since they had started. And the new National Anthem that went *"Jana, mana, gana,"* he couldn't get used to. I also recalled the British and Anglo-Indian boys at Victoria School sniggering when the new anthem was played. Nothing like a rousing, heart-intoxicating "Rule Britannia" and "Land of Hope and Glory" for them! I didn't pay much attention to the Tibetan caretaker's words. I was not interested in politics. Aldous Huxley was far more absorbing.

We left early the next morning. It was sunny, and there was no wind. Everything appeared peaceful, and the surface of the Tsho-go lake was unruffled. It was easy going now, all the way down, and the next day we would be in Gangtok with plenty of oranges to eat. My father would be there, and I would have to discuss with him the career I should pursue. An exciting new world awaited me. And how delightful it would be to see my sisters, Norzin and Norden, and my brother, Norbu. They would be returning to school soon, my sisters to St. Joseph's Convent in Kalimpong and my brother to Victoria. For me, my schooldays were over. Before I mounted my horse, I looked back at the road that led to the Nathö La pass. Beyond that lay Tibet.

## NOTES

1. Headmaster of Victoria Boys School Diary, 1944–1948.
2. "Boney Was a Warrior," Age of Revolution, accessed January 15, 2022, https://ageofrevolution.org/200-object/boney-was-a-warrior-popular-ballad/.
3. "The Artillery Alphabet," Yorkshire Folksongs, accessed January 15, 2022, http://www.yorkshirefolksong.net/song.cfm?songID=26.
4. P. J. O'Reilly, "Drake Goes West," LiederNet Archive, accessed January 15, 2022, https://www.lieder.net/lieder/get_text.html?TextId=22191.
5. P. H. Ditchfield, *Old English Customs* (London: George Redway, 1896), 23.
6. Bell, *Tibet Past and Present*, 285.
7. Harrer, *Seven Years in Tibet*, 45.
8. Pemba Tsering's Diary, 1945.
9. William Shakespeare, *Macbeth*, ed. Cedric Watts (Suffolk: Wordsworth Classics, 2005), 37.
10. William Shakespeare, *Julius Caesar*, ed. Albert Harris Tolman (New York: World Book Company, 1913), 51.
11. William Shakespeare, *As You Like it*, ed. William J. Rolfe (New York: Harper & Brothers, 1878), 65.
12. Edward FitzGerald, *Rubáiyát of Omar Khayyám. A Critical Edition*, ed. Christopher Decker (Charlottesville: University Press of Virginia, 1997), 20.
13. Ibid., 16.
14. Harriet Beecher Stowe, *Uncle Tom's Cabin*, ed. Christopher G. Diller (Ontario: Broadview Press, 2009), 616.
15. Alfred Tennyson, *Poems*, Vol 2. (London: Edward Moxon, 1842), 91.
16. Avram Davidson, *Vergil in Averno* (New York: Doubleday, 1987), 134.
17. Rudyard Kipling, *Poems of Rudyard Kipling* (New York: Thomas Y. Crowell, n.d.), 8.
18. Aldous Huxley, *Antic Hay* (London: Chatto & Windus, 1949), 175.
19. Elliot, *Family Reunion*, 99–100.
20. Charles Dickens, *A Tale of Two Cities* (London: Wordsworth, 1993), 3.

# Epilogue I

$\sim$

# Return to Tibet in 2007

## Riga Lhendup Pemba

To show appreciation for my parents' dedication and support in helping me obtain my medical degree, my wife Yama suggested I do something special. What better way than a magical trip to Tibet, if this could happen at all? I knew how hard it was to get an entry visa to Tibet. Even when one has the Chinese visa, Tibet still requires a special Tibet Autonomous Region (TAR) permit.

Research into the various visas and permits and ways to make it happen finally led us to a travel agent who conducted special guided tours inside China and Tibet. After looking into the finer details and getting some positive reassurance from the agent that it was possible, we finally paid the deposit for the trip, and in return they sent us the itinerary that looked wonderful.

My parents were not aware of our plan, and it was a very pleasant surprise for my dad, who was very excited but, at the same time, still quite skeptical that it was at all possible. Nonetheless, being very detailed in everything he did, he started the process of getting his papers ready for the China visa. I had sent him all the details and documents from the travel agent for the application with strong letters of support from the tour guide office. We were not applying for the TAR permit, as this would have to be done once we got to China. With some help from a family friend who worked for the Bhutanese Embassy in New Delhi and the pages of supporting documents, they were finally granted the Chinese visa. First hurdle crossed.

Since my parents were flying in from India and my wife and I from America, we planned to all meet up in Beijing. After an uneventful flight, they arrived and had a restful sleep. The next day, our Chinese tour guide came to greet us but with some unpleasant news. She said that our papers had been submitted to the Tibet permit office for the TAR permit but had been rejected. Now our tour would have to be adjusted to visiting China only. She did not specify exactly why and whose papers were not approved, but we all knew the answer. Yama argued that we were reassured before we committed to buying the tour package that we would have no problem and that's why we had opted to choose their travel company. The tour guide called their office and said that we could be refunded for part of the trip that excluded Tibet. This was not the answer that Yama wanted to hear, and she asked to speak personally to the tour manager or the owner. It was a long conversation, and I could see that my dad was anxious and looked very disappointed. Not jet lag. After a long chat, we did not get any concrete answers or any promises.

The day after this episode, we visited a few tourist sites in Beijing, which seemed help to uplift my parents' mood. However, the next morning before our visit to the Great Wall of China, we received greater news that our TAR permits had been approved! Yes, Yama had done it! There was to be no floating on a cruise boat up the Yangtze for us; we would be visiting Tibet! My parents were very excited, and the next few days of Beijing and local tour went off very happily in anticipation of our flight to Lhasa.

The flight from Beijing takes about five hours to Lhasa; my dad commented on the difference of speed and convenience from his young days. He really enjoyed the view on the screen that shows Tibetan land below from a camera on the belly of the plane as we approach the airport. Once we landed, picked up our bags, and sailed through the local immigration counter, we were greeted by our Tibetan guide, Pemba Tsering (coincidentally a namesake of our grandfather). He was holding out a card with *Pemba* on it with khatags in his arms for each one of us. He seemed very surprised when we spoke Tibetan. He stated that this was the first time he had ever welcomed a Tibetan family to Lhasa with their tour group. We went on the beautiful ride back to Lhasa, passing the famous bridge that resembles khatags floating in the air. We were greeted by a wholesome, tasty Tibetan and Chinese meal in our hotel accompanied with Tibetan dances and singing.

The next day was another "official" day. Pemba Tsering had to take us to the local Tibetan immigration office to document our arrival and give them our itinerary for the next few days. All of us sailed through smoothly, but when it came to my dad's turn, he had to tackle a full-blown interview. It was almost an hour and a half of grueling questioning. However, the officials, who were Tibetan themselves, were very impressed with the amount of supporting documents that my dad magically produced

*Left to right: Mrs. Tsering Zangmo Pemba, Dhonam (author's grandson), author, Dr. Riga Pemba (author's son), and Mrs. Yama Khandu Pemba (author's daughter-in-law) (Potala Palace, Lhasa, 2007). Courtesy of Dr. Riga Pemba*

from his attaché. He was well prepared, and we were all quite proud to see him come out of the interview room with the officials wishing him a pleasant tour.

The next few days were very interesting and full of sights to see. Dad was very impressed with how much Lhasa had changed to become a full-blown modern city. He walked very briskly up the stairs of the Potala to show us that he had the genes and physiological makeup for the thin Tibetan air. The Potala Palace is very impressive and more majestic than its replica in pictures or postcards, huge rooms with walls adorned with beautiful thangkas and impressive statues. Dad was taking it all in. There was no digital camera; he was loading his camera frequently to take memorable pictures. Pemba Tsering managed to get us a private viewing of the Dalai Lama's chamber both in the Potala and in the Norbulingka, especially for his "Tibetan tourists." When driving through the streets of Lhasa, Dad pointed out a few places he recognized from his childhood days. He pointed out the street where the newly recognized Dalai Lama's official caravan may have passed through. He recalled rubbing the head of the ram extruding from the rock in the Jokhang Temple, indicating doomsday when its body finally emerges. We watched Chinese and Tibetan dancers in the Barkhor. He was impressed with the fast food burger restaurant that contrasted with the old-style shops in the square just as it was years ago. We had coffee and snacks in Makye Ame restaurant, which the Sixth Dalai Lama was rumored to have frequented.

We visited Ganden monastery, and Dad pointed out the house where he had spent a few nights long ago. He said that the monastery looked the same. He had a lot of stories about Ganden and Drepung monasteries, the warrior monks, philosophical debates, and just the size of these mini cities of monks. The visit to Sera was also very nice.

Then we took a long drive from Lhasa to Shigatse and then on to Gyantse via Yamdrok Lake. There were lots of tourists posing with Tibetan mastiffs, gigantic dogs looking even bigger with their decorative collars. Funnily, one of these dogs was kept in a lion cage in a Chinese zoo, mistaking it for one! At the Tashi Lhunpo Monastery, Dad commented on how the hats used to fall off one's head as people tried to look at the tallest Maitreya Buddha statue, measuring about ninety feet.

Gyantse was the place he felt a deep connection with, for it was his birthplace. He had many questions for Pemba Tsering, who did not have many answers to them. As we circumambulated the Kumbum stupa, he took keen interest in the details of the landmarks. He talked about the British Invasion and the Gurkhas who fought against the few Tibetan soldiers. He felt he was home but different, with missing familiarities. This was the *creme de la creme* of the trip for him. Forgotten was the visa anxiety, the grueling immigration interview, and the long drive from

Lhasa. This was it. We had a very entertaining dinner and talked for a long time with the performers, who were from different ethnicities but still performed as a unit. The drive back to Lhasa was very long but enjoyable, taking several breaks, enjoying the scenery and looking at the yak hide boats that were still in use.

Our last night in Lhasa was a grand dinner and an opera show, which was very energetic and entertaining. Dad commented on how Tibetans used to enjoy these very shows long ago during Tibetan New Year. The next morning, we were at the Lhasa train station, taking the train back to Beijing. It was sad to bid goodbye to Pemba Tsering, who was an excellent guide and had helped us get some unique appointments to places that the other tourists would never be able to access. Khatags were in order. Dad sat in his compartment and looked quite sad. He told me he was not going to sleep and would take in all the scenery during the long ride back. However, after a full-course Chinese meal he was taking a nap, probably dreaming if the trip was really a dream. Beijing was a city away from Tibet and its history.

My parents really enjoyed the trip and had many pictures and videos to look at and reminisce, but the memories and the experience can never be matched in words or pictures. I felt that Dad was amazed with the modernization of Tibet and the comforts that come along with this, but were we sacrificing something even greater in order to achieve this balance? It appears that he experienced some of his good old days during this trip and was going to put the old Tibet on paper, and hopefully with this book he has been able to give his readers a glimpse of the Tibet of olden days. *Antiquis temporibus . . .*

# Epilogue II

~

# Return from Tibet

## Diwo Lhamo Pemba

*"Before I mounted my horse, I looked back at the road that led to the Nathö La pass. Beyond that lay Tibet."*

This is the last sentence my father wrote about his home and country in this book, which I found in the attic of our home in Darjeeling. When he left Tibet for studies, he was a young man, on the verge of a career—in fact, a medical career, which his mother and grandmother often associated with compassion. During his education abroad, he was going through a cultural awakening that left him wanting to know more of his own country Tibet, its religion and language. Unfortunately, my father and his siblings lost not only their country but also, after the flood in Gyantse, their parents.

The surprise travel to Tibet in 2007, organized by my brother Riga la and his wife Yama la, was the best gift my father said he had ever received, for he always wanted to go back home. After his return from Tibet, he spent several months sitting outside in the porch of the house, lost in thought. He confessed to me that his visit to Tibet affected him in a way nothing ever did. He temporarily suffered writer's block. For my father, who had written several manuscripts and mostly on a typewriter, this feeling was crippling. The Tibet he had visited in 2007 and the Tibet he grew up in were two completely different entities. One came with memories and experiences that were the core of his being, and the other came with the fast-paced modernization that leaves many places scarred. The two Tibets stood in stark contrast; the Tibet of the twenty-first century highlighted his memories of the traditional Tibet he grew up in. And even though the physical landscape had changed due to developmental modernization, there was still a strong connection between the two Tibets—this place was his home, different, yes, but still home!

Even as he wrote his last novel, *White Crane, Lend Me Your Wings*, suffering from liver cancer, he confessed to me that his last prayer was for his rebirth in Tibet: "That is where I want to be reborn."

# Bibliography

Adjutant-General's Office. *The Queen's Regulations and Orders for the Army*. London: The Superintendence of Her Majesty's Stationary Office, 1868.

Aitchison, C. U., comp. *A Collection of Treaties, Engagements and Sanads. Relating to India and Neighbouring Countries*. Vol. II. Calcutta: Superintendent Government Printing, 1909.

"The Artillery Alphabet." Yorkshire Folksongs. Accessed January 15, 2022. http://www.yorkshirefolksong.net/song.cfm?songID=26.

Bell, Charles. *The People of Tibet*. Oxford: Clarendon Press, 1968.

———. *Portrait of a Dalai Lama*. London: Wisdom Publication, 1987.

———. *Tibet Past and Present*. New Delhi: Motilal Banarsidass, 1992.

———. "A Year in Lhasa." *Geographical Journal* 63, no. 2 (February 1924): 89–101. https://www.jstor.org/stable/1781621.

Baxter, Colin F., comp. *Field Marshall Bernard Law Montgomery, 1887–1976*. London: Greenwood Press, 1999.

Berlin, Irving. "This Is the Army Mr. Jones." Anti War Songs. 2010. https://www.antiwarsongs.org/canzone.php?id=24313&lang=en.

"Boney Was a Warrior." Age of Revolution. Accessed January 15, 2022. https://ageofrevolution.org/200-object/boney-was-a-warrior-popular-ballad/.

Boyce, William. "Hearts of Oak." The Exmouth Shanty Men. Accessed January 15, 2022. https://www.exmouthshantymen.com/songbook.php?id=169.

"The British Grenadiers." Genius. Accessed January 15, 2022. https://genius.com/Traditional-the-british-grenadiers-annotated.

Buchanan, Walter. "A Recent Trip into the Chumbi Valley, Tibet." *Geographical Journal* 53, no. 6 (June 1919): 403–410. https://www.jstor.org/stable/1780416.

Candler, Edmund. *The Unveiling of Lhasa*. London: Edward Allen, 1905.

Camus, Albert. *The Myth of Sisyphus, and Other Essays*. Translated by Justin O'Brien. New York: Random House, 1991.

Chatwin, Bruce. *What Am I Doing Here*. London: Pan Books, 1990.

Churchill, Winston. *The Speeches of Winston Churchill*. Edited by David Cannadine. London: Penguin, 1990.

Coward, Noel. "Mad Dogs and Englishmen." Traditional Music. Accessed January 15, 2022. http://www.traditionalmusic.co.uk/folk-song-lyrics/Mad_Dogs_and_Englishmen.htm.

Darwin, Charles. *The Origin of Species*. New York: P. F. Collier & Son Company, 1909.

Davidson, Avram. *Vergil in Averno*. New York: Doubleday, 1987.

Dickens, Charles. *A Tale of Two Cities*. London: Wordsworth, 1993.

Disney. "Whistle While You Work." University of Pittsburgh. Accessed January 15, 2022. https://voices.pitt.edu/TeachersGuide/Unit7/WhistleWhileYouWork.htm.

Ditchfield, P. H. *Old English Customs*. London: George Redway, 1896.

Drinkwater, John. "Abraham Lincoln." In *The Collected Plays of John Drinkwater*, Vol. 2, 1–100. London: Sidgwick and Jackson, 1925.

Dostoevsky, Fyodor. *Crime and Punishment*. Translated by Richard Pevear and Larissa Volokhonsky. New York: Vintage Books, 1993.

Eliot, Thomas S. *Family Reunion*. New York: Harcourt Brace and Company, 1939.
———. *Poems 1909–1962*. New York: Harcourt, Brace and World, 1963.

Evans-Wentz, W. Y., ed. *Tibetan Yoga and Secret Doctrine*. 2nd ed. New York: Oxford University Press, 1958.

Fields, Gracie. "Wish Me Luck." Genius. Accessed January 13, 2022. https://genius.com/Gracie-fields-wish-me-luck-as-you-wave-me-goodbye-lyrics.

FitzGerald, Edward. *Rubáiyát of Omar Khayyám. A Criticla Edition*. Edited by Christopher Decker. Charlottesville: University Press of Virginia, 1997.

Glahe, Will. "Roll Out the Barrel." Songfacts. Accessed January 20, 2022. https://www.songfacts.com/facts/will-glahe/beer-barrel-polka-roll-out-the-barrel.

Gould, Basil John. *The Jewel in the Lotus: Recollections of an Indian Political*. United Kingdom: Chatto & Windus, 1957.

Harrer, Heinrich. *Seven Years in Tibet*. Translated by Richard Graves. London: Rupert Hart-Davis, 1953.

Harris, Karen. "'I Shall Return': General MacArthur's Promise." History Daily. Accessed January 20, 2022. https://historydaily.org/i-shall-return-general-macarthurs-promise.

Headmaster of Victoria Boys School, Diary, author's copy, 1905–1940.

Hemans, Felicia Dorothea. "Casabianca." In *Best Remembered Poems*, edited by Martin Gardner, 44–45. New York: Dover, 1992.

Hemingway, Ernest. *A Farewell to Arms*. London: Vintage Books, 2005.

Hilton, James. *Lost Horizon*. West Sussex: Summersdale Publishers, 1936.

Hughes, Thomas. *Tom Brown's School Days*. London: Macmillan and Co., 1868.

Huxley, Aldous. *Antic Hay*. London: Chatto & Windus, 1949.

Joyce, James. *Ulysses*. Edited by Hans Walter Gabler. New York: Vintage Books, 1986.

Keats, John. *Poems*. London: Blackie and Son, 1903.

Kipling, Rudyard. *Kim*. New York: Doubleday, Page & Company, 1901.

———. *Poems of Rudyard Kipling*. New York: Thomas Y. Crowell, n.d.

———. *Stories and Poems from Rudyard Kipling*. New York: Grosset & Dunlap, 1909.

Macaulay, Thomas Babington. *Lays of Ancient Rome*. London: Longman, Brown, Green, and Longmans, 1847.

McHugh, Jimmy. "Comin' in on a Wing and a Prayer." University of Missouri–Kansas City. Accessed January 20, 2022. https://dl.mospace.umsystem.edu/umkc/islandora/object/umkc%3A21093#page/1/mode/2up.

Milton, John. *Paradise Lost, Samson Agonistes, Comus, and Arcades*. London: John Sharpe, 1823.

My Learning. "A Wartime Musical Hit." Accessed January 22, 2022. https://www.mylearning.org/stories/its-a-long-way-to-tipperary/764.

Nicolson, Harold. *Curzon: The Last Phase, 1919–1925*. London: Constable & Co., 1934.

O'Reilly, P. J. "Drake Goes West." LiederNet Archive. Accessed January 15, 2022. https://www.lieder.net/lieder/get_text.html?TextId=22191.

Orwell, George. *The Lion and The Unicorn*. London: Penguin Books, 1982.

Powell, Felix. "Pack up Your Troubles." University of Missouri–Kansas City. Accessed January 20, 2022. https://dl.mospace.umsystem.edu/umkc/islandora/object/umkc%3A23228#page/1/mode/2up.

Russell, Bertrand. *Introduction to Mathematical Philosophy*. New York: Dover, 1993.

Sandow, Eugen. *Sandow's System: Sandow on Physical Training*. Edited by G. Mercer Adam. New York: J. Selwin & Sons, 1894.

Scott, Walter. "Lochinvar" In *The Book of Scottish Ballads,* edited by Alexander Whitelaw, 66. London: Blackie and Son, 1857.

Shakespeare, William. *As You Like It*. Edited by William J. Rolfe. New York: Harper & Brothers, 1878.

———. *Julius Caesar*. Edited by Albert Harris Tolman. New York: World Book Company, 1913.

———. *Macbeth*. Edited by Cedric Watts. Suffolk: Wordsworth Classics, 2005.

The Sixth Lama Dalai. "O bird there—white crane—come." In *Songs of Love, Poems of Sadness,* translated by Paul Williams, 117. London: I.B. Tauris, 2004.

*The Spectator, A Weeekly Review of Politics, Literature, Theology and Art*. Vol. 100. London: John Baker, 1908.

Spencer-Chapman, Frederick. *Lhasa: The Holy City*. London: Chatto and Windus, 1940.

Stowe, Harriet Beecher. *Uncle Tom's Cabin*. Edited by Christopher G. Diller. Ontario: Broadview Press, 2009.

Tennyson, Alfred. *Poems*. Vol. 2. London: Edward Moxon, 1842.

Thompson, Kenneth W. *Winston Churchill's World View. Statesmanship and Power*. Baton Rouge: Louisiana State University Press, 1983.

Whittier, John Greenleaf. "Barbara Frietchie." In *Poems of American Patriotism,* edited by J. Brander Matthews, 205–208. New York: C. Scribner's Sons, 1882.

Williamson, Margaret D., and John Snelling. *Memoirs of a Political Officer's Wife in Tibet, Sikkim and Bhutan*. United Kingdom: Wisdom, 1987.

Younghusband, Francis Edward. *India and Tibet: A History of the Relations which Have Subsisted Between the Two Countries from the Time of Warren Hastings to 1910;*

*with a Particular Account of the Mission to Lhasa of 1904*. London: John Murray, 1910.

# Index

# About the Author

**Tsewang Yishey Pemba** was a man of many "firsts"—the first Tibetan to become a doctor in Western medical science and the first Tibetan to publish a full-length autobiography and also the first Tibetan to write a novel in English.

Dr. Pemba was born on June 5, 1932, in Gyantse, Tibet. His father's job at the British mission in Tibet meant that he spent his childhood in Gyantse, Yatung, and also Lhasa, where he was present at the installation of the fourteenth Dalai Lama. Although he received no formal education until the age of nine, he thrived at Victoria School in Kurseong, West Bengal, India, and in 1949 went on to study for his medical degree at University College, London.

Following a short stint working at a hospital in Kalimpong, West Bengal, Dr. Pemba was recruited in 1956 by the future prime minister of Bhutan, Jigme Dorji, to work as a medical officer in the town of Paro. At the time, there were only three modern trained doctors in the country, and, with no electricity, water, modern roads or communications, he had to walk everywhere or ride horses and mules. It was during this period that he wrote his memoir *Young Days in Tibet*, published by Jonathan Cape in 1957, the first autobiographical account by a Tibetan in English.

By 1959, Dr. Pemba was back in Darjeeling, working in Dooars & Darjeeling Medical Association, a hospital under the aegis of the Indian Tea Association. With the uprising in Lhasa, Tibet, against the occupying Chinese forces, thousands of refugees were fleeing to India, many crowding into Darjeeling. Dr. Pemba volunteered for the Tibetan refugee school and the Tibetan refugee Self-Help Centre. He could count every prominent Tibetan refugee, monk and official, who fled from Tibet as one of his patients. His novel *Idols on the Path* (1966) was born in this period, shaped by his memories of Tibet and the experience of the fledgling Tibetan diaspora.

In 1965, Dr. Pemba returned to London to train as a surgeon. He was awarded the Hallett Prize in 1966 for standing first in the primary examinations of the Royal College of Surgeons and, in 1967, obtained their fellowship.

On returning to India, Dr. Pemba worked in Darjeeling; he befriended famous Catholic thinker Thomas Merton in this period and moved back to Bhutan in the mid-1980s to become superintendent of the National Referral Hospital, Thimphu. Until 1992, Dr. Pemba lived in Bhutan and was an appointed United Nations certifying doctor; he sat on the committee devising a Bhutan national formulary and, in 1989, was a member of the Bhutan delegation to WHO in Geneva. He also served as consulting physician to Bhutan's royal family in this period.

After his official retirement in 1992, Dr. Pemba worked privately and traveled extensively to the United States, Europe, and Japan, and he also wrote *Tibet as I Knew It*—his second memoir and account of life in Tibet. Between 2000 and 2005, he made several visits to New York and worked, for a period, as a lecturer in anatomy and physiology. In 2007, Dr. Pemba paid a visit to Tibet after almost sixty years, capturing old memories and renewing ties and seeing a totally changed Tibet.

Beyond the medical profession, Dr. Pemba was an avid follower of the arts, and he never stopped reading and writing, even up to his last days. He passed away on November 26, 2011, leaving behind five unpublished manuscripts. His second novel, *White Crane, Lend Me Your Wings*, was published posthumously in 2017. His wife, Tsering Sangmo, passed away in 2016. They are survived by four children (a fifth child had predeceased them in 2009).

Dechen Pemba